吉田松陰　著

Shouin Yoshida

[留 魂 録] 英完譯書

Soulful Minute

紺野大介　訳

by Daisuke Konno

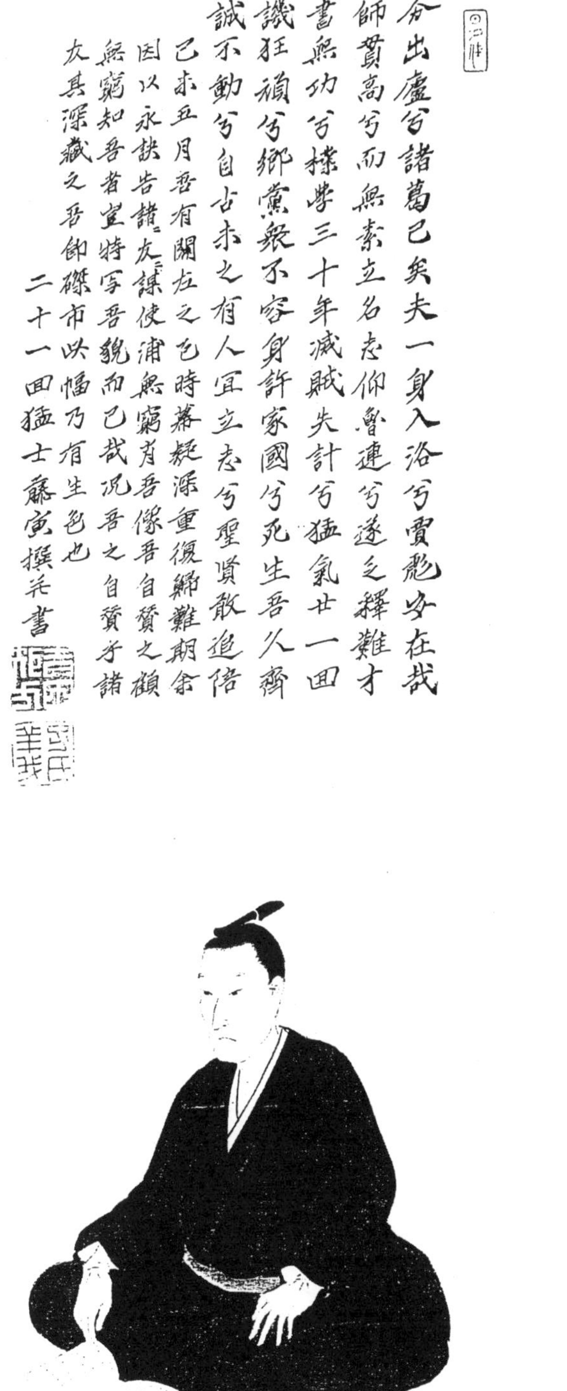

画家松浦松洞（無窮）による吉田松陰

Shouin Yoshida(1830_1859);Portrait by Shoudou Matsuura

目次
contents

1. はじめに……………………………………………………………………4
(preface)

2. 序章：留魂録まで……………………………………………………11
(introduction ; overview of Shouin Yoshida)

3. 本章：留魂録……………………………………………………………107
(main course ; " Soulful Minute")

4. 英国人作家 Robert L. Stevenson の吉田寅次郎…………………188
(Yoshida Torajiro by R.L.Stevenson[1850-1894])

5. 跋文(中国人吉田松陰研究家・郭連友文学博士)…………………222
(contribution by Dr. Guo Lianyou)

6. 跋文(山口県教育会・河村太市会長)………………………………226
(contribution by Mr. Taichi Kawamura)

7. 謝辞………………………………………………………………………228
(acknowledgements)

8. 引用および参考文献……………………………………………………230
(bibliography)

はじめに

「留魂録」は吉田松陰が安政の大獄で処刑される前日のほぼ一日で書き上げた遺書である。薄葉半紙を四つ折りにした縦12cm、横17cm、19面に細書きした約5000字は、不自由な獄舎で書かれたことが想像できるが、その内容は死を目前にした人間とは思えないほどの冷静さで訣別の辞が述べられており、門人への激励や周囲への細心の配慮が示されている。このことがかえって読む人を更なる悲壮感へ誘う、と言えるであろう。

留魂録に限らず、松陰の手紙や上書をみていると、こんなにも他人に優しくなれるのか、こんなにも国を想えるのか、こんなにも自己犠牲が払えるのか...といった魂の叫びが聞こえてくるようであり、重い警鐘を現代の日本人へ与えていると思われる。

この意味で幕末維新の勤王僧・黙霖が「松陰の文章は一字一字が涙であり、一言一言が血だ」と述べているのはけだし名言である。

この度、約 5 ヶ年の歳月をかけその「留魂録」を英完訳した。筆者は作家や小説家ではなく科学技術の世界に身を置く人間なので、奉職の余技として主に休日の土日などを利用しながら取り組んできた。

この動機になっているのは、やはり第一作目となっている幕末の英傑、橋本左内15歳時の著作「啓発録」英完訳を1995年に完成したことに起因している。これには約10年を必要とした。本書を私家製本化し世界の主要大学図書館に寄贈、日頃海外と多く接している為、欧米中国などのほか世界中の方々に対し、日本人の生き方、忠誠心、倫理観、道徳、潔さや美意識などを認識して欲しかったし、事実多大な反響があったと思われる。　また米国クリントン大統領や英国ケンブリッジ大学総長らから感謝状を戴いただけでなく、国内からもかなりな反響があったことも誘因となった。

この書は橋本左内の主君であった越前藩主松平春嶽公の御嫡孫松平永芳氏から宮内庁を通じ、天皇陛下の御手許にも届けられたとのことである。

また特別に印象的だったことは、あの沖縄返還を万感胸に迫る思いで事実上成し遂げ、大作【他策ナカリシヲ信ゼムト欲ス】を遺した国際政治学者若泉敬氏、'82~'87 年代に総理大臣となった中曽根康弘氏、経済界からはGlobal Niche Topで知られる日東電工株式会社中興の祖・山本英樹現会長から深いご感想と過分なご評価を戴いたことであり、心から感謝している次第である。

従って松陰の「留魂録」は私にとって第二作目の英完訳書である。
時代背景は幕末維新であり、左内の「啓発録」とほぼ同時期なので、この点では時間を省略できた。しかし左内の「啓発録」が15歳時の作品であるのに対し、松陰の「留魂録」が30歳の時のものであること、書いた時の環境や位置付けが全く異なること、左内は若干20代前半から春嶽公の指示で政治の表舞台に立ったのに対し、松陰は事実上、成人期の大半

Preface

"Soulful Minute" is Shouin Yoshida's farewell note. He wrote it out in just one day, the day before his execution in the Ansei Purge. The physical size of this missive, 12 cm long and 17 cm wide, coming to about 5,000 characters on 19 pages, is enough to allow us to easily imagine how much inconvenience he had writing it in jail. In "Soulful Minute", he reveals a mind so unruffled enough it is hard to believe that death stared him in the face, as he encouraged his disciples and paid careful and thoughtful attention to his followers. This only increases the pathos we feel upon reading it.

When reading his writings including his letters as well as "Soulful Minute", we cannot help admiring how affectionate he was to others, how anxious he was about the future of his country and how much he sacrificed himself for society. We can almost hear his soulful cry. May it serve as an important warning to modern Japanese as well.

Priest Mokurin, in the last days of the Tokugawa Shogunate, said "Every character written by Shouin Yoshida seems to be filled with his tears, and blood seems to gush out of every word in his letters." Nothing could be more aptly said.

I have spent the last five years finishing the translation of "Soulful Minute" into English. Since I'm not a novelist but a natural scientist, I had to work on it during my holidays, apart from my full-time work.

My motive is derived from my translation and publication of the "Treatise on Enlightenment" written by Sanai Hashimoto, one of the historical heroes in the last days of the Tokugawa Shogunate, in 1995. It took me about 10 years to study his contribution to the country and translate it. After binding it privately, I donated some copies to the libraries of principal universities all over the world.

Because of my fondness for my many friends in overseas countries, I sincerely hope that they have correct understanding of the Japanese mind and our way of life, loyalty, ethics, morals, strict integrity and aesthetic sense. In fact, the response to my translation has been very encouraging. That is, I have received the letters of acknowledgement from many prominent persons including Mr. Bill Clinton, the former US President, and the President of University of Cambridge in the UK, in addition to the heartwarming reaction from intellectuals here in Japan.

I hear from Mr. Nagayoshi Matsudaira, a grandson of Lord Shungaku Matsudaira of the Echizen Domain, Sanai Hashimoto's master, that he presented a book of the "Treatise on Enlightenment " to the current

が監獄生活であったこと、橋本左内という稀代の政治家が[政治に公正さ]を求めたのに対し、一方の吉田松陰は最高の教育者であり[人間の正義]を希求した事が本質的な違いであろう。松陰研究者の殆どが強調しておられるように、「留魂録」に至る幽囚録、士規七則、講孟余話、七生説などからも松陰の本質は至誠の教育者そのものである事が判り、最終作品となった「留魂録」に至っては、遺書にも拘らず「教育とは何か」を深く考察させている。また第八章などの{死生観}は日本人万人の共感を呼ぶと思われる。それは筆者の知っている限りの欧米中国他の多くの人々にとってもおそらく同様であろう。

　何故なら、いわゆる人間としての“民度”が限りなく高いのである。

「留魂録」は松陰を師と仰ぐ幕末の志士達に{聖書}として作用し、“明治維新”という自分達の手で勝ち取った新時代を構築し、新しい日本を主導したのである。

振り返って現代の日本は、政治も経済も教育も混迷の極みにある。一例をあげれば、米国を含めて指摘できることであるが、国会議員は中国をはるかに上回る太子党（親の権力基盤を受け継ぎ、労せずして議員となる人々など）であふれ、民度以前、政治以前に自浄作用が麻痺している。国家財政が破局的状況にある経済、信じられない内容の少年犯罪の多発は、親や学校の教育が殆んど“死に体”に近いことを証明している。

　精神的基盤が無くなってしまった為か、道徳的に降伏してしまっているのか。

人間はたとえ言葉が通じなくとも振舞いを見れば人格は概ね判るものである。

33年間で世界約60ヶ国300都市を回ってきたけれども、誤解を恐れずに言えば、彼等は“日本を知らない”か“知ってるが尊敬してない”のどちらかであった。金はばら撒いてきたが、尊敬される国家戦略、敬意を感じさせる美学、とでもいったものが無かったからであろう。　筆者は“国政の在り方”といった方面に皆目無知なので、その事自体を深く言及することは厳しく自分を控えさせているつもりであるが、世界各国から見て、国政に基づく海外への一挙手一投足はもとより、主要国から見ても、日本は限りなく軽い存在、大国に対し萎縮し、一方で絶対精神が弛緩した状態なのではないかと思われる。

　個々人の“民度”が限りなく下落した結果といえよう。

つまり、言葉を選んで述べる必要があるけれども、それは米国から与えられた平和主義、自分達の手で勝ち取ったものではない民主主義がもたらした“全体”のためなのであろう。米国などよりもずっと歴史の豊かな日本で、過去と全く結びつかず未来を模索することは、表現できないほどの大きな損失である。その損失に個々人が早く気付くべきである。

他方、少なくとも幕末維新まではその対極にあったことを歴史が証明している。正義を貫徹するためには血を流す覚悟があった。凛然とした気概が横溢していたと察せられる。

安っぽい国益や経済援助ではなく、外国人はこういった日本、こうした残像のある日本人にこそ敬意を払っているのだと愚考、愚察している昨今である。　本拙訳書刊行の動機はここにあり、外国人のみならず日本人にもこのことへの再考の一助となれば幸甚である。

Japanese Emperor through the Imperial Household Agency. In addition, it was especially moving for me to receive the praise and comments of Mr. Kei Wakaizumi, an international political scientist in Japan.

Mr. Wakaizumi is responsible for the Okinawa Reversion and is the author of a book entitled "*The Best Course Available*" or "*Tasaku nakarishi wo sinnzemu to hossu*" in Japanese. I also received a letter of thanks from Mr. Yasuhiro Nakasone, former Prime Minister, and Mr. Hideki Yamamoto, the restorer and Chairman of Nitto Denko Corporation, who is well known as Global Niche Top in the Japanese financial circles.

I deeply appreciate their generous compliments and thoughtful reflections on the book.

Accordingly, the translation and publication of "Soulful Minute" from classic Japanese into English is my second effort. Since the historical background is the same as that of Sanai Hashimoto, in that Shouin Yoshida also lived in the closing days of the Tokugawa Shogunate, my background research required less effort this time. However, other conditions between the two men are completely different from each other.

First, while the "Treatise on Enlightenment" by Sanai Hashimoto was written at the age of 15, "Soulful Minute" by Shouin Yoshida was written at the age of 30.

Second, the places and environments where they wrote their respective works are quite different from each other.

Third, their fields of activity were also completely different from each other. Sanai Hashimoto played an active part on the main stage of politics under Lord Shungaku Matsudaira as a political reformer. On the other hand, Shouin Yoshida had to spend the greater part of his lifetime in jails against his will regardless of his situation as a leader of a political movement. While Sanai Hashimoto, a peerless statesman, desired a principle such as "justice in politics", Shouin Yoshida, a superlative educationist, held a creed of the "living heart and soul". This last point is what sets Shouin Yoshida apart from Sanai Hashimoto essentially.

As most scholars who study Shouin Yoshida emphasize, I can also recognize his innate disposition as a devoted educationist from his writings such as "Captivity Document", "*Shikishichisoku*", "Discourses on Mencius", "*Shichishousetsu*" and "Soulful Minute". Although "Soulful Minute", his last piece of writing, is a farewell note, it makes us deeply consider what education is. In addition, Chapter 8, which describes his philosophy on life and death, in particular, will evoke every person's sympathy, regardless of nationality.

This is because what we call the "moral standards" of Shouin Yoshida deserves supreme praise. The fact is that "Soulful Minute" became as "Bible"

日本人の自力による“民度革命”はこれからが本番である。
このことを「留魂録」は限りない優しさと、言葉の最良の意味における愛情で我々に語りかけていると思われる。

2002年12月
東京 つくし野にて　紺野大介

for his disciples and related comrades, and they used it as the blueprint for leading Japan into a new age called the Meiji Restoration.

Reviewing the present state of Japan, the space ship called Japan-maru seems to be drifting in deep space. Some thoughtful people believe the indescribable air of growing crisis about the present state of Japan is due to its people having lost their spiritual base or capitulated to Japanese original moral sense. I often hear that Japanese politics is at its ebb, but it is a matter of course that this phenomenon is derived from the low political awareness of Japanese people ourselves.

Could this be due to a decline in the moral standards embodied by Shouin Yoshida in recent Japan?

At the risk of being misunderstood, I'd like to suggest that the cause may also lie in our receiving pacifism and democracy from the United States on a platter, without our having bled for it ourselves.

In any case, we cannot hope to create a better future for Japan without looking to her longer and more glorious history than United States has had.

Through "Soulful Minute", Shouin Yoshida seems to tell us this with the extreme gentleness and supreme affection expressed in his words.

December, 2002

at Tsukushino Tokyo, Japan
Daisuke Konno

序章：留魂録まで

Introduction ; Overview of Shouin Yoshida

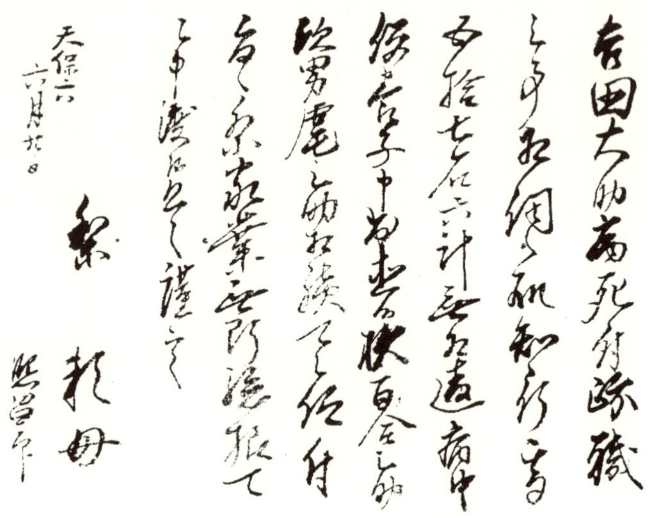

吉田家継嗣奉書写
吉田大助病死に付き、跡職の事之を相い調え候
所、知行高五拾七石六斗相違無く、病中仮養子
申し出置き候、杉百合之助次男虎之助に相続仰
せ付けられるべき旨の条、家業を断絶無き様申
し渡さしむべく候、恐々謹言

(梨羽) 梨　頼母

天保六 六月廿日　　熙昌印

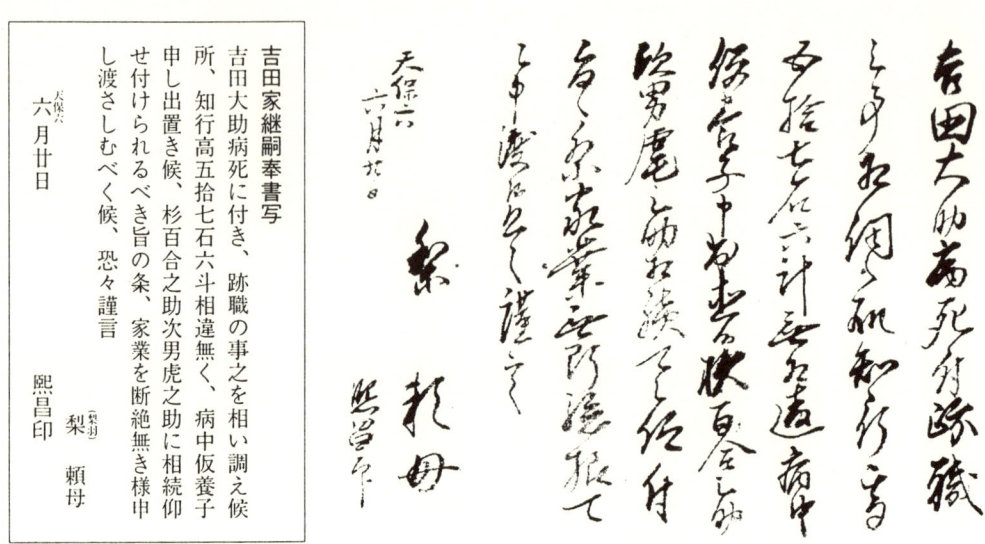

Copy of the written appointment of Yoshida Family successor.

萩（山口県）松本村の下級藩士杉百合之助の次男・杉虎之助（後の松陰）は５歳の時、山鹿流兵学師範である叔父吉田大助(1807 - 1835)の仮養子となったが、翌年大助が死亡したため吉田家を継ぐことになる。これは知行五十七石をそのまま受け藩士となった藩庁からの辞令書の写しである。

Toranosuke (who called himself Shouin after becoming an adult), was the second son of Yurinosuke Sugi, who was a low grade retainer of a daimyo (feudal load) in Matsumoto Village in Hagi (a part of Yamaguchi Prefecture). He was adopted into the family of Daisuke Yoshida, his uncle, who was a master of the Yamaga School of military science. But since the uncle died the next year, Shouin became the head of the Yoshida Family at just age 6. This is a copy of the written appointment issued by the feudal domain office.

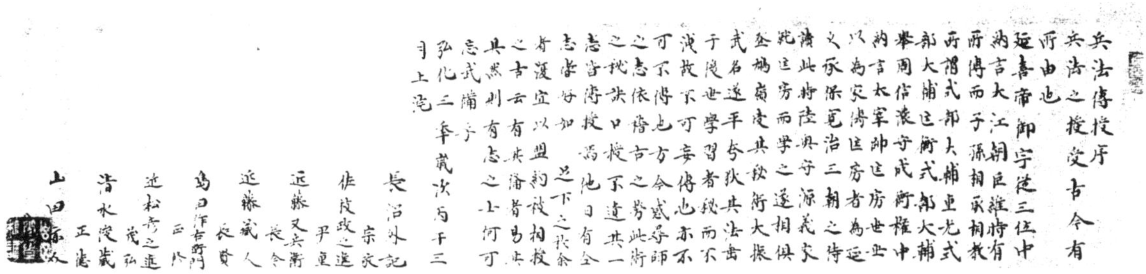

兵法傳授序

兵法之授受古今有所由也延喜帝御宇従三位中納言大江朝臣維時有所傳而子孫相承相教所謂式部大輔重光式部大輔匡衡式部大輔擧周信濃守成衡權中納言太宰帥匡房世世以為家傳匡房者為延久承保寛治三朝之侍讀此時陸奥守源義家就匡房而學之遂相倶登鳩嶺受其秘術大振武名遂平夷狄其法垂于後世學習者秘而不洩故不可妄傳也亦不可不傳也方今尋師之志依稽古之勞此術之秘訣口授不遺其一悉皆傳授他日有同志嗜好如足下之於余者復宜以盟約相授之古云有其備者易其具然則有志之士何可忘武備乎

弘化三季歳次丙午三月上浣

長沼外記宗敬
佐枝政之進尹重
近藤又兵衛長令
近藤蔵人長賢
島田作右衛門正修
近松彦之進茂弘
清水俊蔵正徳
山田亦介公章

兵法伝授序

Foreword in initiating tactics to Shouin Yoshida.

兵法伝授序

兵法の伝授、古今由る所あるなり。延喜帝の御宇、従三位中納言大江朝臣維時伝ふる所あり、而して子孫相承け相教へ、所謂式部大輔重光・式部大輔匡衡・式部大輔挙周・信濃守成衡・権中納言太宰帥匡房、世々以て家伝と為す。匡房は延久・承保・寛治三朝の侍読たり。此の時陸奥守源義家、匡房に就きて之れを学び、遂に相倶に鳩嶺に登りて其の秘術を受け、大いに武名を振ひ、遂に夷狄を平らぐ。其の法後世に垂るるも、学習する者秘して洩さず。故に妄り(みだ)には伝ふべからざるも、亦伝へざるべからざるなり。方今尋師の志に感じ、稽古の労に依り、此の術の秘訣口授、其の一を遺(のこ)さず、悉皆伝授す。他日、同志の嗜好、足下の余に於けるが如き者あらば、復た宜しく盟約を以て之れを相授けらるべし。古に云ふ、其の備ある者は其の具を易(おさ)むと。然らば則ち有志の士、何ぞ武備を忘るべけんや。

弘化三季(ねん)歳次丙午三月上浣

山田亦介公章（判）

長沼外記宗敬　佐枝政之進尹重
近藤又兵衛長令　近藤蔵人長賢
島田作右衛門正修　近松彦之進茂弘
清水俊蔵正徳

吉田大次郎殿

松陰が 16 歳の頃、叔父山田大助の親友、山田亦介(1810_1864)から長沼流兵学についても学び、免許皆伝を授かった。

Shouin Yoshida studied the Naganuma School of coastal defense science at the age of 16 and was conferred full mastership in tactics from Matasuke Yamada, one of his uncle's best friends.

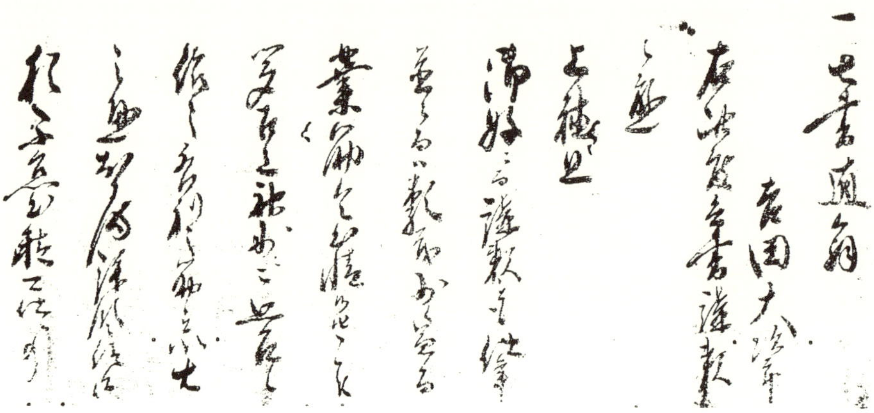

長州藩十三代藩主　毛利敬親

The 13th Lord of the Choushuu Domain; Takachika Mouri

松陰 15 歳時、藩主の親試の際、山鹿素行著「武教全書」を講じた。
この時、特に藩主の好みより、“孫子・虚実編”を予定も無く講じ藩主
敬親はその内容に感嘆し、「七書直解」を松陰に授けた。
七書とは中国の宋代から呼称されるようになった、①孫子②呉子③司馬法
④尉繚子⑤李衛公問対⑥黄石公三略⑦六韜の七種兵法書である。
七書直解とはその解説書のこと。

At the age of 15, Shouin Yoshida gave a lecture on "Bukyou Zensho, Compendium of Military Science," written by Sokou Yamaga to Lord Takachika Mouri.

In addition, he gave a lecture on Chapter “Sunzi・Truthfulness Strategy” at the Lord's request without advance preparations.

Lord Takachika Mouri was struck with admiration at Shouin Yoshida's lecture and gave [7 Chinese handbook for Tactics] to him.

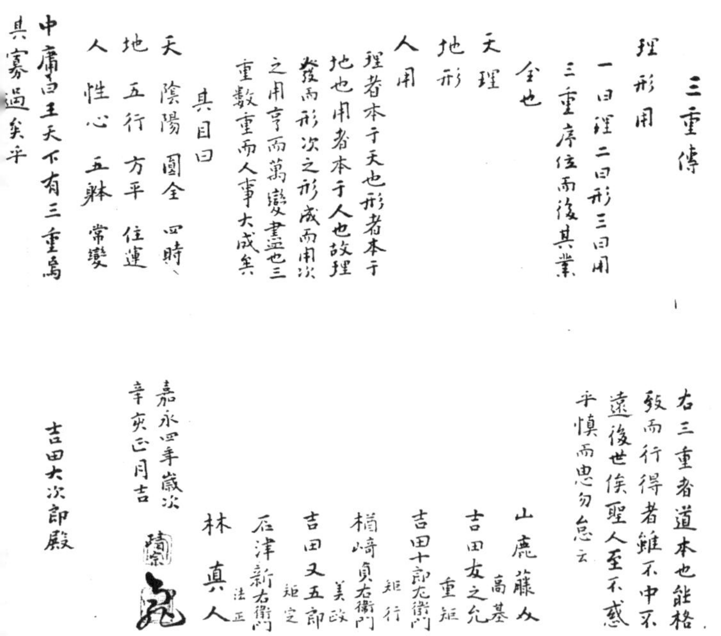
三重傳

理　形　用

一曰理　二曰形　三曰用

三重序位而後其業

全也

天　理

地　形

人　用

理者本于天也形者本于

地也用者本于人也故理

發而形次之形成而用次

之用立而萬變盡也三

重數重而人事大成矣

其目曰

天　陰陽　圓全　四時、

地　五行　方平　往運

人　性心　五躰　常變

中庸曰王天下有三重焉

其寡過矣乎

右三重者道本也能格

致而行得者雖不中不

遠後世俟聖人至不惑

乎慎而思勿怠云

山鹿藤介　高基

吉田友之允　重矩

吉田十郎左衛門　矩行

楢崎貞右衛門　美政

吉田又五郎　矩定

石津新右衛門　法正

林　真人

嘉永四年歳次

辛亥正月吉

吉田大次郎殿

やまが そこう　山鹿素行　1622～85（元和8～貞享2）江戸前期の儒学者。(系)会津藩士町野草仍の食客の貞以の子。(生)陸奥国会津。㊔高興，または高祐，幼名佐太郎，字は子敬，通称甚五右衛門，号は陰山，のち素行。‖6歳で会津より江戸に出る。1630（寛永7）林羅山 の門に入り朱子学を学ぶ。また小幡（勘兵衛）景憲 に甲州流軍学を学んで免許を得，自ら山鹿流軍学を創始。また広田坦斎から忌部神道を，高野山按察院光宥法師からは両部神道を学ぶ。20歳頃には内外の学問を修学しその名声が高まった。'52（承応1）赤穂藩主浅野長直の招きで禄1千石を得て，藩士に軍学を教授。'56（明暦2）「武教要録」「修教要録」「治教要録」の3部作を著わす。儒学は日本の武士社会での日常生活に役立つ実用学であるべきだと主張。'60（万治3）赤穂藩を致仕，声望ますます高くその門は大いに繁栄する。'65（寛文5）「聖教要録」で，朱子学が観念論化して非実用的なことを排斥し，古代聖賢の道にかえることを主張したため，翌年赤穂に配流，配所で「武家事紀」「中朝事実」を著わして，中華思想を排斥，日本の風土や歴史の優秀性を説く。'75（延宝3）許され，江戸の自宅を積徳堂とよび，門人に兵学および儒学を講じた。

山鹿流兵学

江戸初期の儒学者、山鹿素行(1622 - 1685)を学祖とする和流兵学。

会津出身の素行は林羅山の門に入り、朱子学を学んだ後、小幡景憲に甲州流軍学の免許を得、自ら山鹿流軍学を創始した。日本古来の学問をはじめ、儒学のみならず孫子、呉子以来の中国兵法を究め日本文化に立脚した兵学。

松陰は19歳で独立師範となり、22歳で山鹿流最高の極秘三重伝の免許を林真人から受け、明倫館兵学師範としての地歩を確立した。

The Yamaga school of military science was a Japanese style military science originated by Sokou Yamaga. He was a leading scholar in the Edo period, famous for his contribution to Confucian studies, military science, and Japanese history. He studied under Razan Hayashi (1583 - 1657) in a school devoted to the Doctrines of Chu-tzu.

Shouin Yoshida established his base as the tactics master at Meirinkan, a feudal domain school, after being conferred full mastership in top secret strategies in the Yamaga School of military science from Makoto Hayashi in 1851.

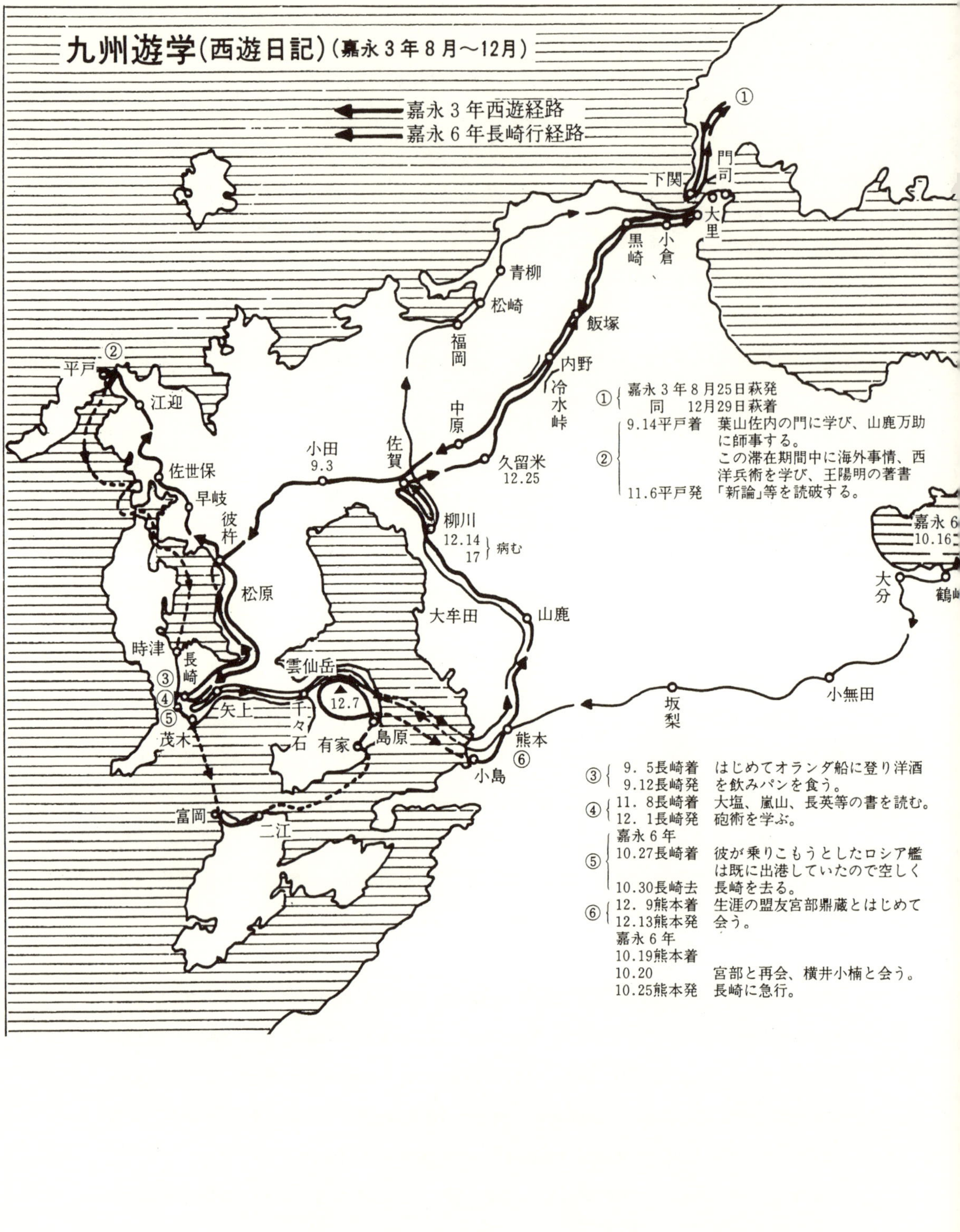
九州遊学（西遊日記）（嘉永３年８月〜12月）
嘉永３年西遊経路
嘉永６年長崎行経路
下関
門司
大里
小倉
黒崎
青柳
松崎
福岡
飯塚
内野
冷水峠
中原
佐賀
久留米 12.25
小田 9.3
平戸
江迎
佐世保
早岐
彼杵
松原
柳川 12.14 17 病む
大牟田
山鹿
時津
長崎
雲仙岳
12.7
矢上
千々石
有家
島原
茂木
熊本
小島
富岡
二江
坂梨
小無田
大分
鶴崎
嘉永６ 10.16
①
②
③
④
⑤
⑥
① 嘉永３年８月25日萩発 同 12月29日萩着
② 9.14平戸着 葉山佐内の門に学び、山鹿万助に師事する。この滞在期間中に海外事情、西洋兵術を学び、王陽明の著書「新論」等を読破する。 11.6平戸発
③ 9．5長崎着 はじめてオランダ船に登り洋酒を飲みパンを食う。 9.12長崎発
④ 11．8長崎着 大塩、嵐山、長英等の書を読む。 12．1長崎発 砲術を学ぶ。
⑤ 嘉永６年 10.27長崎着 彼が乗りこもうとしたロシア艦は既に出港していたので空しく長崎を去る。 10.30長崎去
⑥ 12．9熊本着 生涯の盟友宮部鼎蔵とはじめて会う。 12.13熊本発
嘉永６年 10.19熊本着
10.20 宮部と再会、横井小楠と会う。
10.25熊本発 長崎に急行。

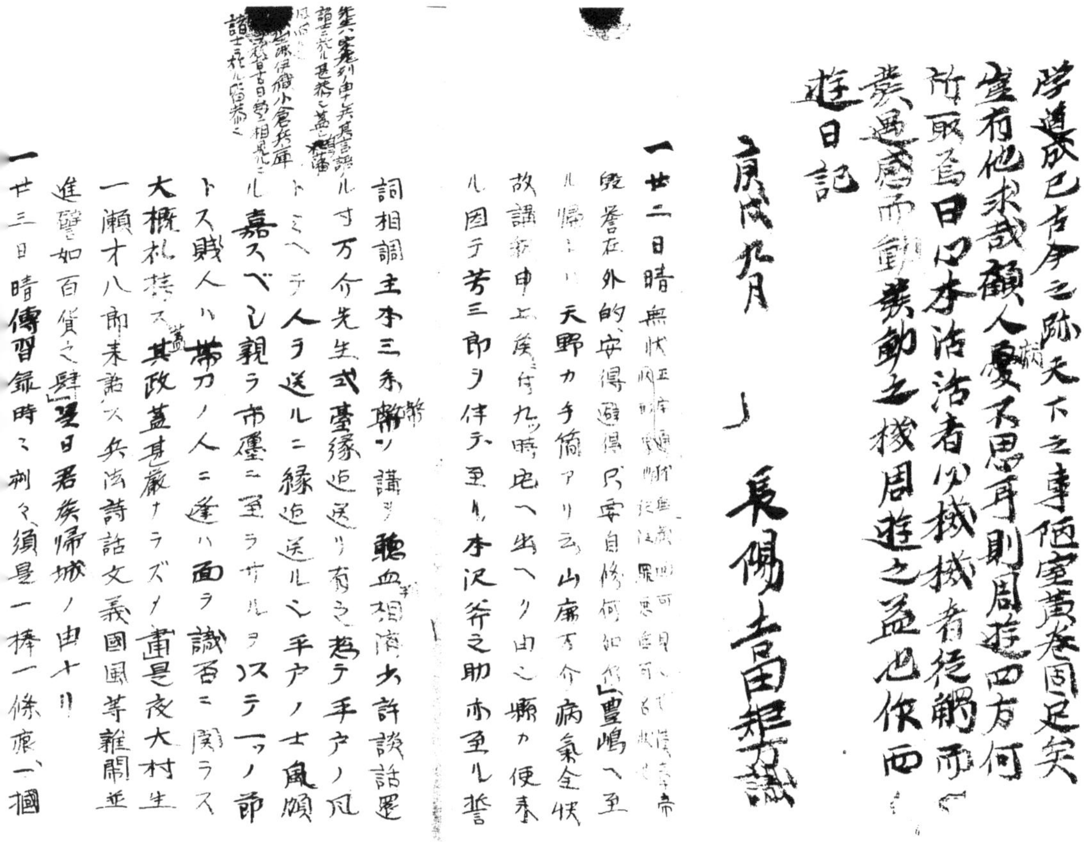
序
學道成己古今之跡天下之事陋室黃卷固足矣
豈有他求哉顧人憂不思耳則周遊四方何
所取焉曰心存活活者少裁裁者徒觸而
萎過而鄙萎動之機周遊之益也依而
遊日記
庚戌九月　長陽吉田矩方識

西遊日記

Kyushuu travel diary

九州遊学時にしたためた西遊日記は肥前平戸藩士・葉山佐内(?_1864)らの厚誼により、さながら読書録の感を呈するほどである。松陰21歳。総計約80冊を50余日で読み、要点は逐一抄録した。その主なものは葉山佐内著「辺備摘案」：アヘン戦争に鑑み、西洋の近代兵器の優秀性を認め、それを取り入れる必要性を説いた。

王陽明著「伝習録」：陽明学からの強い影響。

作者不明「近時海国必読書」：写本として伝えられた稀こう本。日本の蘭学者による翻訳書、西洋の政治、軍事、社会、文化、地理、歴史、国情等の紹介書で、松陰の海外認識を決定的にした。

高野長英著「戊戌夢物語」：江戸後期の蘭学者による1838の著作で、幕府の対外政策を批判、翌年蛮社の獄で永牢。

塩谷宕陰著「阿芙蓉彙聞」：アヘン戦争の清国の論文集。イギリスの植民地政策を詳述した警世書。

陳　炯著「海国見聞録」

僧横川著「日本考略」

ペキサンス著「百幾撒私」：西洋の砲術、砲台など先進的兵器を論じた軍事的著作。今までの和流兵学信望への思い込みを激しく動揺させた。

佐藤一斉著「刻四庫全書簡明」：朱子学と陽明学を折衷し、陽朱陰王と称された先哲の書。

魏　源著「聖武記」：幕末志士に西洋兵学知識などで多大な影響を与えた「海国図誌」を現した著者(1794_1857)によるアヘン戦争後の西洋新兵器との価値ある実践記録。

頼山陽著「新策」

清賀長齢原編「皇朝経世文編」：アヘン戦争でビジネスとして立回った漢奸問題を含め、清国の内政に関するあらゆる政策や意見を集成した記録。

申時行著「書経講義」

大塩平八郎「洗心洞箚記」：著者の代表作で上下巻319条と附録抄からなる全三巻の随筆体の儒学書。

会沢正志齋「新論」：水戸藩藩校弘道館教授頭取による神道と儒学を合わせた大義名分論を基調とした藩政家尊皇攘夷論

During his stay in Sanai Hayama's residence,
Shouin Yoshida read through over 80 books in 50 days.
The main publications are those that follow.

"Henbichakuan" ; by Sanai Hayama (?_1864),a chief retainer of Bizen Hirado Domain (now the city of Hirato in Nagasaki Prefecture)

"Denshuuroku" ; by Wang Yangming (1472_1528), Philosopher and Confucian in Ming Dynasty. The originator of Youmeigaku.

"Kinjikaikoku Hishuusho" ; anonymous

"Bojutsu yume monogatari" ; by Chouei Takano (1804_1850) , Scholar of Rangaku. In 1826 was awarded the degree of "Doktor"

"Afuyouibun" ; by Touin Shionoya (1809_1867), Confucianist in the last days of the Tokugawa shougunate.

"Kaikoku Kenbunnroku" ; by Chen Luntong ,Commander of Emperor Kangxi era in Qing Dynasty.

"Nippon kouryaku" ; by priest Yokokawa

"Kokushikozensho kaimei" ; by Issai Satou (1772_1859) ,Confucian scholar of the late Edo period. His best known work is the collection of essays entitled Genshi Shiroku.

"Seimuki" ; by Yuan Wei (1794_1857), Philosopher and Literary man in Qing Dynasty. Famous for writing the Kaikokuzushi.

"Sinsaku" ; by Sanyou Rai (1781_1832), Historian and Poet, Chiefly famous for writing the Nihon Gaishi.

"Shokyou kougi" ; by Shixing Shen, civil servant in Ming Dynasty.

"Senshin dousatsuki" ; by Heihachirou Oshio (1793_1837), Idealistic Confucian philosopher and teacher of the Wang Yangming School who led a rebellion in Osaka {Tempou Uprising}.

"Shinron" ; by Seishisai Aizawa (1782_1863), Scholar of the Mito school a nationalist school of Confucian study.

不達砲技勿以論兵
孫呉勿以譚砲
辛亥二月

（嘉永四年二月）

村田清風為松陰所贈詩
砲技に達せざれば以て兵を論ずる勿れ。孫呉に通ぜざれば以て砲を譚（たん）ずる勿れ。
辛亥二月

村田清風

村田清風為松陰所贈詩

A poem given to him from Seifuu Murata.

長州藩の改革派の長老村田清風が松陰の前途に期待し、江戸遊学出発に際し贈った詩。藩の財政再建にも功績が大きい。

Seifuu Murata(1783_1855), a senior member of the reform party in the Choushuu Domain, dedicated a poem to Yoshida expecting much of him before going to Edo. Murata contributed to the reconstruction of the economy of the Choushuu Domain

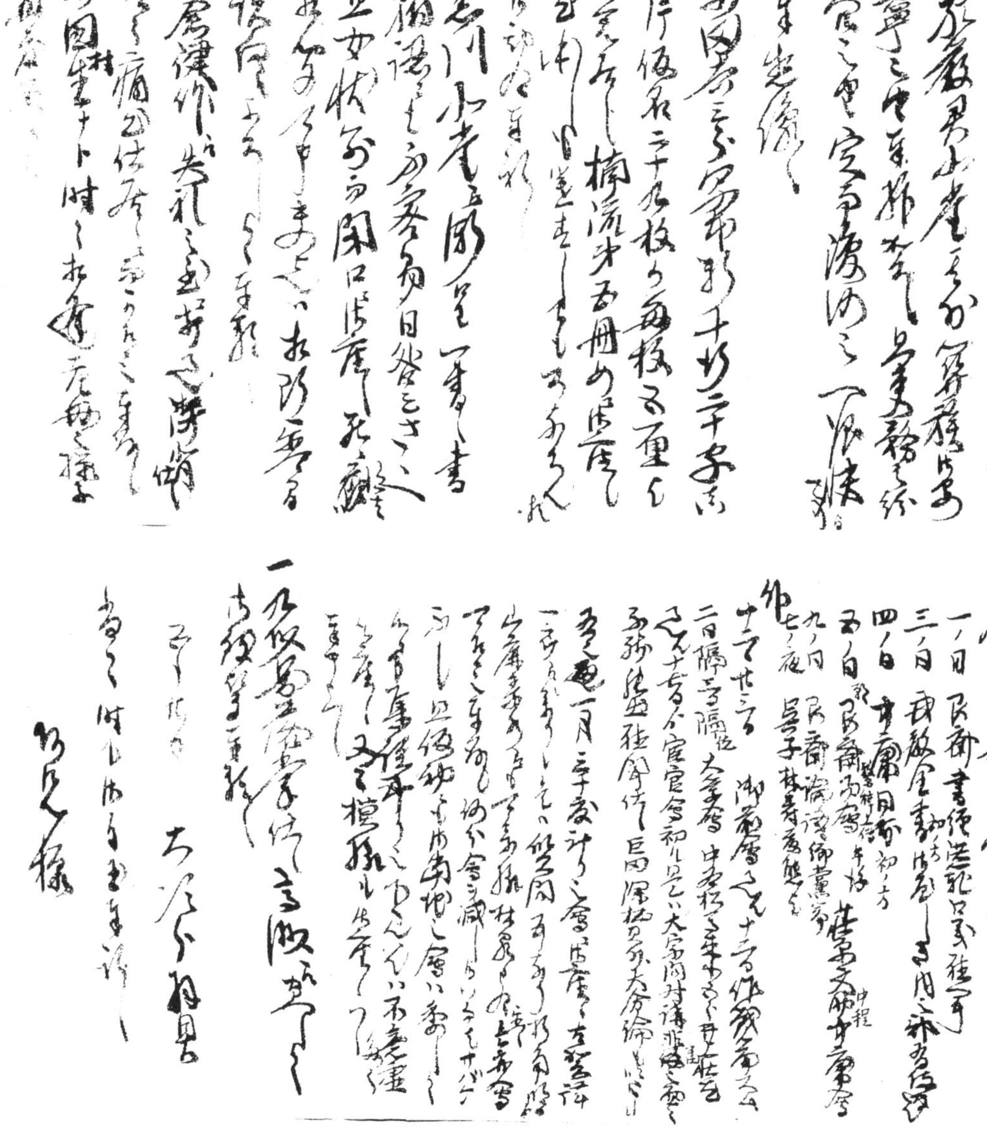

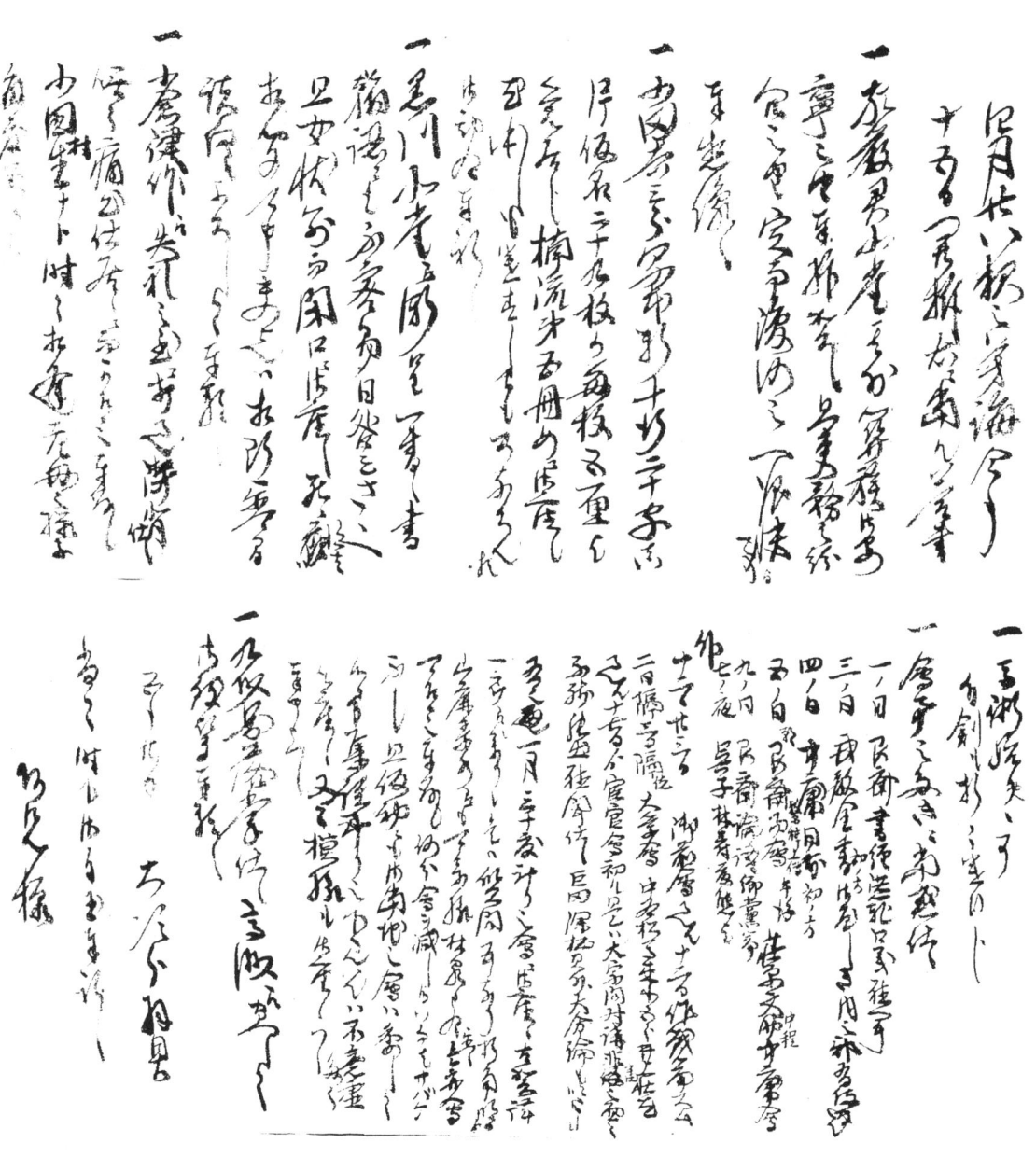

兄宛の書状（江戸での猛勉強ぶりを示す兄宛の手紙）

A letter from Shouin Yoshida to his elder brother, Umetarou Sugi, dated May 20, 1851. This letter is filled with fraternal affection.

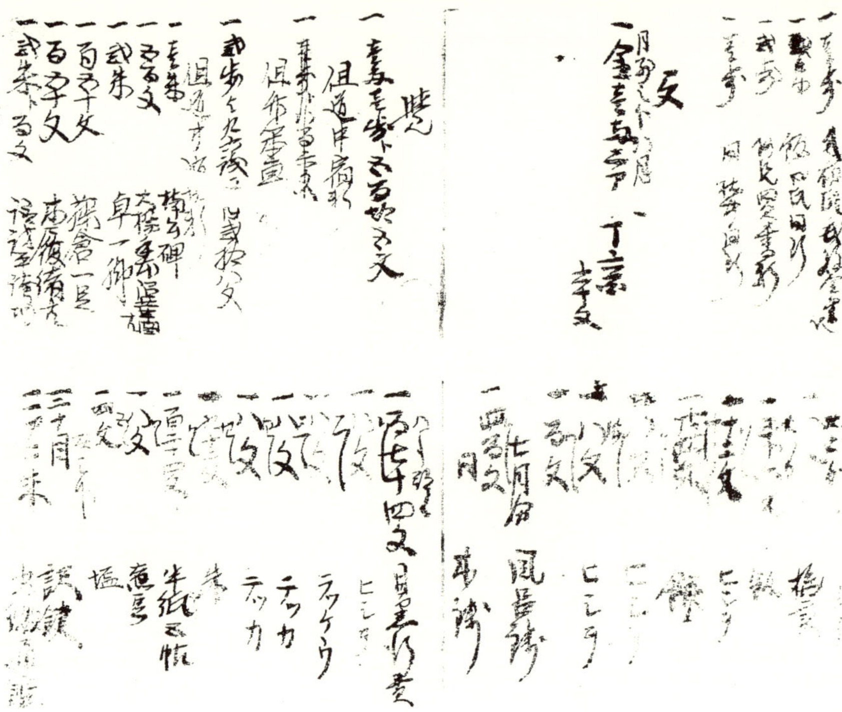

江戸遊学費用録

Memorandum (Ledger) of expenses for studying in Edo (Tokyo)

江戸遊学中費用録

嘉永四年辛亥

費用録

口腹の欲は感に応じて発す、斯の録を見るや泯然として沮喪す。

吉田大次郎

覚

一、壱歩　周布氏武教全書代

一、弐朱　飯田氏同断

一、弐歩　阿兄買書料

一、壱歩　同社中同断

受

一、金壱両二歩□丁六百六十文

月別の分八月□

覚

一、壱両壱歩と五百拾五文
　但し道中宿料

一、四百六拾八文
　但し竹笨車料

一、壱歩と九六銭弐百弐拾八文
　但し道中宿料

一、壱朱　楠公碑

一、五百文　大橋手本、沿革図共

一、弐朱　卓一脚

一、百五十文　藤倉一足

一、百五十文　木履、緒共

一、弐朱と百文　諏訪平袴地

一、四十文　餅

一、（廿七日）八文　梅実

一、（廿八日）五十六文　飯

一、（同日）十二文　ひしほ

一、（廿九日）廿四文　餅

一、（同日）八文　ひしほ

一、（晦日）八文　ひしほ

一、（同日）百文　七月分風呂銭

一、（同日）四百文（七月分）　同　木銭

一、（八月朔日）百七十四文　目黒行費

一、（同日）八文　ひしほ

一、（二日）八文　らっけう

一、（三日）八文　てっか

一、（四日）八文　てっか

一、（四日）九十二文　朱

一、（同日）百二十四文　半紙五帖

一、（同日）八文　煮豆

一、（五日）四文　塩

一、（此じ下）二十目　訳鍵

一、一歩二朱　少微通鑑

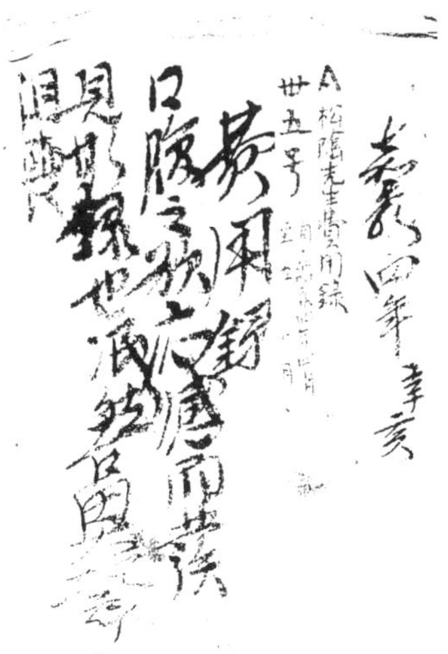

「江戸遊学願」の許可がおり、藩主の参勤の列に従って行く藩士
中谷忠兵衛の「冷飯」となった。「冷飯」とは藩主の行列には加わらず
藩士の食客として行列を共にするものである。
上表は松陰が嘉永四年即ち 1851 年 3 月 5 日　萩出発から江戸に到着後
8 月 25 日までの金銭出納帳である。遊学の身として実に倹約な生活とし、
書籍や学用品に最も費やしている。記録中の「訳鍵」とはオランダ語の字
典であり、兵学者の松陰が蘭学を研究していたことが判る。

Shouin Yoshida, when allowed by the Lord to study in Edo, went to Edo as a "Hiyameshi" of Chuubei Nakaya, a retainer, who was a member of the procession of Sankin-koutai, a rule or system of the Tokugawa Shogunate, whereby feudal lords had to reside in Edo in alternate years. "Hiyameshi" is not a regular member of the procession, but a person who takes part in the procession as a dependant on the retainer. The above list is a cash book which Shouin Yoshida kept from March 5th when he departed Hagi to August 25th after he reached Edo in 1851. This cash book shows that he was quite economical and spent money mainly for books and school supplies. "Yakuken" in the cash book is a dictionary for Dutch. It shows that Shouin Yoshida, a strategist, had studied "Rangaku (Western learning)".

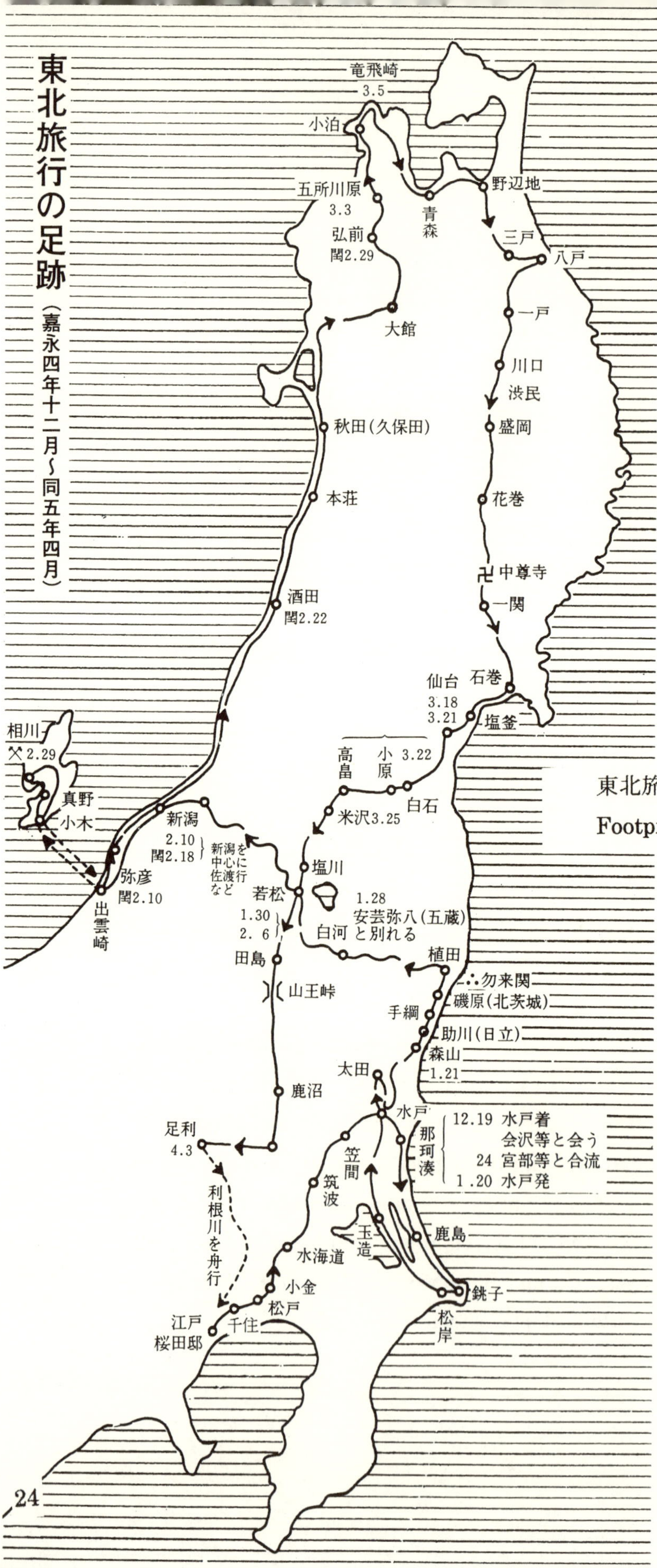

東北旅行の足跡
Footprint in Trip Tohoku.

東北旅行の足跡

The course Shouin Yoshida followed when he traveled in the Tohoku district (the northeast part of Japan).

東北遊日記は江戸遊学中の松陰が嘉永四年 1852 年 12 月 14 日から翌年 4 月 5 日まで友人の肥後藩士宮部鼎蔵(1820_1864)と同行して東北を遊歴したときの旅行記録である。出発前に友人江幡五郎の仇討援助（南部藩内訌）問題に関係し、過書(幕府の通過証明書)を待たずに出発、藩邸を亡命する形となった。

旅自体は水戸学にも接し国史へ開眼するなど収穫は大きかったが、江戸藩邸に戻ったあと、直ちに帰国命令が出され世禄は没収、一介の浪人となった。脱藩が如何に重大な罪になるかを知悉していた松陰が、何故この挙に出たのかは現在でも謎とされている。

"A Sketch of My Journey in the Tohoku District" is a record of travel written by Shouin Yoshida when he made a trip to the Tohoku district together with Teizou Miyabe, who was one of his friends and a retainer of the Higo Domain (now Kumamoto Prefecture) from December 14, 1852 to April 5, 1853 during his stay in Edo. This trip resulted in Yoshida's secession from his feudal domain because of his leaving Edo without a passport. The real reason was that, before leaving Edo, he concerned himself with the problem of revenging Gorou Ebata, who was one of his friends.

The trip itself gave him a deep understanding of the Mito school and opened his eyes to the history of Japan. But as soon as he returned to Edo, a command was issued... an order that he return to Choushuu domain. In addition, he forfeited his salary and was dismissed by his Lord. It is a mystery why he behaved so unwisely though he had a full knowledge of how his feudal domain dealt with the crime of secession.

東北遊歴のため亡命(脱藩)した松陰に対し、藩が下した裁断の申渡書。
父杉百合之介の「育」(ハグクミ)の身となった。

The Domain Government passed judgment on Yoshida's leaving Choushuu and travellling in the Tohoku district without the permission of the Lord. This is the written judgment. He was placed in "Supervision" under his father.

亡命裁断書

右軍学稽古の為め江戸差登され居り候処、去る亥の十二月十四日稽古切手を以て御門外罷り出で、暮に及び候ても帰り申さず候に付き、揚り切手に相成り候。尤も固屋内其の外只今迄懸り合之れなき段支配証人役より申出で候由、同十五日御目付方より申出で之れあり、（猶ほ居合せの親類児玉初之進よりも右に付き心当りの先々相尋ね候へども、一向行衛相分かり申さず候由、同日申出で候。）

（中略）

（之れに依り重き仰付けられ方も之れある儀に候へども）、前非を悔い立ち帰り、且つ宮部鼎蔵より内々断りの趣も之れあり、御不審の筋之れなく候に付き、格別の御了簡を以て御家人召放たれ候事。

右、申渡さるべく候。

The Domain's judgment on his leaving Choushuu without the Lord's permission

示諸友詩

余逋亡の罪を以て、壬子（嘉永五）十二月八日籍を削られ禄を奪わる。此れを賦して諸友に示す。

士窮して節義を見、世乱れて忠臣を識る。
二語吾れ常に愛し、服膺してこれを紳に書す。
四海鏡と澄みて二百春、豊禄幾人か祖勲を襲ぐ。
時平かにして復た将を斬り、旗を搴るの事なし。
政清くして寧んぞ闥を排し、裾を曳くの人あらんや。
魚は躍り龍は潜み皆自得し、恩波浩蕩として豈に垠あらんや。
嗟吾れ狂頑家門を覆し、俯仰何の面あって乾坤に対せん。
吾が罪万死猶お尚お軽し、放逐況や自在の身を賜わるをや。
艱難崎嶇は問うところに非ず、誓って節義を蓄い国恩に報いん。
人の与に傭作す匡衡にあり、弟子の都養となる乃ち児寛。
孫敬は戸を閉ざして縄を頸に繋け、仲舒は帷を下して園を窺わず。
青史に記載するところ、一々吾が真を養う。
一朝業成らば故山に臥し、松陰梅下の烏角巾。
時に世事に向って頽波を廻らし、且つ古道のために糾紛を解かん。
君を致し民を沢むはやんぬると雖も、説を立て世を済うは尚お言うべし。
是れありてこそ死後祖に謝すべく、是れありてこそ生前君に負かざらん。
敢えて途に窮し窮に堪えざるがために、節を屈し義を失いて徒らに沈淪せんや。
客あり我れを誡む語諄々、努力して恩光の新たなるを邀うべしと。
主人答えず愧面に満つ、此の言吾れに到るは果して何の因ぞ。
寧んぞ忍びんや百年報国の志、翻って一身禄利の間に陥るに。　未定

示諸友詩

Poetry to friends

亡命の罪で浪人の身となった松陰がその感懐を諸友に示した詩。

原本は鎌倉の瑞泉寺にあり、伯父の竹院和尚に示した模様である。

Shouin expressed his feelings to his friends when he was a lordless samurai (having been dismissed by his Lord) due to his leaving his Domain without permission of the Lord. The original work is in custody of Zuisenji temple in Kamakura. It seems that he showed it to Priest Chikuin, his uncle.

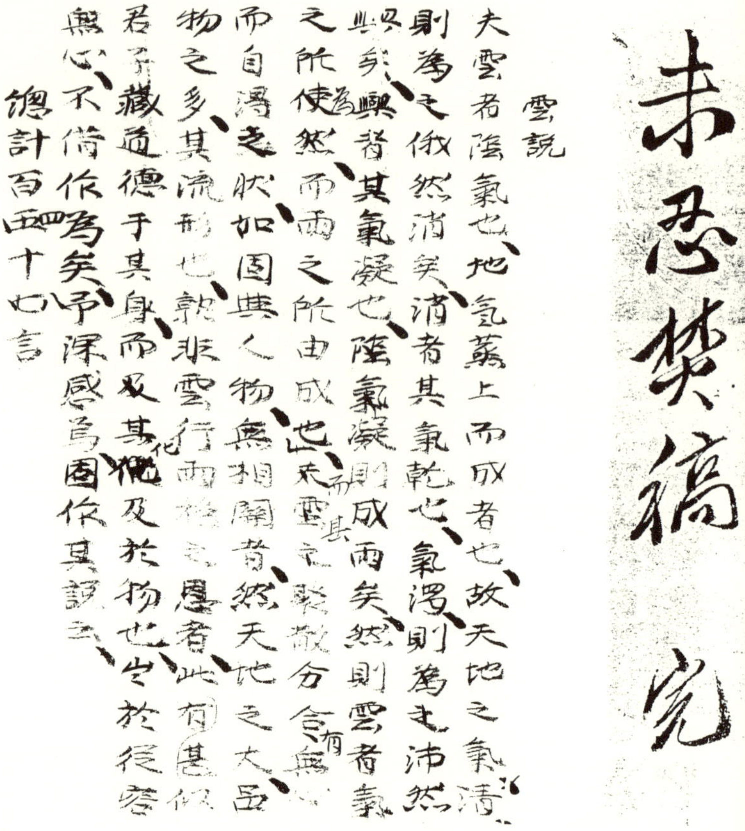
未忍焚稿

雲説

夫雲者陰氣也、地氣蒸上而成者也、故天地之氣清則為之俄然消矣、消者其氣乾也、氣濁則為之沛然興矣、興者其氣凝也、陰氣凝則成雨矣、然則雲者氣之所使然、而雨之所由成也、夫雲之聚散分合、無心而自得之於如固與人物無相関者、然天地之大、品物之多、其流形也、孰非雲行雨施之恩者、此有甚似君子蔵道徳于其身而及其化及於物也、豈於従容無心、不借作為矣、予深感焉、因作其説云、

總計百四十七言

未忍焚稿

雲の説

夫れ雲は陰気なり、地気蒸上して成りしものなり。故に天地の気清まば、則ち俄然消ゆ。消ゆるは其の気乾けるなり。気濁ならば則ち沛然と興る。興るは其の気凝れるなり。凝らば則ち雨と成る。然らば則ち雲は気の為る所にして、雨の由つて成る所なり。而して其の聚散分合、無心にして自得の状あり、固より人物と相関なきもの、如し。然れども天地の大なる、品物の多き、其の形を流くや、孰れか雲行雨施の恩に非ざるものならんや。此れ甚だ君子の道徳を其の身に蔵して、其の化の物に及ぶや、従容無心にて出でて作為を借らざるに似たるあり。予、深くこれに感ず、因つて其の説を作ると云ふ。

未忍焚稿

The anthology called “Mininfunkou”

家に伝わり代々収めてきた世襲的な特定の学問(家学)に関する詩文集。

松陰 16 歳から 21 歳までの作品で、学問の態度を知る重要文献である。

This is one of the anthologies on the hereditary and specific learning (Family learning) handed down from generation to generation.

This work was written by Shouin Yoshida from the ages of 16 to 21 and is considered to be very important and essential for his finding his academic approach.

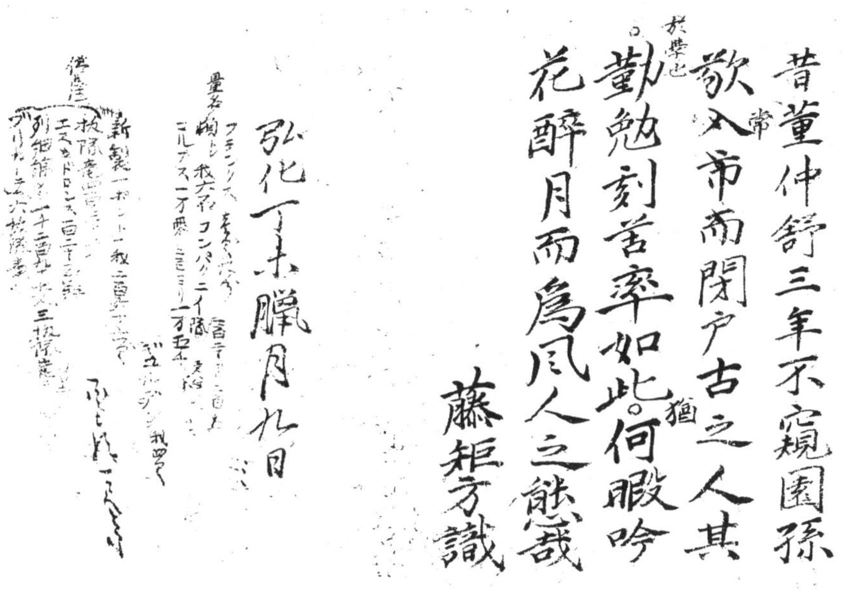
昔董仲舒三年不窺園孫
敬常入市而閉戸古之人其
勤勉刻苦卒如此猶何暇吟
花酔月而為風人之態哉
藤矩方識
弘化丁未臘月九日

自警語

A note of self-caution

中国・前漢時代の大学者で「新儒学の創始者」である董仲舒(BC179_BC104)らの｛研究のためには三年間庭を眺めず｝とか｛常に戸を閉ざして刻苦勉励す｝といった逸話、故事に松陰は痛く感じ、当時の風流文雅の風潮に抗し、大いに実学に励むことを決意したときのもの。

Shouin Yoshida was strongly impressed by anecdotes and historical sayings such as “Study hard without looking at your garden for three years.” and "Work diligently with the door always closed." These are mottoes of Dong Zhongxu (179 BC - 104 BC), who was a scholar in Former Han (Old China) and the founder of New Confucianism. He resisted the trends of taste and elegance at that time and decided to study practical hard science.

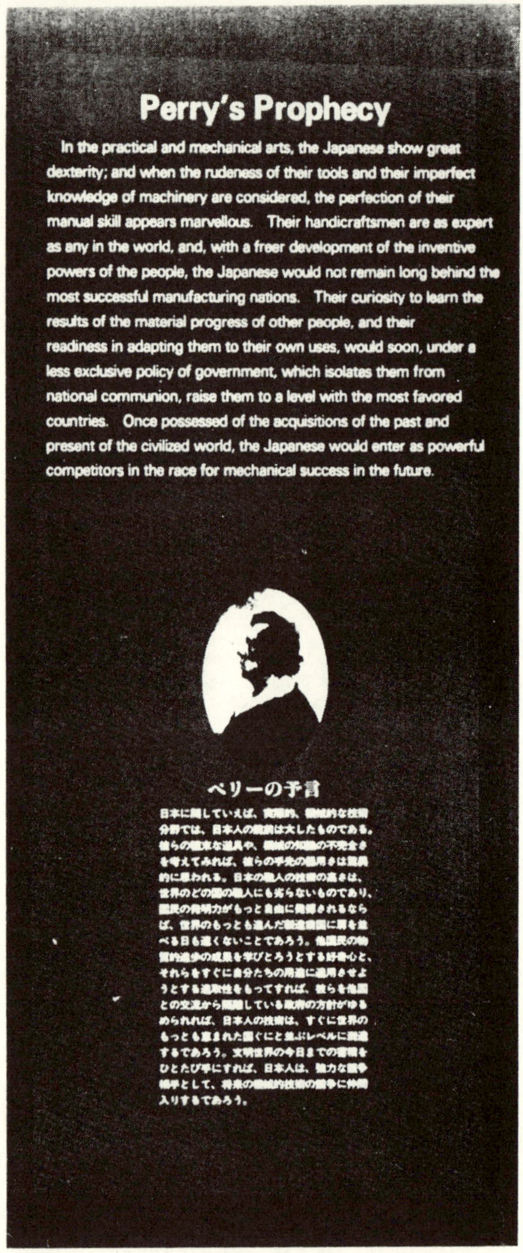

ペリー来航。
Visit of Commodore
M.C. Perry to Japan (1794_1858)

M.C. Perry was a U.S. naval officer who urged Japan to open the country to the Western world more than 200 years after the beginning of national seclusion. Perry, a veteran of the Mexican War, was appointed in 1852 to lead a fleet to urge Japan to open its country to diplomatic and commercial exchange between the United States and Japan. Perry set sail late in 1852 and arrived at Edo Bay on July 8, 1853, subsequently delivering his credentials and his president's letter with great pomp and ceremony.

THE ILLUSTRATED LONDON NEWS.

THE UNITED STATES EXPEDITION TO JAPAN.

Illustrated London News, 7 May 1853.

Perry drawn by a Japanese
at the reception, Yokohama,March 1854.

日本の国情に無関係に、ペリー来航の目的は、一つは太平洋で操業しているアメリカ捕鯨船の安全確保であった。何故なら当時米国は世界一の捕鯨国であったからである。もう一つの目的は中国でアヘン戦争が勃発し、アメリカも東洋進出のバスに乗り遅れないため、先ず日本と通商を確立し極東に足場を築くためである。この目的遂行のため大蒸気船を建造させ、大砲には弾丸をこめ、兵士達に最高の戦闘体制をとった。

The Perry visit to Japan had two purposes, apart from the state of affairs in Japan. One was to ensure the security of U.S. whaling ships operating in the Pacific at that time, since the US was the biggest whaling country in the world. Another purpose was to establish a framework for a trade relationship with Japan in the Far East so as to keep up with other countries making inroads into Oriental markets. To achieve these goals, Perry came to Japan at the head of a fleet with artilleries loaded with shells and troops in their highest combat readiness.

蓮台寺の松陰

Shouin Yoshida in Rendaiji Temple

人物画、歴史画、武者画などをよく描いた日本画家・前田青邨(1885_1977)が、松陰の下田出国事件を題材として 1967 年 82 歳時に描いたもの。
下田近郊の蓮台寺温泉の村山家にあった松陰の机や行燈から画想を得た。
机上の書物は松陰が江戸から携行した「唐詩選掌故」である。

This portrait of Shouin Yoshida was drawn by the Japanese painter and artist Seison Maeda (1885 - 1977), who is famous for portrait painting, history painting, warrior painting, and so on. It was done in 1967, when he was 82 years old. He drew this portrait using the incident of Yoshida's attempting to go abroad from Shimoda as material for a painting based on a painting image from his desk and "andon (oil lamp stand with wood frame and paper shade)" which were kept in custody by the Murayama family in the spa of Rendaiji Temple in the suburb of Shimoda.

The book in the painting is [Tangshixuan Zhanggu], which Shouin Yoshida brought from Edo.

将及私言

Private suggestion to the Lord

ペリー来航を　浦賀で直接視察、久里浜の日米会見を観衆の一人として見学した松陰は、日本の危機を傍観できず、浪人の身でありながら意見書を藩主に匿名で上書した。

ここでペリーの要求に対する幕府の外交姿勢を批判している。ただこの時点では幕府をまだ敬重すべき権威として認めているものの、同時に幕府に対置する朝廷の存在を示し、日本国は幕府の私領ではないと明言した。長い封建体制で定着している諸概念を根底から覆す新しい国体観を提示した。

将及私言

謹んで按ずるに、外夷の患由来する所久し、固より今日に始まるに非ざるなり。然れども今般亜美理駕夷の事、実に目前の急、乃ち万世の患なり。六月三日、夷舶浦賀港に来りしより、日夜疾走し彼の地に至り其の状態を察するに、軽蔑侮慢、実に見聞に堪へざる事どもなり。然るに戦争に及ばざるは、幕府の令、夷の軽蔑侮慢を甘んじ、専ら事穏便を主とせられし故なり。然らずんば今已に戦争に及ぶこと久しからん。然れども往事は姑く置く。夷人幕府に上る書を観るに、和友

（後略）

Shouin Yoshida observed the Perry fleet in Uraga firsthand with his own eyes and was a spectator to the progress of the Perry meetings at Kurihama. He couldn't sit as a spectator to the crisis that Japan confronted, however, and presented a statement of his views on July 3, 1853 to his former Lord anonymously though he was a lordless samurai (having been dismissed by his Lord). In his statement, he criticized the diplomatic attitude of the Shogunate toward Perry's demands regarding the opening of ports of Japan.

At this point in time, he recognized the Shogunate as a respectable authority, and at the same time, he touched on the existence of the Court confronting the Shogunate, and asserted that Japan was not the private property of the Shogunate. He illuminated a new national structure which might radically overthrow the various concepts that had held the Japanese people down under a long feudal system.

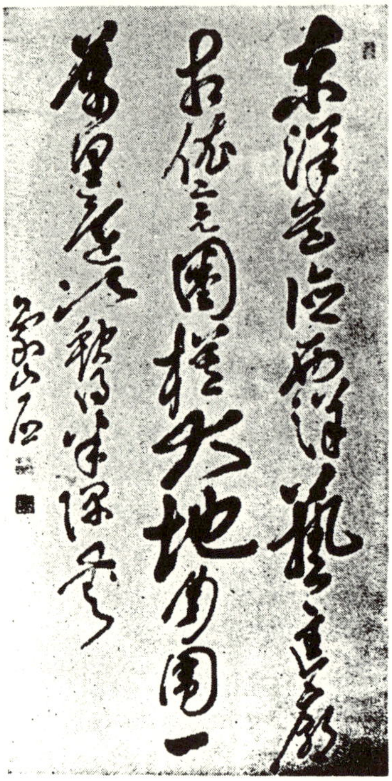

佐久間象山の書と絵

Poem and painting of Shouzan Sakuma.

松陰の師であり、思想的に大きな影響を与えた佐久間象山は開国論者であった。幕末期に生涯、終始開国論を主張したのは象山だけの模様である。「東洋の道徳、西洋の芸術」とは佐久間象山の言葉（左上/像山書幅）で、西洋の科学技術（芸術）を積極的に取り入れようとした。
ペリー来航に際し、「急務十条」を老中阿部正弘に献策し、海軍と沿岸防備を主張、海防に定見を持つ兵学者であった象山に対し、砲術の教えをうけるため橋本左内、吉田松陰、河井継之助、勝海舟、坂本竜馬など幕末の諸国の俊英達がその門を叩いている。当時、海防こそ国の要と心を砕き、海軍の設置を念ずるあまり、書斎を「海舟書屋」と名付けたほどである。下田で国禁を犯して事件をおこす直前、象山は松陰に物心両面にわたる細かな世話をした。松陰と金子重輔の密航未遂事件に連座して伝馬町に投獄させられたが、あくまで鎖国の愚かしさを主張し、毅然としてその非を認めようとはしなかった。象山は国禁を犯す松陰に対し

「法は人間が作り、それは時代と共に変わるものだ」と説いていた。

Shouzan Sakuma (1811_1864), who was a mentor of Shouin Yoshida and greatly influenced him in his ideology, wanted to get rid of the policy of seclusion and open the country to the world. It seems to be only Shouzan Sakuma who kept such a policy unchanged until he died in the last days of the Tokugawa Shogunate.

Since Shouzan Sakuma was a strategist having a definite view on coastal defense, extraordinary characters of the whole country in the last days of the Shogunate called on him to ask for instruction on gunnery- many young brilliant persons including Sanai Hashimoto, Shouin Yoshida, Tsugunosuke Kawai, Kaishuu Katsu, Ryouma Sakamoto.

He always racked his brains about how to complete armaments for coastal defense and called his den "Kaishuu Shoya (Navy Office)" because of his obsession with the establishment of the navy.

Just before the incident at Shimoda in which Shouin Yoshida tried to violate the national prohibition on going abroad, Shouzan Sakuma warmly took care of Shouin Yoshida and Juusuke Kaneko both physically and spiritually. Although he was also arrested on suspicion of being implicated in the incident and thrown into prison, he insisted on the stupidity of a policy of seclusion and resolutely refused to acknowledge his and their behaviors as wrong.

Shouzan Sakuma asserted to Shouin who violated the national prohibition as follows:

"Laws are made by man and vary with the times."

佐久間象山

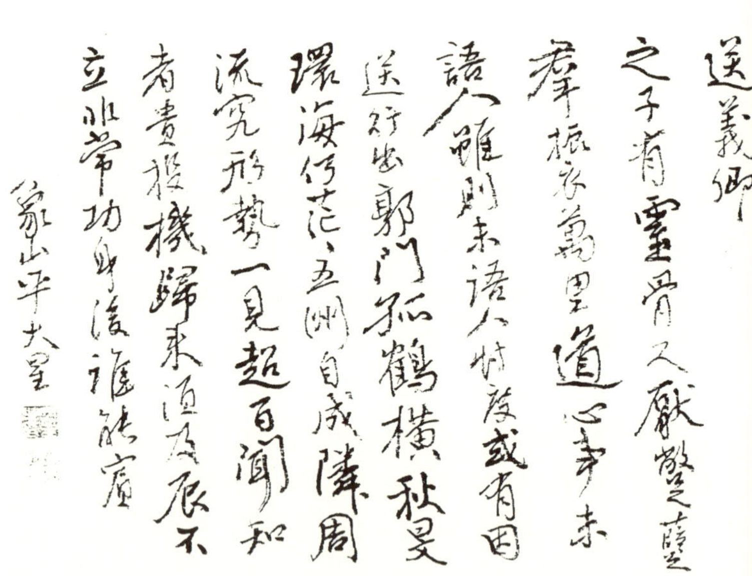

送義卿
之子有靈骨久厭蹩躄羣
振衣萬里道心事未語人
雖則未語人忖度或有因
送行出郭門孤鶴横秋旻
環海何茫茫五洲自成隣
周流究形勢一見超百聞
知者貴投機歸來須及辰
不立非常功身後誰能賓
象山平大星

義卿を送る

之の子霊骨あり、久しく躄躄の群を厭う。
衣を奮う万里の道、心事未だ人に語げず。
則ち未だ人に語げずと雖も、忖度或は因るあり。
行くを送って郭門を出ずれば、孤鶴秋旻に横たわる。
環海何ぞ茫々たる、五州自ら隣を為す。
周流形勢を究めよ、一見は百聞に超ゆ。
智者は機に投ずるを貴び、帰来須らく辰に及ぶべし。
非常の功を立てずんば、身後誰れか能く賓せん。

象山平大星

佐久間象山送別詩

A farewell poem dedicated to Shouin Yoshida from Shouzan Sakuma in 1853.

オランダ文字（嘉永四年七月以降）

松陰のオランダ語研究は萩に居たころから始まっており、藩医田原玄周に手ほどきを受けた。江戸に出て「遊学日記」中にもあり、五月二十八日から蘭語を学び始め佐久間象山に学ぶようになったのは七月二十日からである。松陰は身辺多事で余り熱心ではなかった。これは故紙中から発見されたもの。ここにあるオランダ語を日本語に釈すと、下のようになる。

behooren	（属する）
eigenlyk	（固有の）
ongefruikelyke	（使用せざる異常の）
enkelvouduc	（単数の）
eerste	（第一の）

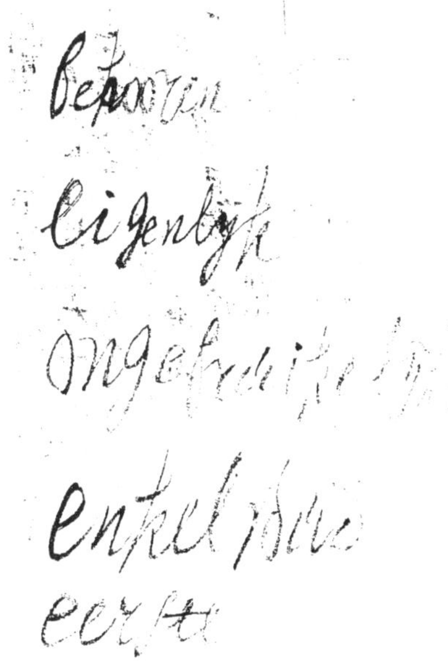

松陰のオランダ文字

Dutch literature of Shouin Yoshida

さくま しょうざん　佐久間象山　1811～64（文化8～元治1）幕末期の思想家・兵学者。㊋信濃国松代藩5両5人扶持の給人佐久間国善の子。妻順子（瑞枝）は勝海舟の妹。㊤信濃国埴科郡松代。㊔国忠、のち啓、幼名啓之助、通称修理、字は子迪・子明。〈ぞうざん〉ともいう。‖16歳で藩老鎌原桐山の門に入り、経義・文章を学び、1833（天保4）江戸に出て佐藤一斎に詩文を学ぶ。'35帰藩して御城付月並講釈助を命ぜられた。'39再び江戸へ出て神田お玉ヶ池に塾を開設。'41藩主真田幸貫が老中となり、翌年海防掛となると、命をうけて海外事情を研究して「海防八策」を上書。また江川太郎左衛門（英龍）に入門して砲術を修める。'43郡中横目付となり、洋学による殖産興業を藩に建議し、翌年黒川良庵に蘭学を学ぶ。沓野村など3か村利用掛となって山村の開発に着手したが農民の反対にあって失敗。'53米艦の来航により藩の軍議役に任ぜられ、また「急務十条」を老中阿部正弘に上書した。またガラスを製し、砲を鋳造、「増訂和蘭語彙」の出版計画をたて、牛痘種の導入を図るなど多角的な活躍を示す。'54吉田松陰の事件に連座して江戸小伝馬町の獄に入り、松代に蟄居を命ぜられる。'62蟄居赦免となり長州・土佐藩より招聘を受ける。'64幕命により上洛、山階宮・一橋慶喜に謁し時務を論ず。また将軍徳川家茂・中川宮にも謁す。7月京都三条木屋町で暗殺され、知行・屋敷地とも召上げられた。「省諐録」「礮学図編」などの著作がある。㊢「増訂象山全集」全5巻，

投夷書（安政元年三月十一日）

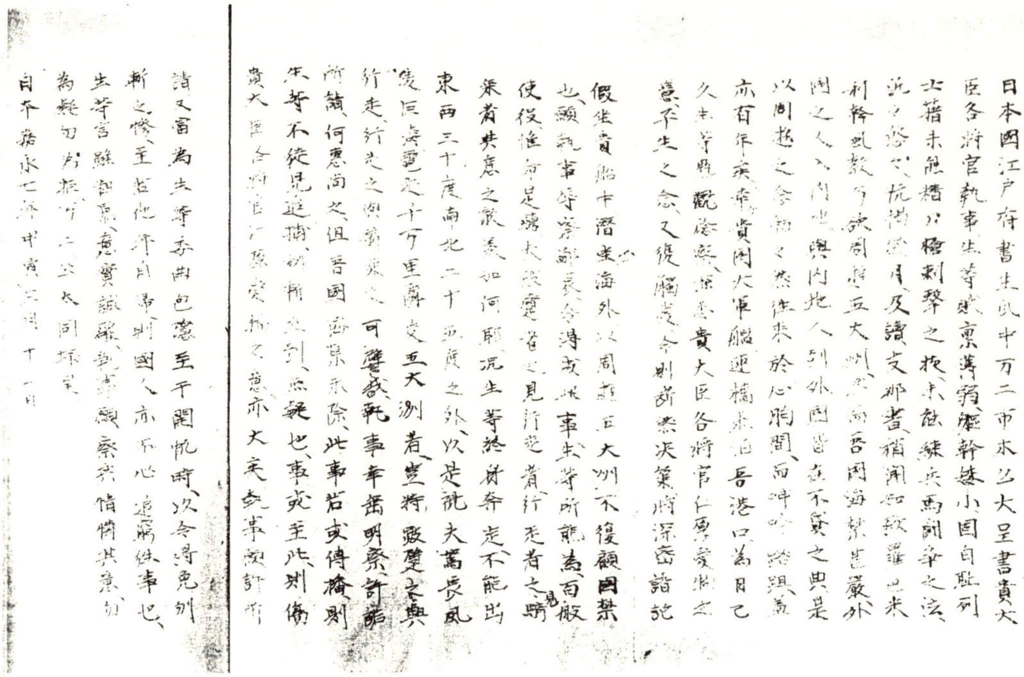
日本國江戸府書生瓜中万二市木公太呈書貴大
臣各將官執事生等賦稟薄弱軀幹矮小固自恥列
於士籍未能精刀槍擊刺之技未能練兵馬鬪爭之法
汎汎悠悠玩愒歳月及讀支那書稍聞知歐羅巴米
利幹風教乃欲周遊五大洲然而吾國海禁甚嚴外
國之人入内地與内地人到外國皆在不貸之典是
以周遊之念勃勃然往來於心胸間而呻吟躑躅蓋
亦有年矣幸貴國大軍艦連檣來泊吾港口爲日已
久生等熟觀縱察深感貴大臣各將官仁厚愛物之
意平生之念又復勃發今則斷然決策將深密請託
假坐貴船中潛出海外以周遊五大洲不復顧國禁
也願執事等容鄙衷令得成此事生等所能爲百般
使役惟命是聽夫跛躄者之見行走者行走者之見騎
乘者其意之欣羨如何耶況生等終身奔走不能出
東西三十度南北二十五度之外以是視夫駕長風
凌巨濤電走千万里鄰交五大洲者豈將跛躄之與
行走行走之與騎乘也可譬哉執事幸垂明察許諾
所請何慮尚之但吾國海禁未除此事若或傳播則
生等不徒見追捕刎斬無疑也事若至此則傷
貴大臣各將官仁厚愛物之意亦大矣執事願許所
請又當爲生等秘此事至于開帆時以令得免刎
斬之慘至若他年自歸則國人亦不必追究往事也
生等言雖粗鹵意實誠確執事願察其情憐其意勿
爲疑勿爲拒万二公太同拜呈
日本嘉永七年甲寅三月十一日

投夷書

A letter to the US fleet asking permission to travel with them to overseas countries

この書状は安政元年3月6日に草稿を書き、翌日、佐久間象山に加筆してもらった。そして3月27日、伊豆下田にて米軍将校のポケットに入れて立ち去り、当日夜、停泊中の米軍艦にむけ出国の挙を決行した。

This letter was written by Shouin Yoshida as a draft on March 6, 1854, and was touched up by Shouzan Sakuma. The next day, on March 27, at Shimoda, Shizuoka prefecture, he secretly left it in the pocket of a U.S. officer. During the night of the same day, he actually attempted to go abroad on a U.S. Flagship.

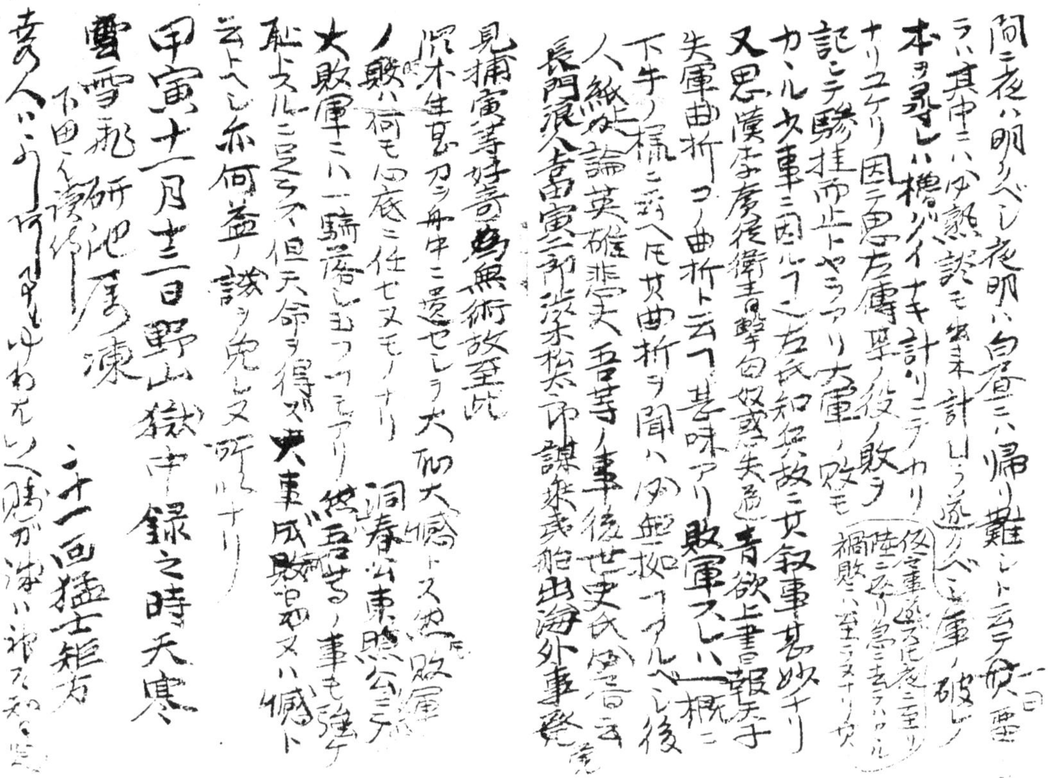

3 月 27 夜記

Record of the incident in the night of March 27.

松陰は金子重之助(1831_1855)と共に下田の米旗艦の船上に足跡を印した。しかしこの国禁を犯してまでの海外脱出には失敗した。松陰は野山獄でこの夜記を書いて事件の曲折と心情を明らかにした。

＊（文献 72 の中の「下田渡海考」によれば、松陰の黒船密航の目的は海外脱出より、むしろペリー刺殺の意図があったとの説を考察している)。

Shouin and Juusuke Kaneko(1831_1855) left their mark on the US Flagship in Shimoda. However the plan to oversea escape banned by state law was crushed. Shouin made the incident clear his heart and complications on this achieves at Noyama Jail, Hagi, Choushu(Now part of Yamaguchi prefecture).

[Depending on the study "Consideration stowed away to US black ship in Shimoda port" in bibliography 72 mentioned, the purpose Shouin stowed away did not get out of Japan but intend to stab Perry to death.]

下田獄中歌

A poem composed in Shimoda Jail

牢屋内で当時の心情を発露したもので、有名な詩歌が認めてある。
The following poem is famous for fully expressing his feelings at that time.

「かくすれば、かくなることと知りながら、止むに止まれぬ大和魂」

“ Even knowing that the end could come,
It could’t be held back the Yamato spirit !”

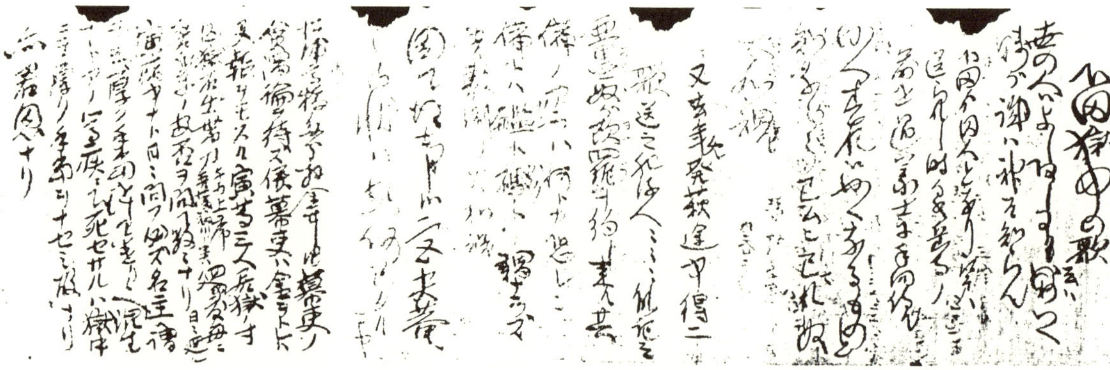

深いキリスト教信者であり、明治・大正期の教育家である新渡戸稲造(1862_1933)の歴史的英文名著「武士道」(Bushido; The Soul of Japan／1899年出版:文献46) によれば、上記の詩歌は次のごとく記されている。

“Full well I knew this course must end in death;
It was Yamato spirit urged me on
To dare whate’er betide” ____________________by Inazo Nitobe

本書中、武士道/Chivalryの道徳的体系で no-bless o-blige(ノーブレス・オブリージュ；高い身分に伴う義務)を詳述し、日本特有の語義として義／Rectitude or Justice,勇／courage,仁／Benevolence,礼／Politeness,誠／Veracity and Sincerity, 忠義／The Duty of Loyaltyなどの英語彙を使用している。

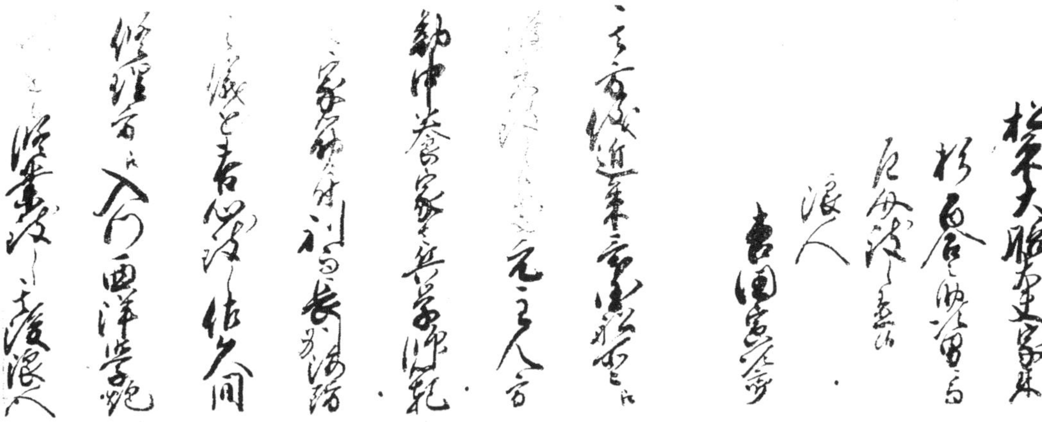

かねこ じゅうすけ　金子重輔　1831～55(天保2～安政2) 幕末期の志士。系長門国萩津守町の商人金子茂左衛門の長男。名貞吉、重之輔(助)、別称渋木松太郎，市木公太。‖初め萩で足軽奉公のあと，江戸に出て毛利藩邸の小者になる。学問に志して鳥山塾に入り，諸藩の志士とも交わる。やがて吉田松陰 に学び，1854(安政1)松陰と共に，伊豆国下田からアメリカ軍艦に乗り密航を企てたが失敗し，江戸へ送られたが，病気のため藩地に護送され，萩で獄死した。墓萩市沖ノ町の保福寺。参福本椿水「踏海志士金子重輔伝」1928。

幕府裁決書写

A Copy of the written verdict of the Shogunate

下田渡海事件で揚屋（未決囚用牢屋）に6ヶ月おり、9.18日幕府は松陰、重之助、象山ら連携者らに裁決を下し処罰した。松陰が予想していたより罪が軽かった。

On September 18, 1854, the Shogunate handed down a verdict of guilty on the Shimoda case to Shouin Yoshida, Shouzan Sakuma, Juusuke Kaneko and other persons concerned with the Shimoda affairs.

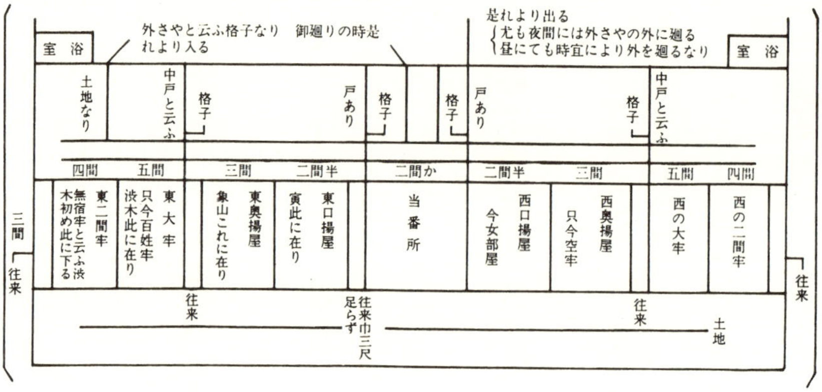

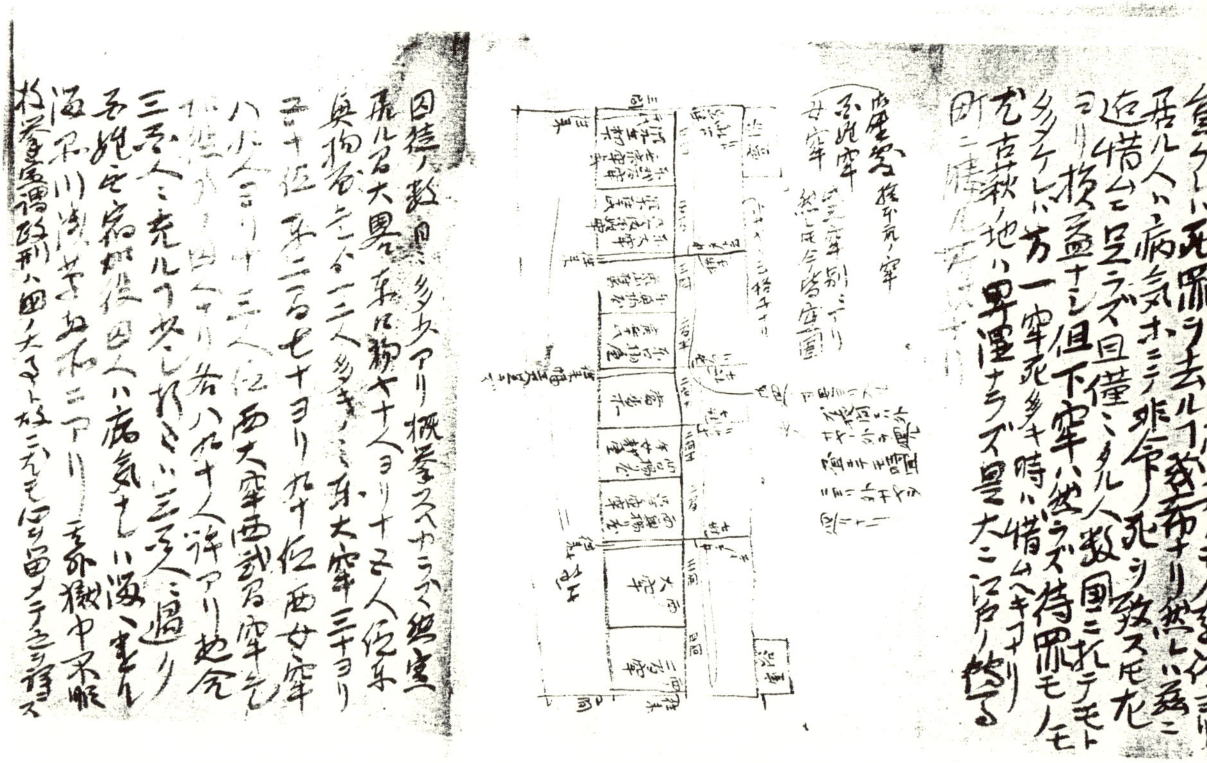

父あて書状の中の江戸獄舎

Edo Jail sketching in the letter to his father

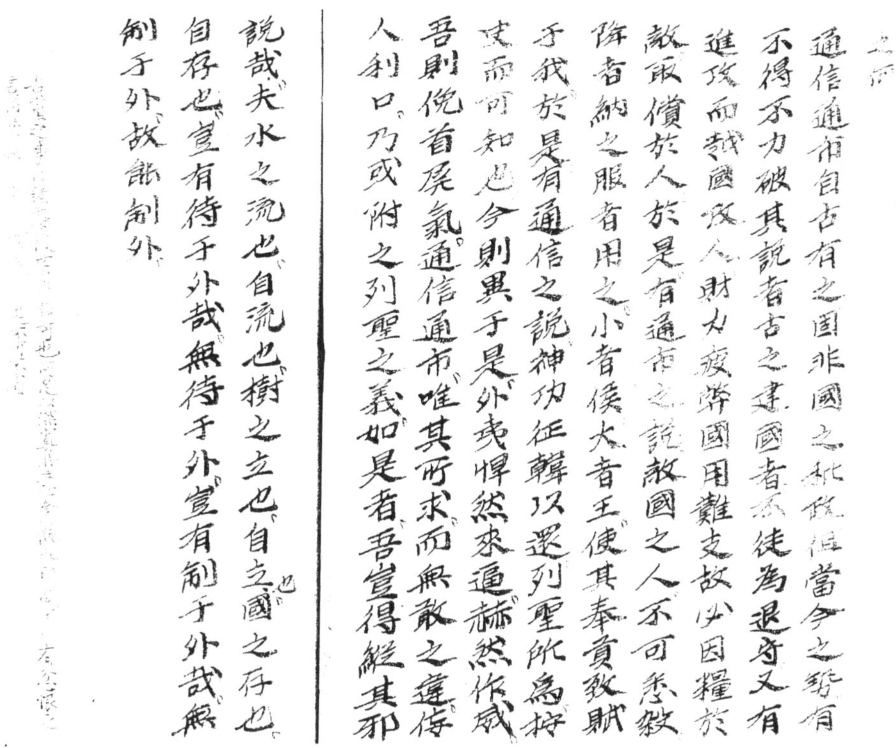
通信通市自古有之国非國之秕政但當今之勢有
不得不力破其説者古之建國者不徒為退守又有
進攻而裁國攻人財力疲弊國用難支故必因糧於
敵取償於人於是有通市之説敵國之人不可悉殺
降者納之服者用之小者侯大者王使其奉貢致賦
于我於是有通信之説神功征韓以還列聖所爲按
史而可知也今則異于是外夷悍然來逼赫然作威
吾則俛首屏氣通信通市唯其所求而無敢之違傍
人利口乃或附之列聖之義如是者吾豈得縱其邪
説哉夫水之流也自流也樹之立也自立也國之存也
自存也豈有待于外哉無待于外豈有制于外哉無
制于外故能制外

幽囚録

Captivity Document

幽囚録は、安政元年江戸獄から萩の野山獄へ移された後、松陰が下田出国事件の動機、思想的根拠、当時の国情を述懐したもので、著作中最も重要なものの一つである。積極的自主外交など国策の大要を述べている。
この書は松代で蟄居中の師の佐久間象山へ贈られた。このため最後に象山の添削批評が加えられている。

After having been transferred to Noyama Jail (Hagi)from a jail in Edo in the autumn of 1854, Yoshida wrote down his motivations and and the background to his idea about going to overseas countries from Shimoda and the state of national affairs at that time in the so-called "Captivity Document" in Noyama Jail. This is one of the most important documents in his literary works. In it, he proposed his own national policy for an assertive and independent diplomacy.

He presented this note to Shouzan Sakuma, his mentor, who was placed in confinement by the Shogunate in Matsushiro in Nagano Prefecture. Thus, Shouzan Sakuma corrected this document and added his comments to it in the final section.

二十一回猛士説

吾れ庚寅の年を以て杉家に生れ、已に長じて吉田家を嗣ぐ。甲寅の年、罪ありて獄に下る。夢に神人あり、与うるに一刺を以てす。文に曰く、二十一回猛士と。忽ち覚む。因つて思うに、杉の字二十一の象あり、吉田の字も亦二十一回の象あり。吾が名は寅、寅は虎に属す。虎の徳は猛なり。吾れ卑微にして孱弱、虎の猛を以て師と為すに非ずんば、安んぞ士たることを得ん。吾れ生来事に臨みて猛を為せしこと、凡そ三たびなり。而るに或は罪を獲、或は謗を取り、今は則ち獄に下りて復た為すあること能わず。而して猛の未だ遂げざるもの尚お十八回あり、其の責も亦重し。神人蓋し其の日に益々孱弱、日に益々卑微、終に其の遂ぐる能わざらんことを懼る。故に天意を以て之を啓きしのみ。然らば則ち吾れの志を蓄え気を並する。豈に已むことを得んや。

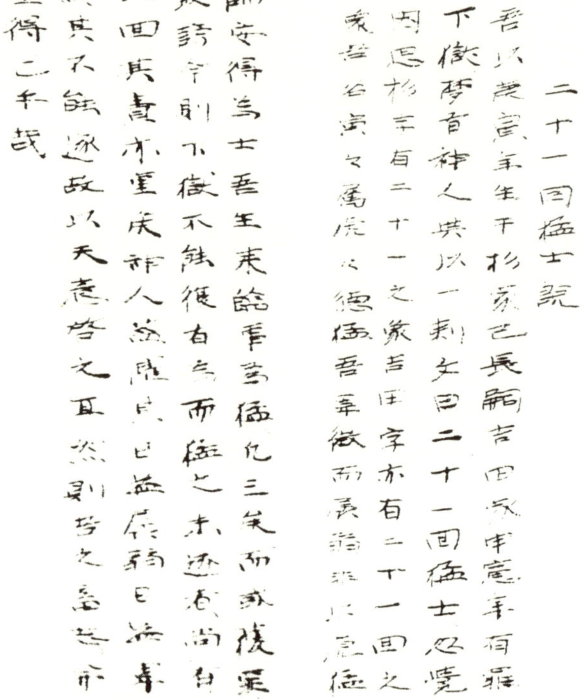

吉田松陰の名は矩方、字は子義または義卿。通称は幼時には虎之助、後に大次郎、松次郎といい最後に寅次郎と改めた。松陰は号である。
下田での出国未遂事件以後、二十一回猛士の別号を用いるようになった。

The first name of Shouin Yoshida was actually Norikata, which could be written with the kanji for Shigi or Gikei.

He was commonly called Toranosuke in his childhood. Later he was called Daijirou or Matsujirou, and in the end he changed his name to Torajirou. Shouin is a pen name. After he failed to go abroad at Shimoda, he used “Nijuikkai_moushi” as another pen name of his.

蘭の画稿

A sketch of an orchid

獄中の松陰は絵心を筆に託そうとした形跡がある。
この絵は 1855 年、清狂上人に贈る詩を中断し余白に蘭の花を描いたもの。

There is a sign that Yoshida, while in jail, wanted to convey his aptitude for painting in the trace of his paintbrush. This orchid was painted in the blank space made by discontinuing the writing of a poem, which was dedicated to the Seikyou holy priest in 1855.

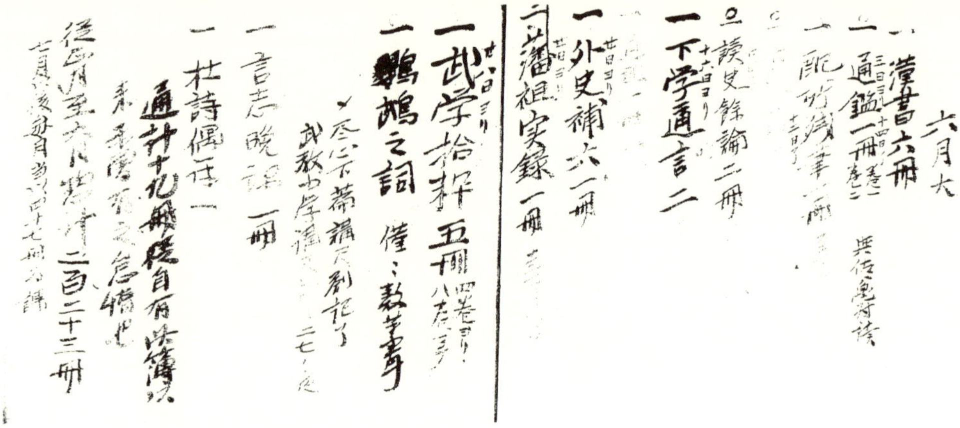

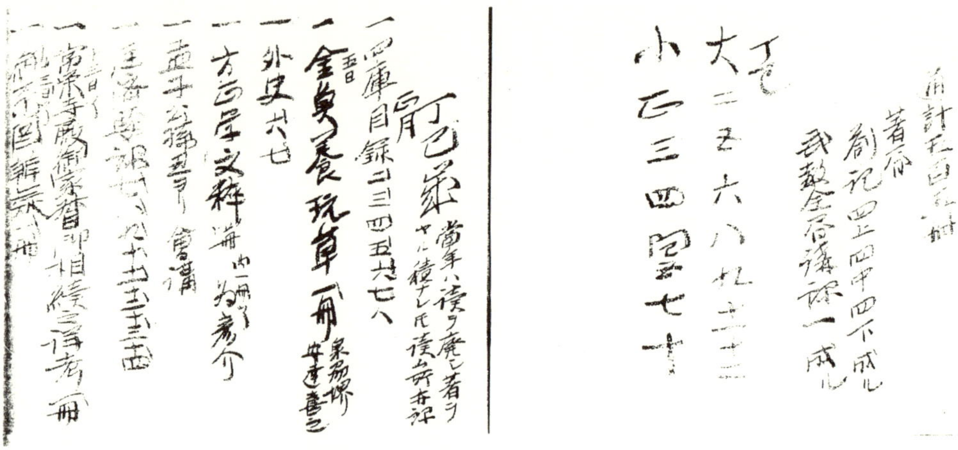

（前略）

六月大

〇一、漢書六冊　了

〇一、通鑑一冊巻三　佐々亀と対読す　三日より　十四日了

一、配所残筆一冊　七月に至り乃ち卒る

〇一、下学邇言三　一冊　家兄と校讎す　八日より　十二日了

〇一、読史余論二冊　了　二十日了

〇一、下学邇言二　一冊　十六日より　晦了

一、通鑑一冊巻三四

一、外史補六　一冊　二十日より

一、藩祖実録一冊　二十日より　七月に至り乃ち卒る

〇一、武学拾粋五冊四巻より八巻まで　二十八日より　晦了

〇一、鸚鵡の詞　僅々数葉のみ　了

〆尽心下篇講釈、劄記了る

武数小学講釈初る　二七の夜

〇一、言志晩録一冊　晦了

〇一、杜詩偶評一　晦了

通計十九冊　自ら此の簿を有してより以来、未曽有の怠惰なり

正月より六月に至る総計二百二十三冊、七月以後は毎月当に四十七冊を以て課す。

通計五百五冊

著書　劄記四上四中四下成ル　武教全書講録一成ル

丁巳

大　二五六八九十一十二

小　正三四閏五七十

丁巳歳　当年ハ読ヲ廃シ著ヲヤル積ナレトモ読ム所亦録

正月

一　四庫目録　二三四五六七八九　上帙子

一　（五日）金魚養玩草一冊　泉州堺 安達喜之

一　外史　六七

一　方正学文粋四冊内一冊了　為彦介

一　孟子公孫丑ヨリ会講

一　（了）経済要録七八九十十一十二十三十四

一　（十三日了）常栄寺殿御家督御相続之詳考一冊

一　（十三日了）御系図弁疑一冊

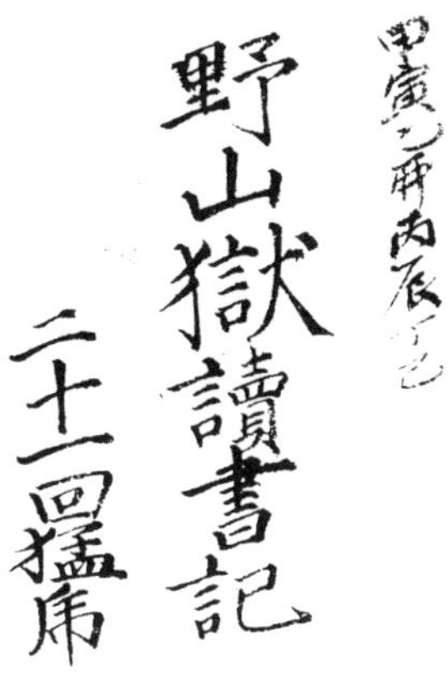

野山獄読書記

Notes on readings in Noyama Jail

松陰は野山獄においても学問に対する情熱は頗る旺盛で、結果的に最も充実した時期となった。囚人の好奇心もそそり、驚くべきことは牢屋が獄中座談会、読書会、学習会へと変遷し、松陰は次第に獄舎を学舎に変えてしまったことである。獄司までもが松陰に弟子入りし受講した。
彼の読書量も又安政元年 10 月からの約 3 年間で約 500 冊に及んだ。

While in Noyama Jail, Yoshida was full of enthusiasm for study. Consequently, the time in Noyama Jail was the richest in his life. His academic passion so influenced other inmates that it changed from an ordinary prison into something like Shouin Yoshida's private school for discussion, reading, and learning.

Eventually, even jail officers became his disciples and attended his lectures. He read approximately 500 books in three years beginning in October 1854.

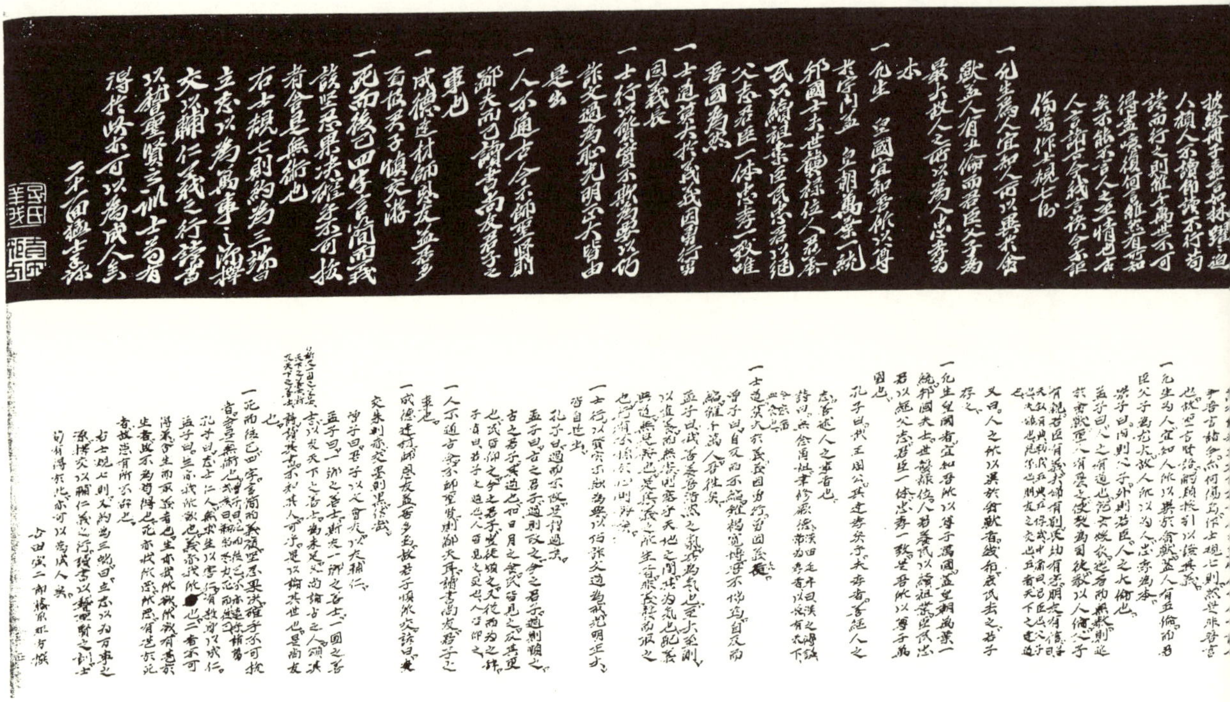

たまき ぶんのしん　玉木文之進　1810～76(文化7～明治9)幕末期の長州藩士。㊔吉田松陰 の父杉百合之助の弟。玉木氏を継ぐ。㊔正韞，字は蔵甫。‖藩校明倫館都講，異船防御手当掛，代官を歴任。勤王家で，1842(天保13)松下村塾(松陰開塾のものとは別)を開き松陰に影響を与える。'69(明治2)塾を復活するが，'76一門・子弟のうち萩の乱に関係するものが多く，責任をとって自害した。

士規七則

"Shiki shichisoku"

野山獄での思索中に執筆したものを叔父の玉木文之進(1810_1876)の添削を経て、従弟の玉木彦介の元服時に贈ったもの。　長州藩出身の乃木希典将軍(1849_1912)もその師玉木文之進から松陰自筆の草稿を贈られ、修養指針としていた。第一則は人間の人間たる所以、第二則は皇国民(わが国の旧称)の立場、第三則並びに第四則は個人としての士道の在り方、　第五則以降は士道確立へ向けた心がけについて述べている。

士規七則

冊子を披繙せば、嘉言林の如く、躍々として人に迫る。顧ふに人読まず。即し読むとも行はず。苟に読みてこれを行はば、則ち千万世と雖も得て尽すべからず。噫、復た何をか言はん。然りと雖も知る所ありて、言はざる能はざるは人の至情なり。古人これを古に言ひ、今我れこれを今に言ふ。亦詎ぞ傷まん、士規七則を作る。

一、凡そ生れて人たらば、宜しく人の禽獣に異る所以を知るべし。蓋し人には五倫あり、而して君臣父子を最も大なりと為す。故に人の人たる所以は忠孝を本と為す。

一、凡そ皇国に生れては、宜しく吾が宇内に尊き所以を知るべし。蓋し皇朝は万葉一統にして、邦国の士夫世々禄位を襲ぐ。人君、民を養ひて以て祖業を続ぎ、臣民、君に忠して以て父志を継ぐ。君臣一体、忠孝一致、唯だ吾が国を然りと為す。

一、士の道は義より大なるはなし、義は勇に因りて行はれ、勇は義に因りて長ず。

一、士の行は質実欺かざるを以て要となし、功詐過を文るを以て恥と為す。光明正大、皆是れより出づ。

一、人古今に通ぜず、聖賢を師とせずんば、則ち鄙夫のみ。読書尚友は君子の事なり。

一、徳を成し材を達するには、師恩友益多きに居り。故に君子は交游を慎む。

一、死して後已むの四字は言簡にして義広し。堅忍果決、確乎として抜くべからざるものは、是れを舎きて術なきなり。

右士規七則、又約して三端と為す。曰く、「志を立てて以て万事の源と為す。交を択びて仁義の行を輔く。書を読みて以て聖賢の訓を稽ふ」と。士苟に此に得ることあらば亦以て成人と為すべし。

二十一回猛士手録

This was written by Shouin Yoshida while he stayed in Noyama Jail in 1855, and edited by Bunnoshin Tamaki, his uncle. He presented this note to his cousin, Hikosuke Tamaki, as a congratulatory gift when a ceremony was held to celebrate his coming of age. General Nogi (1849_1912), who came from Choushuu, was presented with Shouin Yoshida's original draft by Bunnoshin Tamaki and used it as a guiding principle to cultivating his mind. The 1st principle refers to the essence of human beings, the 2nd principle refers to the ideal way of the Japanese people, the 3rd & 4th principles refer to the ideal way of a warrior as a private person, and 5th to 7th principles refer to the mental attitude aiming to establish the ideal way of warriors.

獄中俳諧

恐れながら公御参勤を祝い奉りて　九月朔日

短歌行

障りなき月明るさの秋深し　花廼屋
　千代を祝ぐ渡来し鶴　花逸
糊附の袷衣を孫にきせ替て　節洞
　拾捨る苧くず糸くず　花廼屋
此ごろは絶へず折々下り舟　逸
　綿に連たる安売の米　松陰
一酔の夢に世渡るみぞれ酒　蘇芳
　冬枯ながら話物真似　花逸
都ニハ近頃あじな流行事　松陰
　彼所ハ神社ここは仏閣　蘇芳
晴もよし霞にうもる花と花　同
　利茶の会に客の待受　花廼屋
洗たる髪もあだなる妄　蘇芳
　散らし書なる口紅の文　花廻屋
問屋場ハ早晩もどさくさ鬧に　蘇芳
　雨が揚れは乾く沙道　同
人情は兎角田舎が律義ニて　松陰
猫の首ねの鈴のからから　蘇芳　（中略）
花ハ今盛りと誰も喜びて　松陰
　青柳誘ひ謡ふ春風　琴鳴

各詠

杯の手元ハ軽き新酒哉　琴鳴
落鮎に易く越なん一瀬哉　花逸
大手振て行道広し星月夜　蘇芳
荊葉の枯てさわぐや秋の暮　谷遊
初鴨や夜ハほのほのと水の色　節洞
落栗のいかの取付袂かな　城木
松杉の木立ハ高し露しぐれ　和暢
色を見て鴉のとまる熟柿哉　豊浦
楓する中ニも朱の鳥井哉　久子
朝霧や見習ぬ嶋の五ツ六ツ　松陰

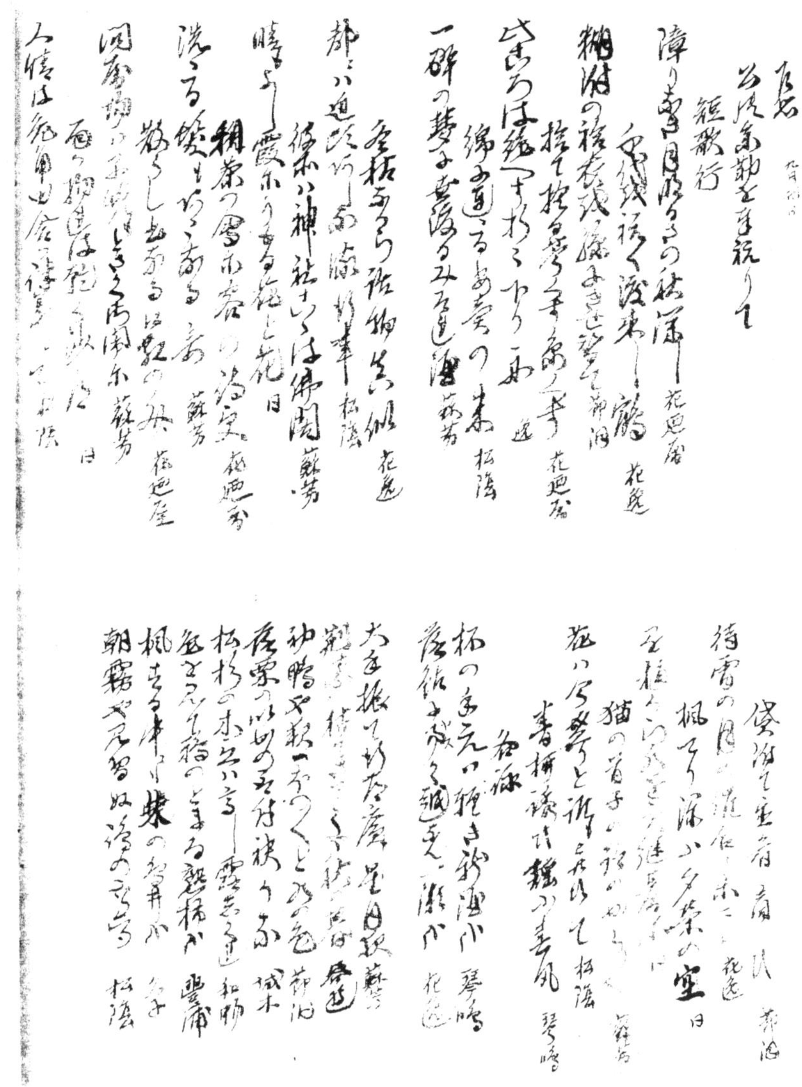

獄中俳諧

Haikai (seventeen-syllable verse) made in jail

獄中における短歌行と各詠の記録。獄中にあっても藩主の動静に想いをはせ、同様に囚人にも情操を育もうとした。俳諧に優れた囚人には教えを請い、獄内の分け隔てない親睦を図った。

This is the record of “haikai” made by Shouin Yoshida in jail. While he was much concerned about the actions of his Lord even in jail, he tried to cultivate the artistic sentiments of his fellow inmates. He asked a fellow jail inmate noted for excellence in “haikai” to instruct him in it. He tried to promote mutual friendship without discrimination.

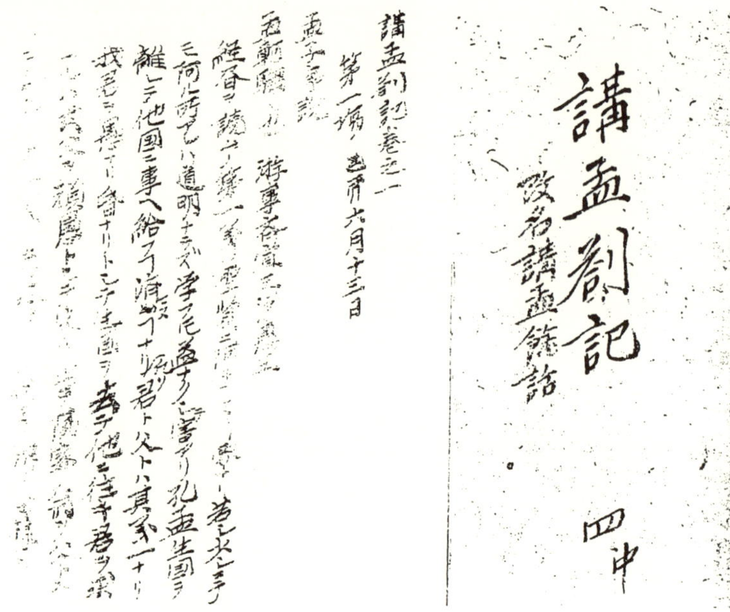

講孟余話

Discourses on Mencius

「講孟余話」は安政二年 6 月 13 日から翌年 6 月 13 日まで、前半は野山獄で囚人に、後半は幽囚先で肉親の人達に講義、一年間で孟子全巻を読み終えた記録である。本著作は松陰の全著述中、主著の第一と見做してよく、所謂「孟子」の訓解の書ではない。時に孟子に共感し、時に孟子を批判しており、松陰の人生観、国家観、政治、教育、外交思想などに対する態度の全体を鮮明としている。これに 55 回の講義を要した。

This discourse on Mencius was delivered from June 13, 1855 to June 13, 1856. The first half of his lecture was made to inmates in Noyama Jail, and the latter half was for his blood relations at a confined facility after being released from the jail. This proves that he read through the whole volume of Mencius in one year. This book can be regarded as one of the most monumental of Mencius's original works, and is not merely an interpretation of the moral discourse of Mencius.

Shouin Yoshida shows his sympathy with Mencius in some parts in the Discourses and criticizes Mencius in other parts. In the Discourses, Yoshida made his views clear on life, patriotism, politics, education, diplomacy and so on through 55 lectures.

志

天地大徳君父至恩報徳以心
復恩以身此日難再此生難復
此事不終此身不息

藤寅

松陰の報徳訓（23,October,1856）

Teaching of Shouin Yoshida for repaying the favor bestowed by one's country. He wrote to express his philosophical conception.

七生説

“Shichishosetsu”

南北朝時代の武将楠木正成(1294 _1336)の七生報国の精神が、明から渡来した儒学者朱舜水(1600 _1682)に、また自分に受け継がれていることを実感した松陰が、精神の不滅を確信し、儒学の理気説を借りて自分の信念を表明したもの。松陰の人生観、士道観、国体観が一応確立したのは講孟余話以降と言われるが、七生説とは七たび生まれ変わって国恩に報いるという説。(欄外行間に黙霖の朱筆が認められる)

七生説

天の茫々たる、一理ありて存し、父子祖孫の綿々たる、一気ありて属く。人の生るるや、斯の理を資りて以て心と為し、斯の気を稟けて以て体と為す。体は私なり、心は公なり。私を役して公に殉ふ者を大人と為し、公を役して私に殉ふ者を小人と為す。故に小人は体滅し気竭くるときは、則ち腐爛潰敗して復た収むべからず。君子は心、理と通ず、体滅し気竭くるとも、而も理は独り古今に亙り天壌を窮め、未だ嘗て暫くも歇まざるなり。

余聞く、贈正三位楠公の死するや、其の弟正季を顧みて曰く、「死して何をか為す」。曰く、「願はくは七たび人間に生れて、以て国賊を滅さん」。公欣然として曰く、「先づ吾が心を獲たり」とて耦刺して死せりと。噫、是れ深く理気の際に見ることあるか。是の時に当り、正行・正朝の諸子は則ち理気並び属く者なり。新田・菊池の諸族は気離れて理通ずる者なり。是れに由りて之れを言はば、楠公兄弟は徒に七生のみならず、初めより未だ嘗て死せざるなり。是れより其の後、忠孝節義の人、楠公を観て興起せざる者なければ、則ち楠公の後、復た楠公を生ずる者、固より計り数ふべからざるなり。何ぞ独り七たびのみならんや。

余嘗て東に遊び三たび湊川を経、楠公の墓を拝し、涕涙禁ぜず。其の碑陰に、明の徴士朱生の文を勒するを観るに及んで、則ち亦涙を下す。噫、余の楠公に於ける、骨肉父子の恩あるに非ず、師友交遊の親あるに非ず。自ら其の涙の由る所を知らざるなり。朱生に至りて則ち海外の人、反つて楠公を悲しむ。而して吾れ亦朱生を悲しむ、最も謂れなし、退いて理気の説を得たり。乃ち知る、楠公・朱生及び余不肖、皆斯の理を資りて以て心と為す。則ち気属かずと雖も、而も心は則ち通ず。是れ涙の禁ぜざる所以なり。余不肖、聖賢の心を存し忠孝の志を立て、国威を張り海賊を滅ぼすを以て、妄りに己が任と為し、一跌再跌、不忠不孝の人となる、復た面目の世人に見ゆるなし、然れど斯の心已に楠公諸人と、斯の理を同じうす。安んぞ気体に随つて腐爛潰敗するを得んや。必ずや後の人をして亦余を観て興起せしめ、七生に至りて、而る後可と為さんのみ。噫、是れ我に在り。七生説を作る。

文尾に

「是の文其の患節を観るに足る、僕輩之を読み壮快し襟を正す」

の黙霖の朱筆あり。

Shouin Yoshida believed that he had inherited the spirit of General Masashige Kusunoki (1294_1336) as well as Shushunsui (1600_1682), a Confucian scholar, who came from the Ming dynasty. He believed firmly that spirits are immortal. He expressed his faith by means of “Shichishosetsu” in which he uses the Confucian view of the reasonable spirit. "Shichishosetsu” refers to the idea that every one should be regenerated seven times to repay one’s country for the favor that one has had bestowed upon one by his country.

松下村塾聯
万巻の書を読むに非ざるよりは、
寧んぞ千秋の人たるを得ん。
一己の労を軽んずるに非ざるよりは、
寧んぞ兆民の安きを致すを得ん。
丙辰秋日（安政三年）　藤寅書

松下村塾聯

Slender bamboo boards for “Shoukasonjuku School” (166cm x 18cm)

この聯は松陰が書き、久保五郎左衛門が彫ったもので、松下村塾に掲げられた。簡潔に松陰の学問態度や教育精神が示されている。

Handwriting on the bamboo boards is by Shouin Yoshida, and was carved by Gorouzaemon Kubo. It was exhibited in the school. This shows his approach to study and educational spirit.

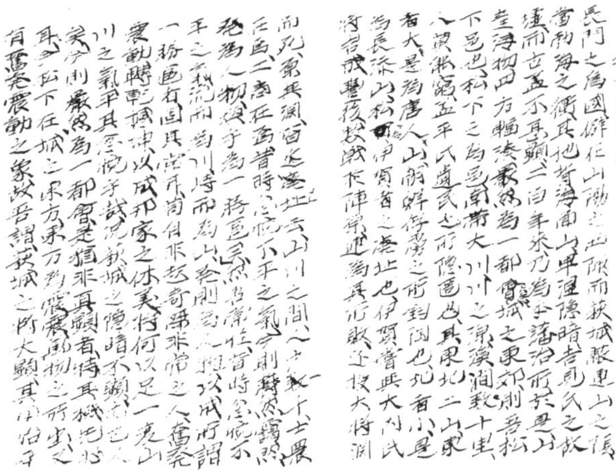

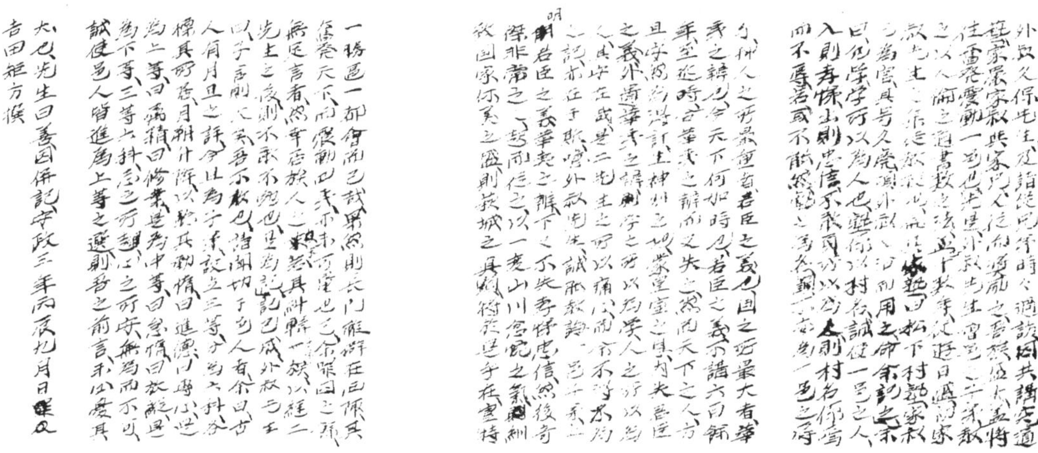

松下村塾記

Record of the “Shoukasonjuku School”

講孟余話の後、引き続き望まれて講義。松陰の関心は次第に兵学から「日本外史」、「春秋左氏伝」、「資治通鑑」など日本や中国の史書に関心が移っている。

After the Discourses on Mencius, Shouin Yoshida continued lecturing in Hagi at the request of his disciples. His interest gradually moved from military tactics to the histories of Japan and China.

高杉晋作(1839_1867)
Shinsaku Takasugi

久坂玄瑞(1840_1864)
Genzui Kusaka

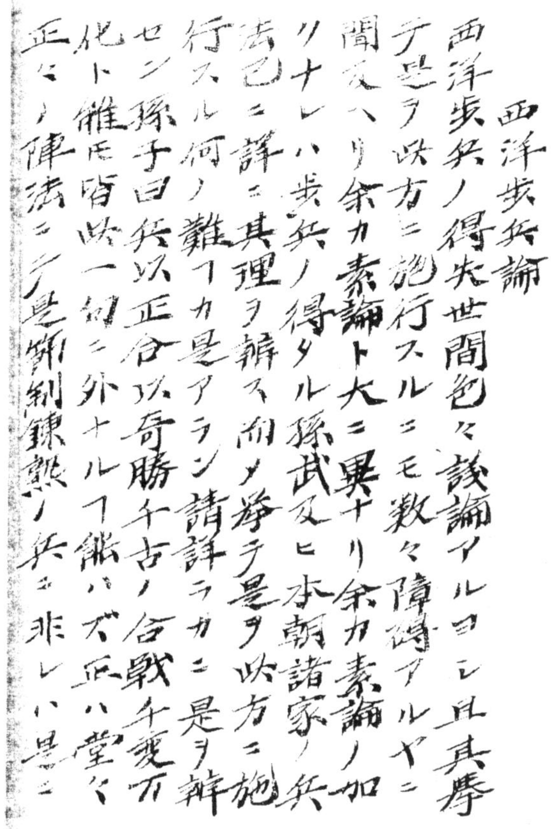
西洋歩兵論
西洋歩兵ノ得失世間色々議論アルヨシ且其擧テ是ヲ此方ニ施行スルニモ数々障碍アルヤニ聞及ヘリ余カ素論ト大ニ異ナリ余カ素論ノ如クナレハ歩兵ノ得タル孫武及ヒ本朝諸家ノ兵法已ニ詳ニ其理ヲ辨ス而メ擧テ是ヲ此方ニ施行スル何ノ難キコトカ是アラン請詳ラカニ是ヲ辨セン孫子曰兵以正合以奇勝千古ノ合戦千変万化ト雖皆此一句ニ外ナルコト能ハズ正ハ堂々正々ノ陣法ニシテ是節制錬熟ノ兵ニ非レハ是ニ

西洋歩兵論

西洋歩兵の得失、世間色々の議論あるよし。且つ其の挙げて是れを此方に施行するにも数々障碍あるやに聞き及べり、余が素論と大いに異なり。余が素論の如くなれば、歩兵の得たる、孫武及び本朝諸家の兵法已に詳かに其の理を弁ず。而して挙げて是れを此方に施行する、何の難きことか是れあらん。請ふ、詳かに是れを弁ぜん。孫子曰く、「兵は正を以て合ひ、奇を以て勝つ」と。千古の合戦、千変万化と雖も、皆此の一句に外なること能ばず。正は堂々正々の陣法にて、是れ節制錬熟の兵に非ざれば、是れに当ること能はず。

（後略）

西洋歩兵論

Comment on Western Infantry

松陰は和流兵法を打破し、西洋の組織的歩兵制の導入を論説した。
門下の高杉晋作や久坂玄瑞らが後に組織した奇兵隊の根拠をここに見出すことができる。

Shouin Yoshida proposed to overthrow Japanese style tactics and organize a Western style systematic infantry corps. In his comment, we can find the historical basis of the Kiheitai corps (the first Japanese infantry corps including persons who didn't belong to the samurai class) that was later organized by his disciples such as Shinsaku Takasugi, Genzui Kusaka, and so on.

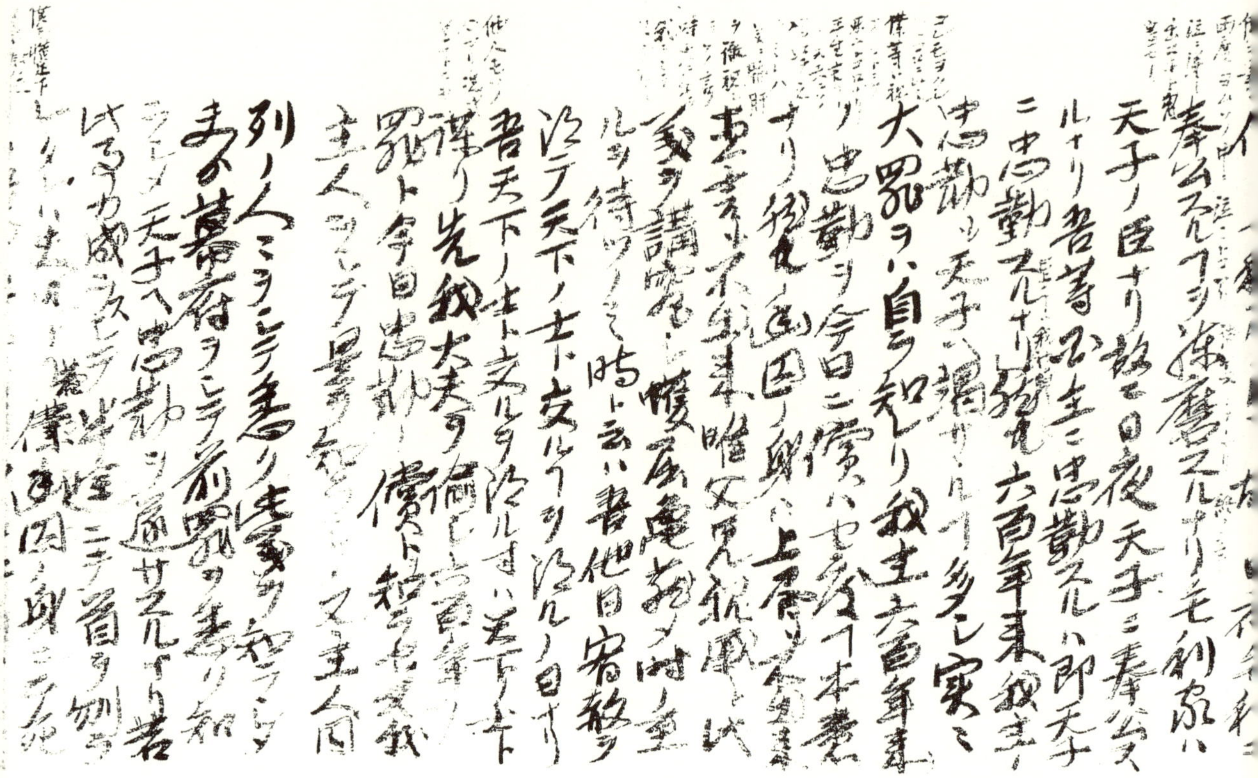

うつのみや もくりん　宇都宮黙霖　1833～1906（天保4～明治39）幕末・維新期の勤王僧。㊋僧峻嶺の子。㊓安芸国賀茂郡長浜。㊔字は絢夫，別号を史狂，僧名覚了・鶴梁。1866（慶応2）還俗して宇都宮真名介雄綱と称す。‖幼時から僧としての修業を積むとともに詩文をよくした。22歳の時，本願寺に籍を置いたまま諸国を遍歴，やがて尊王攘夷を唱えるにいたった。1858（安政5）一旦は捕えられたが，その後も長州藩討幕派と結び，'64（元治1）幕府の第1次長州征伐には広島に潜入して捕えられ，再び投獄される。維新後は湊川神社・男山八幡宮の神官を歴任した。'77（明治10）より10数年をかけて大蔵経の和訳にあたった。㊥「回天詩史」，「幽後集」1869。

黙霖との往復書簡

Letters exchanged between Shouin Yoshida and Priest Mokurin

勤王僧黙霖(1833_1906)は安政二年獄中の松陰と文通、翌年萩に再来訪し松陰と面会を求めたが、謹慎中であったため書簡の往復だけとした。
黙霖は急進的な討幕論を松陰にぶつけ、思想的転換を促す重要な影響を与えた。また黙霖も

「松陰の文章は一字一字が涙であり、一言一言が血だ」と述べている。

默霖との往復書状　（本文松陰、行間及び文末細字默霖）

（前略）

僕は毛利家の臣なり、故に日夜毛利に奉公することを練磨するなり。毛利家は天子の臣なり、故に日夜天子に奉公するなり。吾れ等國主に忠勤するは即ち天子に忠勤するなり。（以上のことは我れ初めよりしる）然れども六百年來我が主の忠勤も天子へ竭さざること多し。實に大罪をば自ら知れり。我が生六百年來の忠勤を今日に償はせ度きこと本意なり。然れども幽囚の身は上書も出來ず直言も出來ず、唯だ父兄親戚と此の義を講究し蠖屈亀藏して時の至るを待つのみ。時と云ふは吾れ他日宥赦を得て天下の士と交はることを得るの日なり。吾れ天下の士と交はるを得る時は天下の士と謀り、先づ我が大夫を諭し六百年の罪と今日忠勤の償とを知らせ、又我が主人をして是れを知らしめ、又主人同列の人々をして悉く此の義を知らしめ、夫れより幕府をして前罪を悉く知らしめ、天子へ忠勤を遂げさするなり。若し此の事が成らずして半途にて首を刎ねられたれば夫れ迄なり。若し僕幽囚の身にて死（なば、吾れ必ず一人の吾が志を繼ぐの士をば後世に殘し置くなり。）

（後略）

「欄外の默霖書簡」

○僕此の書を兩度よむ、其の中に泣きし所あり、微笑したる所あり。終りに至りて泣くにも涕も出ぬほど胸塞がれり。

○これもよくしるところに候なり。僕等は祖先のことにて惡むところなり。平生言へることならぬゆゑに、その心を以て之れをみれば實に肺肝を徹視して、その言の味大いに出で我れをして泣かしむるなり。

Priest Mokurin (1833_1906), a royalist, wrote to Shouin Yoshida, who stayed in the jail, in 1855. After Shouin Yoshida was released from the jail, the Priest called on him in Hagi in 1856. But since he was placed under house arrest by the Shogunate, the Priest couldn't see him. They could only exchange letters.

Priest Mokurin expressed the radical view of overthrowing the Shogunate and influenced Yoshida enough to remold his thought. Mokurin said,

"It seems that every character written by Shouin Yoshida is filled with his tears, and blood is about to gush out of every word in his letters."

久坂玄瑞あて書状

A Letter Addressed to Genzui Kusaka from Shouin Yoshida

江戸遊学中の久坂玄瑞(1840_1864)に、松陰が松下村塾の盛んな勉強振りを知らせたもの。文中、「利介(後の伊藤博文)も中々周旋家のようだ」などと記している。

久坂玄瑞あて書状

伊佐塾にて頻りに読む様子なり。茂十郎山口へ行き留守中なり。正亮九州より戻り大いに叱る故頗る憤励の機あり。来原の姪(めい)岡部は兄の品鑑(ひんかん)の如し。福原一向来らず。近来の勉強家は岡部の外有吉熊次郎・木梨平之允等なり。中井の姪の由天野清三郎中々奇物、他人未だ深くは取らず、僕独り之れを愛す。芸生富樫文周頻りに読むなり。此の五生皆寄宿。提山坊主大いに進む、利介(後の伊藤博文)亦進む、中々周旋家になりさうな。南は館中にて勉強の由、山根も定めて勉強ならん。兄去後山根は両三度来る。南は絶えて来らず。人各〻志あり、兄決して人に強(し)ふるなかれ。○松洞貎する所の松桂老人四月十日物故、栄太にも知らすべし。○口羽へは絶えず往復、口羽の識見益〻進み、詩眼大いに進む。清狂稿論定は口羽へ託し候。跋(ばつ)は兄早々御認(したた)め然るべく候。松洞が貎せし図を巻首へ出したし。刻手彼れ是れ撰び置き候様御相談下さるべく候。蕭海、伝を作る筈、是れは像の傍へ附け置くべし。中谷へ託し拙堂へも選択と敍とを頼み置き候。江戸にて藤森へとも一敍を乞うては如何、是れも清狂生前の知己なればなり。委細は中谷より申上げ候筈なれども、思ひ出し候所丈(た)け書附け置き候。御考合下さるべく候。淡水(あわみ)へも御相談下さるべく候。○直八も折々塾へ来て食を炊(かし)ぎて宿する組の者、中々の奇男子なり、愛すべし。(風(ふ)と思ひ出し候。岩国の二宮小太郎へ良蔵より遣はし候拙記の事、如何御取計らひ下され候や。先日良三嘮致したり。)

六月十九日　　松陰生

実甫老兄

松洞へ別に書付を遣はさず、此の書御対読勿論なり。

「村塾寄宿生有吉熊次郎頗(すこぶ)る読書出来さふなり気あり」

(この行反対に記す。反故であろう)

Shouin Yoshida wrote to Genzui Kusaka in Edo to inform him of the hard work of students at the Shoukasonjuku School. In this letter, he touched upon Risuke (later called Hirobumi Itoh, the first Japanese prime minister) to the effect that Risuke seems to be excellent in mediation.

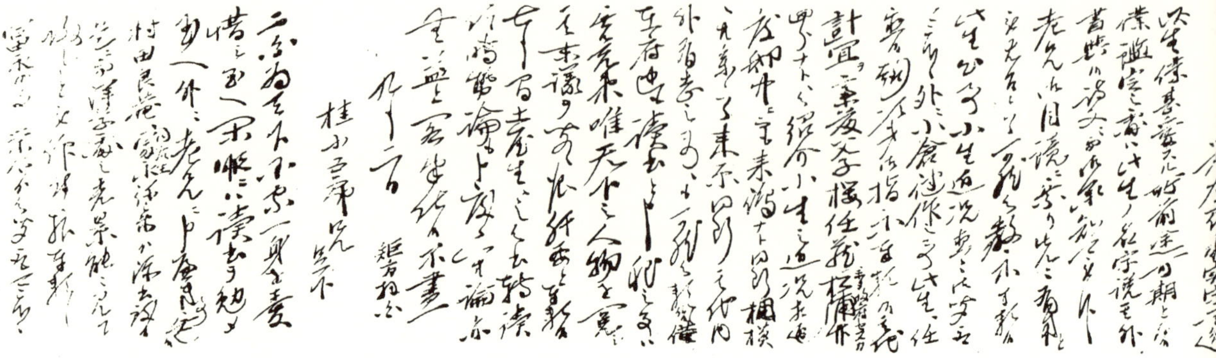

桂小五郎あて書状

A letter to Kogorou Katsura (later called Takayoshi Kido) from Shouin Yoshida

桂小五郎（後の木戸孝允;1833_1877）は嘉永二年 17 歳で松陰の兵学門下となって以来、松陰に兄事して教えを受けた。書状は安政四年のもので、門人吉田栄太郎を紹介し、江戸における指導を頼んだもの。松陰は門人が他国へ行くとき等、常に極めて懇切で、強い愛情をかけた。

桂小五郎あて書状

杉原辰之助組の者、自称吉田氏
栄太郎秀実、字は無逸

此の生僕甚だ愛する所、前途期すべしと存じ候。僕鑑定の処は此の生の名字説其の外書き与へ候詩文にて御承知下さるべく、老兄御目鏡に乗り先々有用と思召され候はば、然るべく御教示頼み奉り候。此の生心事、小生近況、直々御聞取り下さるべく候。外に小倉健作の事、此の生へ任せ置き候。趣次第御指示頼み奉り候。其の他宜しきを計り斎藤父子・桜任蔵・松浦竹四郎など（未だ帰府せぬか。）へ御紹介、小生の近況相通じ度く、邸中にても来嶋など同断、相模へども参り候はば来原同断、其の他内外有志のものへも然るべく御頼み仕り候。僅かの在府、迚も読書と申す程の事は覚束なく、唯だ天下の人物を閲し、其の末議を聞き候儀肝要と頼み奉り候。七月の間土屋生への御書転読仕り候。時勢論も申し度く候へども、論も亦無益と閣筆仕り候。不尽。

九月二日　　矩方拝白

桂小五郎兄　足下

二白、天下国家の為め一身を愛惜し給へ。閑暇には読書を勉め給へ。外に老兄に申すべき事これなく候。村田良菴へ富永弥兵衛（同居生）より添書致し候。是れにて洋学処の光景能々見て帰れと仰せ付けられ候様頼み奉り候。富永が事、栄太より御聞取り下さるべく候。

Since becoming a disciple of Shouin Yoshida at the age of 17 in 1849, Kogorou Katsura regarded Shouin Yoshida as his lifelong mentor. Shouin Yoshida introduced another young disciple, Eitaroh Yoshida, to Kogoroh Katsura through this letter and asked him to guide Eitarou Yoshida in Edo. Whenever his disciples made a trip to other places, he would warmly look out for their welfare this way.

月性あて書状

letter from Shouin to Gesshoh.

松下村塾派と周布政之助率いる明倫館派とで激しい対立、議論があった時藩内の対立を回避するため、周防の妙円寺住職だった月性(1817_1858)に調停を依頼したときのもの。月性は来萩し両者の諒解を取り付けた。

月性あて書状

調停一事御心頭に懸けられ候段、実に感銘致し候。右に付き、何卒折角の御厚情徒事に相成らず候様にと種々案労仕り候より同志へ申し談じ候処、孰れも同意に御座候。其の段は他事に之れなく、江南・松下相和睦する〳〵と申したる計りにては真情は終に貫徹仕らざる事に付き、松下生悉く周布を主盟とし毎々会集仕るべく、書生の妄論も尽し、政府諸君事実上の様子も承り候はば、真情相通じ真の和睦に相成り申すべくと存ぜられ候、と申し候とも、松下社中も先日御面会の中谷・高杉・尾寺・久保等の数子、且つは所謂有隣子等のみに御座候。何卒上人の御紹介を以て御帰在前に一夕周布へ会する様の事出来申す間敷くや。此の段成就仕り候へば誠に御調停も真功相顕はれ誠に妙々に御座候。全体僕も一囚室に坐し黙々仕り居り候内に、松下の議論などと人に目せられ候ては人聞きも如何敷く

（以下闕）

This letter was sent to Gesshou (1817_1858), who was the chief priest of Myouenji Temple, to request mediation between the Shoukasonjuku Party and the Meirinkan Party led by Masanosuke Sufu (1823 - 1864), political leader of Choushuu Domain. It asks help in avoiding antagonism between the two opposing parties in the Domain.

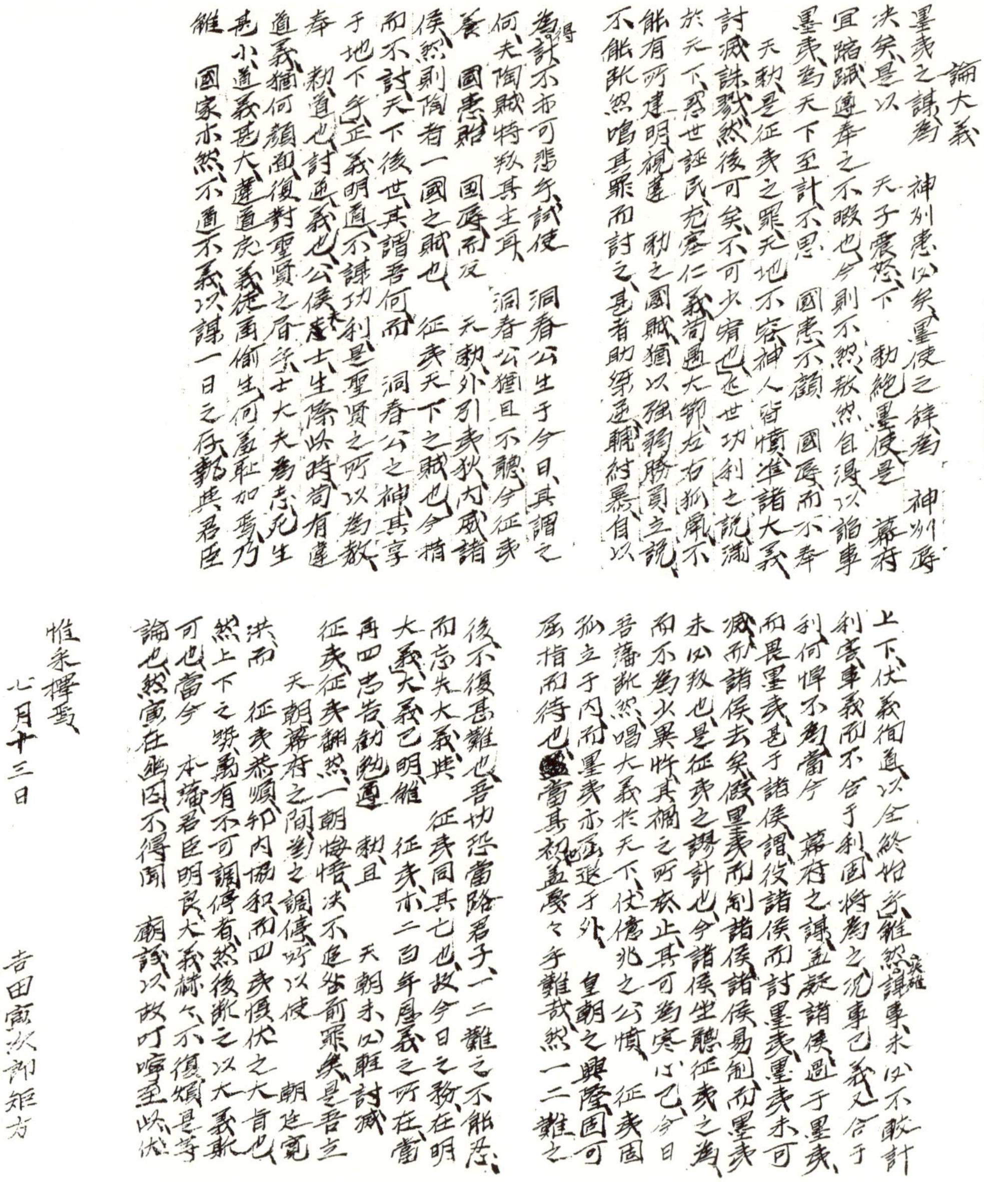
論大義
惟采擇焉
七月十三日
吉田寅次郎矩方

論大儀

Comment on righteousness

井伊直弼大老は米国との通商条約問題を一挙に解決するため、勅許を待たずに独断で調印。松陰はこれを聞いて大いに憤慨し「大義を論ず」という一文を用意し藩主に上(ﾀﾃﾏﾂ)ろうとしたが、しかし最早時すでに遅く敢然と討幕論に思想転換した。

大義を論ず

墨夷の謀は神州の患たること必せり。墨使の辞は神州の辱たることを決せり。是を以て天子震怒し、勅を下ろして墨使を絶ちたまふ。是れ幕府宜しく蹜蹙遵奉これ暇あらざるべし。今は則ち然らず、敖然自得、以て墨夷に諂事して天下の至計と為し、国患を思はず、国辱を顧みず、而して天勅を奉ぜず。是れ征夷の罪にして、天地も容れず、神人皆憤る。これを大義に準じて、討滅誅戮して、然る後可なり、少しも宥すべからざるなり。（中略）

試みに洞春公をして今日に生れしめば、其れこれを何とか謂はん。夫の陶賊は特だ其の主に叛けるのみ。洞春公猶ほ且つ聴かず。今征夷は国患を養ひ、国辱を貽し、而して天勅に反き、外、夷狄を引き、内、諸侯を威す。然らば則ち陶なる者は一国の賊なり、征夷は天下の賊なり。今措きて討たざれば、天下後世其れ吾れを何とか謂はん。而して洞春公の神、其れ地下に享けんや。（中略）

今日吾が藩断然として大義を天下に唱へ、億兆の公憤に仗らば、征夷固より内に孤立し、而して墨夷も亦外に屈退し、皇朝の興隆、固より指を屈して待つべきなり。其の初めに当つてや、蓋し戛々乎として難きかな。（中略）

大義已に明かなるときは、征夷と雖も亦二百年恩義の在る所なれば、当に再四忠告して、勉めて勅に遵はんことを勧むべし。且つ　天朝未だ必ずしも軽々しく征夷を討滅したまはず、征夷翻然として一朝悔悟せば、決して前罪を追咎したまはざるなり。是れ吾れの　天朝・幕府の間に立ちて、これが調停を為し、天朝をして寛洪に、而して幕府をして恭順に、邦内をして協和に、而して四夷をして慴伏せしむる所以の大旨なり。然れども上下の勢、万調停すべからざるものあり、然る後これを断ずるに大義を以てせば、斯ち可なり。当今本藩は君臣明良にして、大義赫々、復た是れ等の議を煩はさざるなり。然れども寅の身幽囚に在りて、廟議を聞くことを得ず、故に以て叮嚀此に至る。伏して惟ふ采択せられることを。

七月十三日　　吉田寅次郎矩方

In order to solve the problem of the commercial treaty with the U.S. at a stroke, Lord Naosuke Ii, Chief Minister of the Shogunate, signed the treaty arbitrarily on June 19, 1858 without Imperial sanction. Hearing this, Shouin Yoshida was enraged by his arbitrary decision and execution of the Chief Minister. Consequently, he prepared a paper entitled “Comment on Righteousness” with an intention to address it to his Lord. However, it was too late.

It was then that he resolutely changed his political ideology to that of overthrowing the Shogunate.

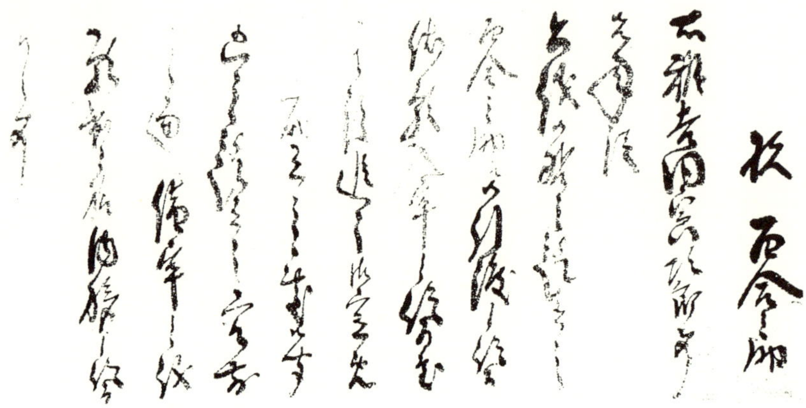

再入獄内命書
右育吉田寅次郎事、先年公儀より
御咎めの趣之れあり、百合之助へ
御引渡し仰付けられ、願ひに依り
入牢仰付け置かれ、其の後追々御
宥免の筋之れあり候処、御聞込の
趣之れあり、最前の通り借牢の儀
願ひ出で候様内移仰付けられ候
事。

再入獄内命書

Secret Order for Re-imprisonment

安政の大獄による粛清は、橋本左内や梅田雲浜、頼三樹三郎などの逮捕により恐怖政治の度合いを急速に深めていた。安政 5 年 11 月萩では江戸から帰国した松陰門下の赤川淡水が村塾を訪れ、京都の政情を報告。薩摩と水戸の者が井伊直弼大老の暗殺を計画、密かに長州にも助勢を求めている模様との話をした。この報告は松陰をひどく刺激した。
丁度この頃、井伊大老の指示で老中間部詮勝(1802_1884)が朝廷内の反幕府勢力を粛清するため京都へ上る情報も入っていた。薩摩や水戸が井伊大老をやるなら、長州は老中間部を暗殺すべしと考察。　松陰は長州藩政府の重鎮・周布政之助らに宛て、暗殺に必要な武器を藩政府で用意して欲しい旨の願書を提出。驚いた藩は受け付けるはずも無く、松陰に好意的であった筈の周布もほとほと手を焼き、野放しにすれば藩にも災いが及ぶのを恐れ松陰の名代玉木文之進に出したのがこの「再入獄内命書」である。

The extent of the terrorism in those days was rapidly increased by a purge, referred to as a "wholesale arrest" in the Ansei Era, that was represented by the arrest of Sanai Hashimoto, Unpin Umeda, Mikisaburou Rai and so on. In November 1858, Tansui Akagawa, a disciple of Shouin Yoshida, returned to Hagi from Edo to visit the Shoukasonjuku School and reported on the political situation in Kyoto.

In addition, he recounted how groups in Satsuma and Mito Domains plotted for the assassination of Lord Naosuke Ii, Chief Minister of the Shogunate, and seemed to want the secret assistance of Choushuu. This report greatly agitated Shouin Yoshida.

At about that time, he also knew that Akikatsu Manabe (1802 _1884), a senior councilor of the Shogunate, was going to Kyoto to purge the factors against the Shogunate in the Imperial Court. He thought that if the Satsuma and Mito Domains would assassinate the Chief Minister of the Shogunate, the Choushuu should have assassinated Manabe, a senior councilor of the Shogunate. Thus, he wrote a letter to Masanosuke Sufu, one of the leading opposition figures, to ask the Choushuu government to prepare weapons for such an assassination. The Choushuu government was shocked and refused his assassination proposal immediately.

Masanosuke Sufu, who was previously amicable to him, was also disgusted by his behavior. Sufu was afraid that leaving Shouin Yoshida to his own devices would harm the Domain itself. Then he prepared this Secret Order for Re-imprisonment and sent it to Bunnoshinn Tamaki as Shouin Yoshida's representative.

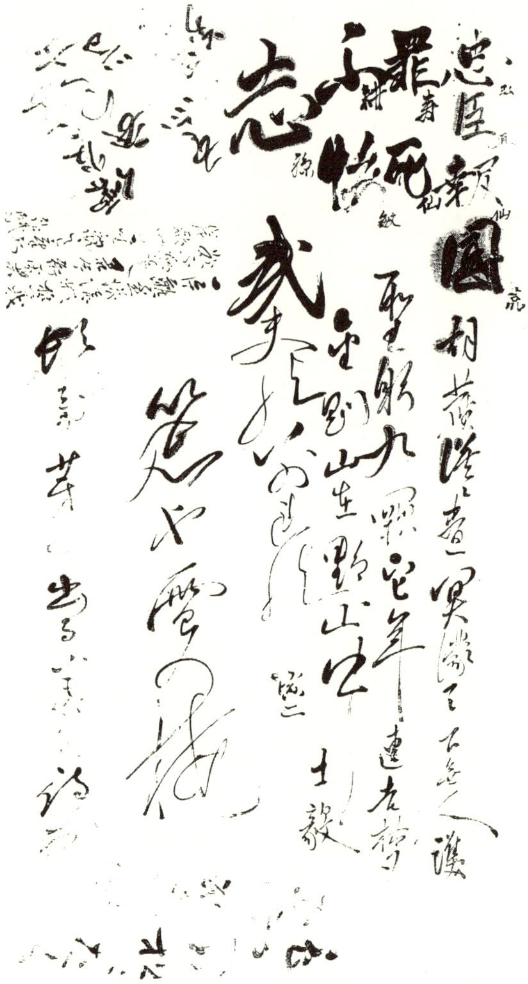

別宴寄せ書。

Letters of support written at the farewell dinner

入江杉蔵ら門下生は藩邸に松陰の罪状を問うたが自宅謹慎となった。

この寄せ書は松陰の野山再入獄日に親戚門人20余名が集まった時のもの。

別宴寄せ書

忠臣報国　胡塵漠々尽冥濛、天下無人護
罪死　聖躬、九闕它年遭吉夢、
不悔　金剛山在野山中　士毅
志　武夫の別れの筵や雪の梅　寅二

色かへぬ松のたぐゐし武夫の
頓て芽の出る春を待友　作

一片離盃涕涙頻、誓我欲不恥古人。
君今衝雪去岸獄、何日重観意気新。
徳民
再拝

吾亦一男児
儒官之子武門之士

Several disciples of Shouin Yoshida. including Sugizou Irie, pressed the Domain Government to say why Shouin Yoshida was imprisoned only to be ordered to be confined to their houses.

This letter of support was made by twenty and odd men including relatives and disciples of Shouin Yoshida on December 26, 1858, when he was imprisoned in Noyama Jail again.

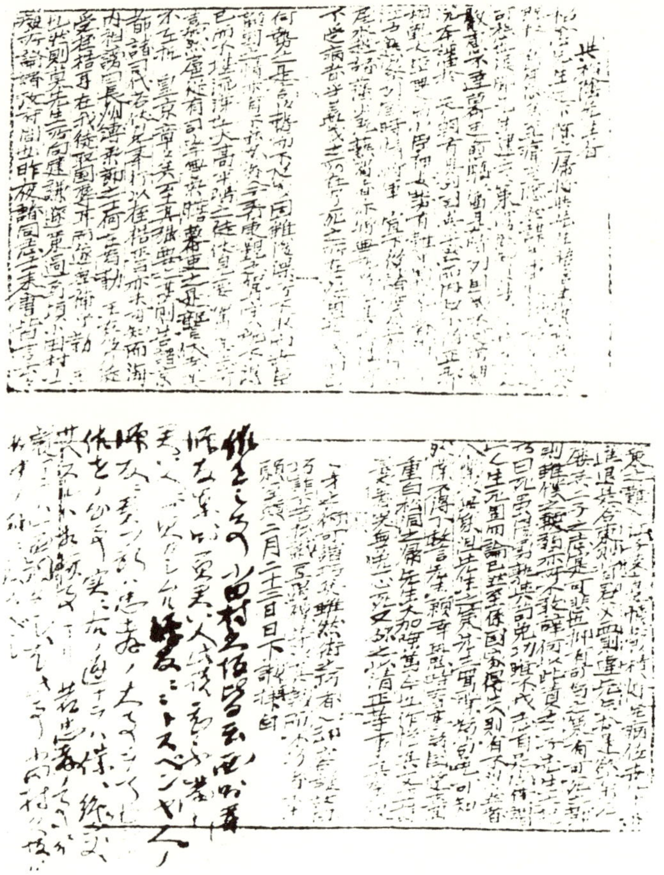

与松陰先生書

A letter sent to Shouin Yoshida from Genzui Kusaka

これは再度の野山獄入獄で藩の政策に激情する松陰に江戸の久坂玄瑞が送った書状。松陰が画策していた「間部詮勝要撃策」や藩主毛利敬親参勤の途上を利用して京都・伏見に留め、反幕府派の公卿、三条実美らと会わせて旗揚げさせる所謂「伏見要駕策」について、門下の久坂玄瑞が師の松陰に対し時期早尚と諌めている。文尾の書き込みは松陰のもの。

松陰はこれらの画策を高杉晋作や久坂玄瑞にも知らせ同調を呼びかけ、江戸の門下生の返事に強い期待をかけていた。しかしこのような画策は長州藩自体を危機に追い込むので自重すべきとの“勧告書”となった。松陰は信頼していた門下生が次第に離れ、孤立した自分の立場に気付き怒りと悲しみに打ち震えていったのもこの時期である。

This is a letter sent from Genzui Kusaka to Shouin Yoshida, who was raging against the policy of the Domain in Noyama Jail. In this letter, because time was not yet ripe for them, Kusaka dissuaded Shouin Yoshida, to whom Kusaka looked up as his mentor, from executing the "Manabe assassination scheme" and "Army-raising program at Fushimi" in Kyoto that Yoshida had maneuvered.

This latter program involved holding a conference with Lord Takachika Mouri, anti-Shogunate party (represented by Sanetomi Sanjoh, a court noble) at Fushimi in Kyoto to ally Chouchuu with court nobles, taking the opportunity of the Lord's travel to Edo for Sankin-Koutai, and to raise arms to overthrow the Shogunate.

The postscript on the left side was written by Shouin Yoshida.

Yoshida informed his disciples, including Takasugi and Kusaka who stayed in Edo at that time, of these plans and asked them for their support. He fully expected them to reply that they would act with him. But they replied to the effect that since these schemes might drive Choushuu itself into a crisis, and remonstrated with him to be more prudent.

He was enraged realizing that his disciples whom he had trusted had left him one by one and that he had become isolated.

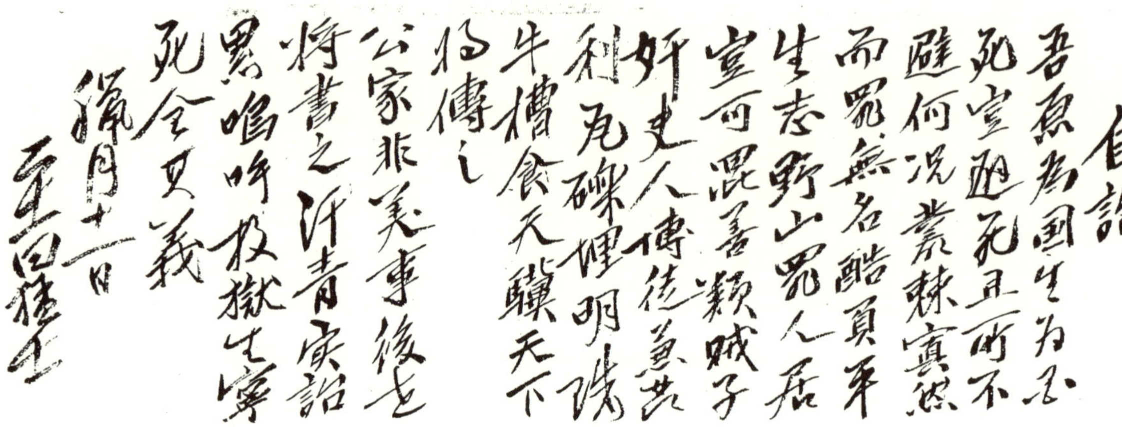

自詒

Convicted Again

再入獄の命令が降りた後、父百合之介の病を看護するため投獄の延期を請願し許可された。その代わりに幕府への罪状を明確にせよとの彼の主張は取り下げるここととなった。この詩はその時の心情を表したもの。

「獄に投じて生きるよりは、死んでその義をまっとうしたい」

自詒

吾れ原(も)と国の為めに生く、
国の為めに死する豈(あ)に避けんや。
死すら且つ避けざる所、
何ぞ況や叢棘(そうきよく)に寘(お)かるるをや。
然り而して罪名あらず、
酷(はなは)だ平生の志に負(そむ)く。
野山は罪人の居、
寧んぞ善類を混(まじ)ふべけんや。
賊子と奸夫人と、
博(ば)鶉徒悌と姦利と。
瓦礫、明珠を埋め、
牛槽(そう)、天驥(てんき)を食(やしな)ふ。
天下将にこれを伝へんとす、
公家の非美事。
万世将にこれを書せんとす、
汗青(かんせい)累なきを得んや。
嗚呼、獄に投じて生きんよりは、
寧ろ死して其の義を全うせん。

(十二)臘月十一日　　二十一回猛士

After the issue of the Secret Order for Re-imprisonment, Shouin Yoshida petitioned the Choushuu Government to put off his imprisonment to allow him to care for his father who had taken ill, and the petition was accepted. In return for this postponement, he had to withdraw his demand that the Shogunate clarify the reason for his conviction.

The following poem expresses his sentiment at that time.

" I would rather die fulfilling my duties than live thrown in jail."

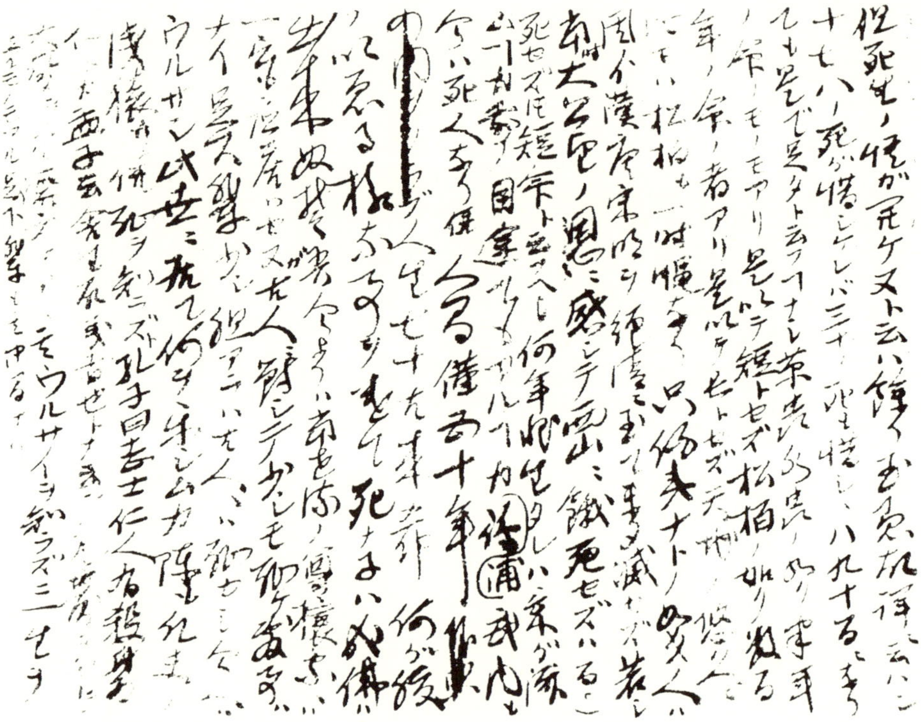

品川弥二郎あて書状

A letter addressed to Yajirou Shinagawa from Shouin Yoshida.

安政六年四月、愛弟子の一人品川弥二郎（後の内務大臣）に与えた「死生の悟り」の手紙。　“人生七十古来希なり、何か腹の癒えるようなことを遣って死なななければ、成仏は出来ぬぞ“と叱咤している。

絶食之辞

正月二十四日

吾れの尊攘は死生これを以てす。自ら謂えらく、以て天地に対越すべしと。豈に図らんや、初めや小人俗吏これを憚り、中ごろは正人君士これを厭い、終に平生の師友最も相敬信する者、交々吾れを遺棄し、交々吾れを沮抑せんとは。尊攘為すべからざるに非ず、吾れの尊攘を非とするなり。尊攘自ら期して而も尊攘に非ず、吾が事已んぬ。然らば則ち何如せん、其れ積誠より始めんか。吾れの尊攘は誠なきなり、宜なり人の動かざるや。今より逐件、刻苦すること左の如し、誠あらば則ち生き、誠なくんば則ち死せん。然らずんば何を以て天地に対越せんや。

吉田矩方謹識。

無用の言を言わず。戯言妄語は論ずるまでもなく、乃ち憂世の言と雖も、蔵否の論は皆無用なり。吾が性多言なり、多言は敬を失し誠を散ず、故に無用の言を言わざるを第一戒と為す。（下略）

絶食之辞

Fasting address

再入獄後も松陰は門人知人達に諸処指示していたが、彼らは師を敬遠するようになった。このことは松陰を絶望の淵に追いやり、遂には絶食して死生を天に聴くべく決心するところとなった。

当時の痛切悲壮な心境を表明している。

Even after being imprisoned again, Shouin Yoshida gave instructions to his disciples and other acquaintances from the jail. But, they began to keep him at a distance. This threw him into despair. At last, he decided to fast to ask God whether he should live or die. This address expresses his grievous and pathetic state of mind at that time.

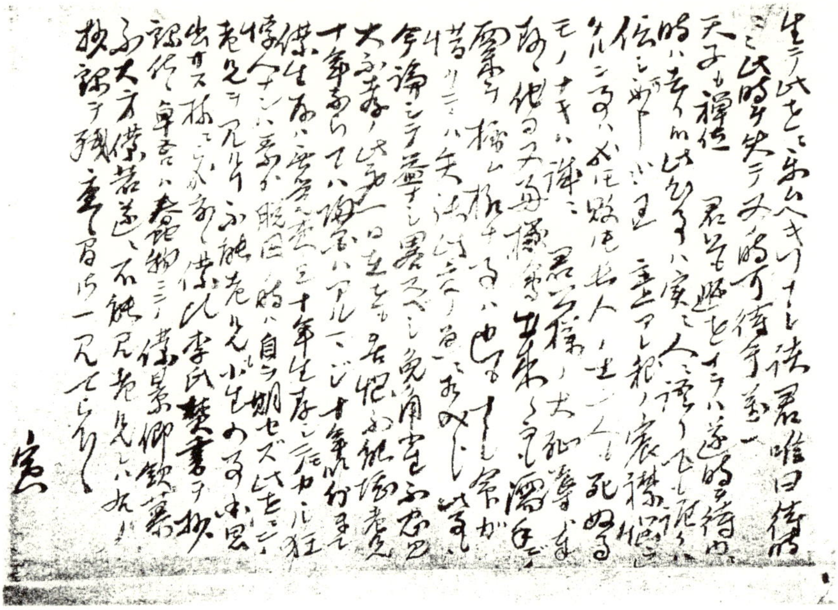

高杉晋作あて書状

A letter to Shinsaku Takasugi.

一時は死を覚悟した行状があったが、安政六年四月にはようやく落ち着きを取り戻した。暗殺計画に藩からの武器供与願いなど応じる筈もない事位理解していたとすれば、時勢から目をそむけている長州藩に喝を入れたとの見方(野村和作宛書状)もある。

北山安世(佐久間象山の甥)に出した書状では、以下述べている。

「今の幕府も諸侯も最早酔人なれば扶持の術なし。
草莽崛起の人を望む外頼みなし」

次第に藩に見切りを付け始め、草莽(民間力)へ傾斜していく。死生問題を含め、この晋作への手紙は心の悲しみと素直な自分の心情を述べている。

高杉晋作あて書状

生きて此の世に楽しむべきことなし。諸君曰く、「唯だ時を待て時を待て」と。此の時を失うて又の時待つべけんや。万一　天子も禅位、君公も遯世あらば遂に時を待つ内に時は去り候。此の心事は実に人に語りても誰れかは信じ申すべくや。且つ　主上あれ程の宸襟悩ませられたるに、事は成るとも敗るとも長門の士一人も死ぬるものなきは、誠に君公様の大恥辱と存じ奉り候。他日又機会出来候ても漏手で粟を握む様な事は迚もなし。命が惜しくては失張り此の度の通りに相成り申し候。此の事は今論じて益なし、略すべし。兎角小生不忠且つ大不孝の此の身、一日世に在るも苦悩堪ふる能はず。老兄十年ならでは帰国はあるまじ。十年以外まで僕生存は覚束なし。且つ十年生存してもかかる狂悖人なれば素より脱囚の時は自ら期せず、此の世にて老兄を見ること能はず。老兄にも小生の事必ず思ひ出さぬ様成され度く候。僕頃ろ李氏焚書を抄録仕り候。卓吾は蠢物にて僕、景仰欽慕大方ならず。僕若し遂に老兄に見ゆる能はざらんも、右の抄録を残し置き候間御一見下さるべく候。

寅

Although Shouin Yoshida had once prepared for death, he regained his presence of mind in April 1859 at long last. If he had realized that the Choushuu Domain would not comply with the demand to furnish weapons for an assassination plan, he might have revitalized the Choushuu Government, which had been ignoring the trends of the times. A letter to Wasaku Nomura from Yoshida suggests the above point of view.　In a letter to Ansei Kitayama (a nephew of Shouzan Sakuma), Shouin Yoshida disclosed his feelings as follows:

"All of the dignitaries of the Shogunate and feudal lords have already become mere drunkards and are unable to support the people. Civilian revolt is the only hope for disrupting the status quo under these circumstances."

He began to give up on the Domain Government as hopeless gradually from this point in time and set his mind toward civilian power. This letter to Shinsaku Takasugi shows his deep lamentation and feelings straightforwardly, including about the problem of life and death.

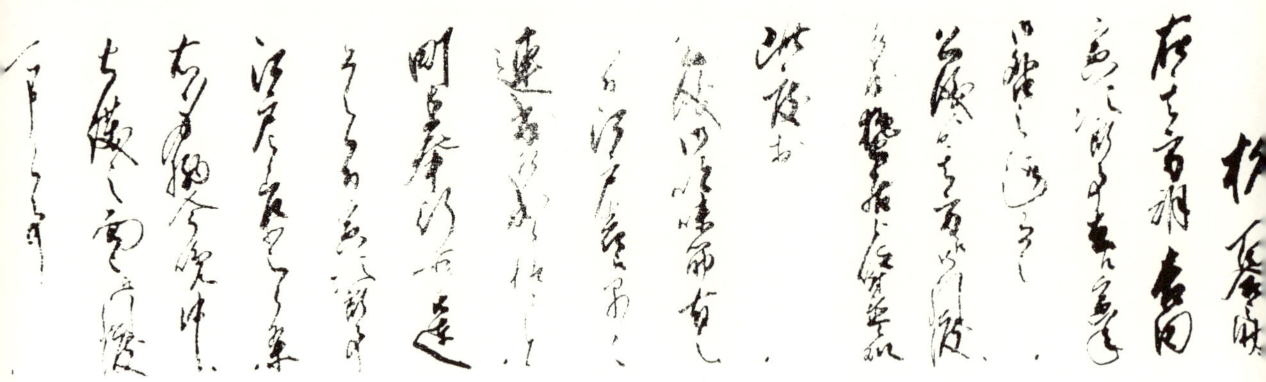

東送命令書

杉百合之助

右其の方育吉田寅次郎事去る寅年御咎めの趣之れあり、公儀より其の方へ御引渡し相成蟄居仰付け置かれ候処、此の度公儀に於て御吟味筋之れあり候に付き、江戸表へ早々連出し相成り候様にと、町奉行所より御達し之れあり候に付き、寅次郎事江戸差登され候條、右身柄今晩中守護の面々へ引渡し申すべく候事。

東送命令書

Command to Transfer Shouin Yoshida to Edo

幕府からのこの命令は長州藩の長井雅楽(1819 - 1863)らを経由して安政六年５月に松陰の父、杉百合之助に内命された。松陰は即座にこの機会を捉え、「尊攘の大儀を法廷で説き、幕政転換に役立てることが長州藩のためでもある」と考えた。

This Shogunate command was given to Yurinosuke Sugi, his father, through Utanokami Nagai (1819_1863) of the Choushuu Government in May of 1859. Hearing this command, Shouin Yoshida promptly hit upon the idea that it would also be beneficial for the Choushuu Government to elucidate the righteousness of the principle of revering the Emperor and expelling the foreigners in a court of law, if he were called upon to convert to Shogunate policy.

東行前日記

志

かけまくも君の国たに安からは身を捨るこそ賤がほゐ也
五月雨の曇りに身をハ埋むとも君の御ひかり月と晴てよ
今更ニ言の葉草もなかりけり五月雨晴る丶時をこそ待て

五月十四日　午後、家兄伯教至り、東行の事を報じて云はく、「長井雅樂、之れが爲め故ら特に國に歸りしなり」と。薄暮、家兄復た至り、飯田正伯・高杉晋作・尾寺新之允連名の書を致す。云はく、「幕府有志の官員佐々木信濃守・板倉周防守等、水府及び諸藩の正士の罪を寛くせんことを請ひ、聽かれず、是れに坐して罷免せらる。今先生幕逮を蒙る。願はくは身を以て國難に代り、且つ懇ろに公武を合體するの議を陳べられなば社稷の大幸なり」と。家兄の初め至りしときは事未だ確定せず。乃ち一絶を作る。

密使星馳事若何　　密使星馳す事若何、
人傳縛我向秦和　　人は傳ふ我れを縛して秦に向つて和すと。
武關一死寧無日　　武關の一死、寧んぞ日なからんや、
何倣屈平投汨羅　　何ぞ倣はん屈平汨羅に投ずるに。

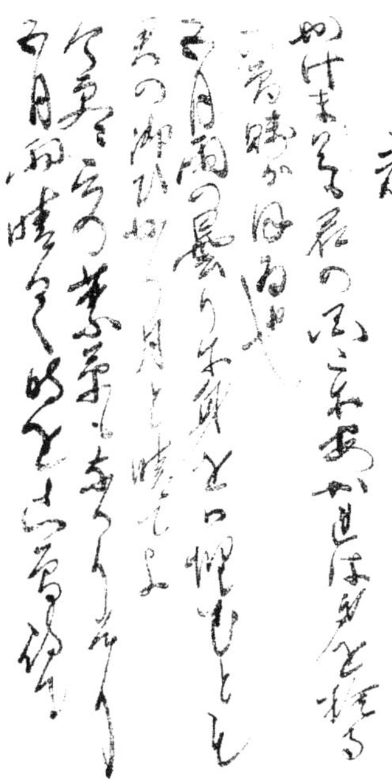

東行前日記

Diary before going to Edo

松陰は十数年後の計画を高杉晋作宛に書いていたが、東送命令書を受け、出発前に筆をとることにした。内容は日々の記事並びに家族、親戚、知人、門人に遺した詩歌文から構成されており松陰の思想哲学を知る貴重な文献である。

Though he wrote to Shinsaku Takasugi sometimes about the schemes that would be achieved after ten-odd years, he decided to put his ideas into shape before going to Edo.

The content consists of daily incidents and poems and writings dedicated to his family, relatives, acquaintances and disciples and is valuable in learning his ideology and philosophy.

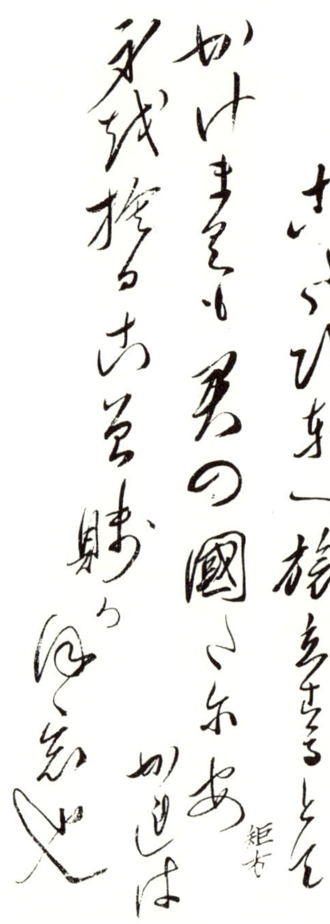

養母に遺した和歌

こたび東へ旅立するとて

かけまくも君の国だに安かれば

身を捨(すつ)るこそ賤(しず)がほゐ也

矩方

養母へ遺した和歌

A tanka (31 - syllable Japanese poem) dedicated to his foster mother

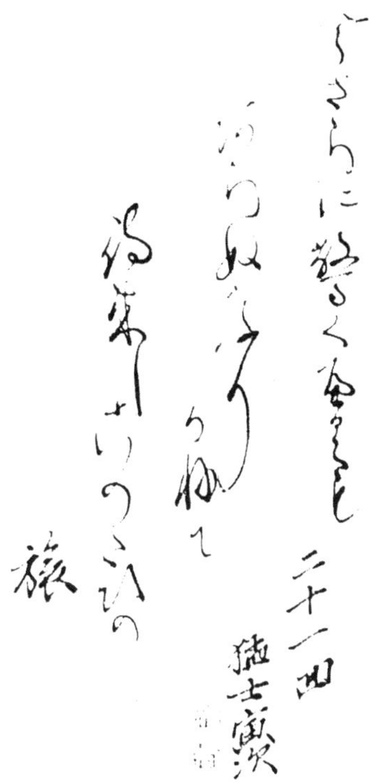

留別久坂玄瑞和歌
今さらに驚くべくも
あらぬなり
かねて
待来しこのたびの旅
二十一回
猛士寅次

留別久坂玄瑞和歌

A tanka dedicated to Genzui Kusaka

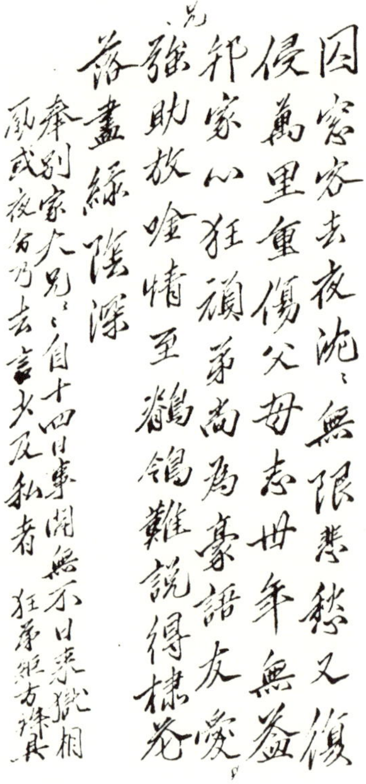
囚窓容去夜沈々無限悲愁又復
侵萬里重傷父母志廿年無益
邦家心狂頑弟尚為豪語友愛
兄強助放唫情至鶺鴒難説得棣花
落盡緑陰深

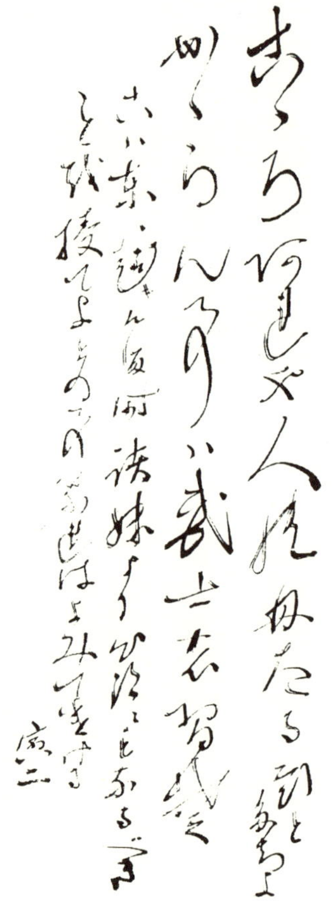

兄である杉梅太郎へ別れを告げる詩
（安政六年五月二十二日）
A poem dedicated to Umetarou Sugi.

諸妹に遺した和歌
（安政六年五月十七日）
A Tanka dedicated to his sisters.

諸友に語ぐる書

吾れ甲寅の挙（下田出国事件）、自ら万死を分とす。図らざりき、幕府寛貸以て死せざるを得たり。是れ今日宜しく幕府の為めに死すべきの一なり。甲寅の後、幽囚せられて国に在り、而も吾が公眷顧衰へず。是れ今日宜しく吾が公のために死すべきの二なり。加之、聖天子宵衣旰食、夷事を軫念したまひ、去年来の事豈に普率（全国の人々）の宜しく旁観坐視すべき所ならんや。是れ今日宜しく天子の為めに死すべきの三なり。三の宜しく死すべきありて死す、死すとも朽ちず。亦何ぞ惜しまん。吾が藩多士、最も卓犖を称する者は僧清狂なり、而して清狂は則ち死せり。最も忠貞を称する者は口羽徳祐なり、而して徳祐も亦死せり。此の二人の者は人士の望を属する所、而も疾病の犯すや死より貰されず。是れ死は人の免れざる所、吾が迂愚に於て益々惜しむに足らざるなり。

水戸の鵜飼幸吉・越前の橋本左内・京師の頼三樹三郎の諸人は皆当世の名士にして、年歯皆壮、吾れと伯仲す。今皆死して不朽の人となる。吾れ豈に独り諸人に後るべけんや。

漢の朱雲・宋の施全・明の楊継盛、吾れ嘗て仰いでこれを慕ふ。今吾れ幸に一死を得ば亦以て三賢の亜あるべし。

今茲五月、檻輿国を去る、平生の心事具さに諸友に語げ、復た遺欠なし。諸友蓋し吾が志を知らん、為めに我れを哀しむなかれ。我れを哀しむは我れを知るに如かず。我れを知るは吾が志を張りてこれを大にするに如かざるなり。

　吾れの将に去らんとするや、子遠（入江杉蔵）吾れに贈るに死の字を以てす。吾れこれに復するに誠の字を以てす。子遠の言大いに是れ理あり、若し誠の字にして未だ透らずんば、或は頭巾の氣習あらん。但し

（後文闕）

諸友に語ぐる書（弟子達に対する辞世の書）

Letter to his disciples ;

A farewell document written on October 20, 1859, the eve of his death, addressed to his disciples

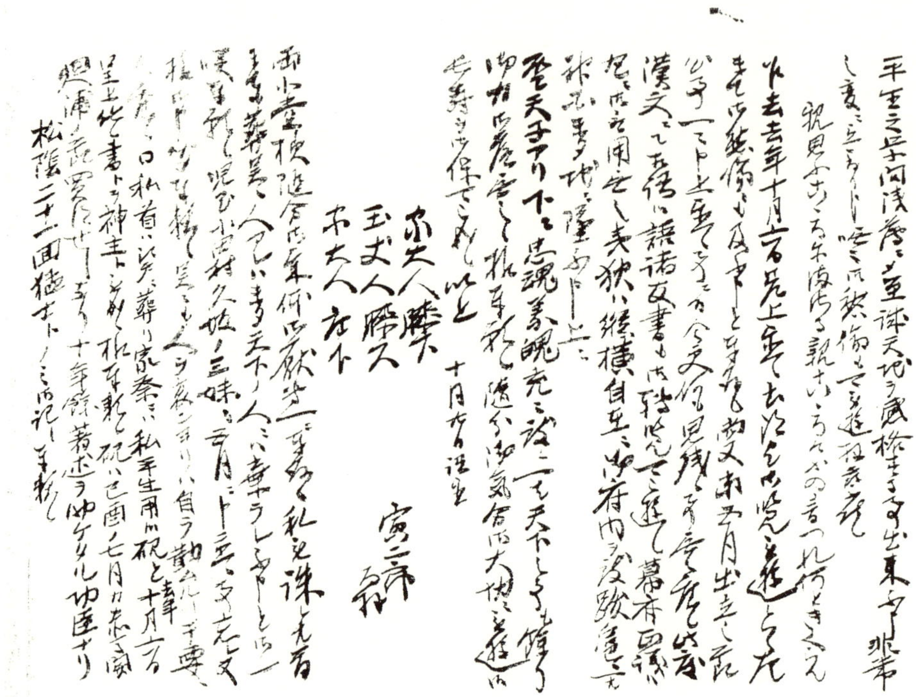

A farewell document written on October 20, 1859, the eve of his death, addressed to his family

永訣書

平生の学問浅薄にして至誠天地を感格すること出来申さず、非常の変に立到り申し候。嘸々御愁傷も遊ばさるべく拝察仕り候。

　親思ふこころにまさる親ごころけふの音づれ何ときくらん

さりながら去年一月六日差上げ置候書、得と御覧遊ばされ候はば左まで御愁傷にも及び申さずと存じ奉り候。尚ほ又当五月出立の節心事一々申上げ置き候事に付き、今更何も思ひ残し候事御座なく候。此の度漢文にて相認め候諸友に語ぐる書も御転覧遊ばさるべく候。幕府正議は丸に御取用ひ之れなく、夷狄は縦横自在に御府内を跋扈致し候へども、神国未だ地に墜ち申さず、聖天子あり、下に忠魂義魄充々致し候へば、天下の事も余り御力落し之れなく候様願ひ奉り候。随分御気分大切に遊ばされ、御長寿を御保ち成さるべく候。　以上。

十月二十日認め置く。　寅次郎百拝

家大人　膝下

玉丈人　膝下

家大人　座下

両北堂様随(兄)分御気体御厭ひ専一に存じ奉り候。私誅せられ候とも、首までも葬り呉れ候人あれば、未だ天下の人には棄てられ申さずと御一咲願ひ奉り候。児玉・小田村・久坂の三妹へ五月に申し置き候事忘れぬ様申し聞かせ頼み奉り候。呉々も人を哀しまんよりは自ら勤むること肝要に御座候。○私首は江戸に葬り、家祭には私平生用硯と、去年十(一)月六日呈上仕り候書とを神主と成され候様頼み奉り候。硯は己酉の七月か、赤間関廻浦の節買得せしなり、十年余著述を助けたる功臣なり。

　松陰二十一回猛士とのみ御記し頼み奉り候。

永訣書

His final letter to family

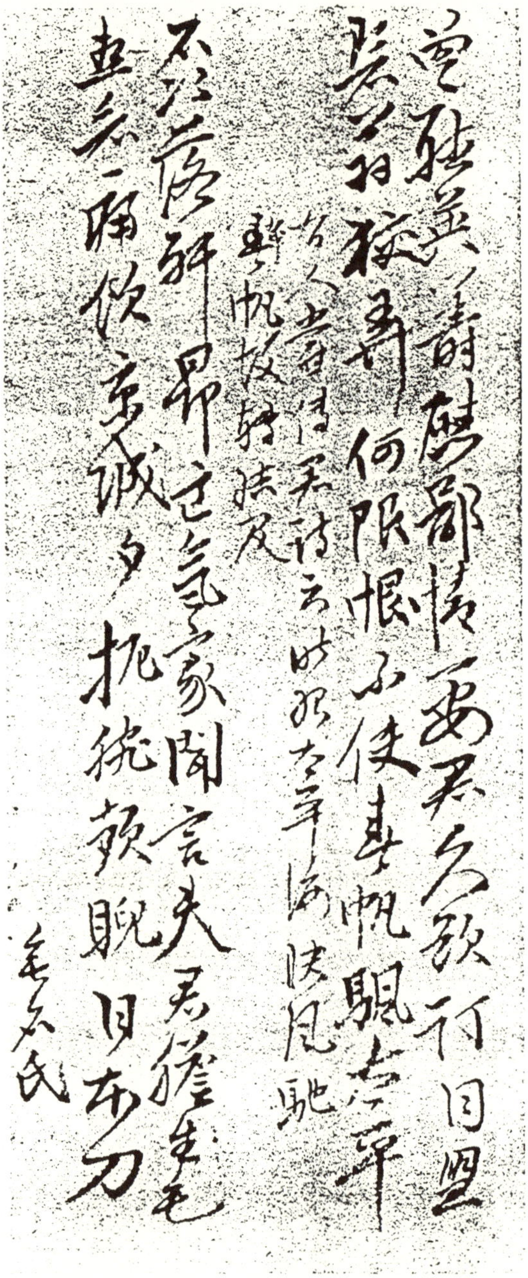

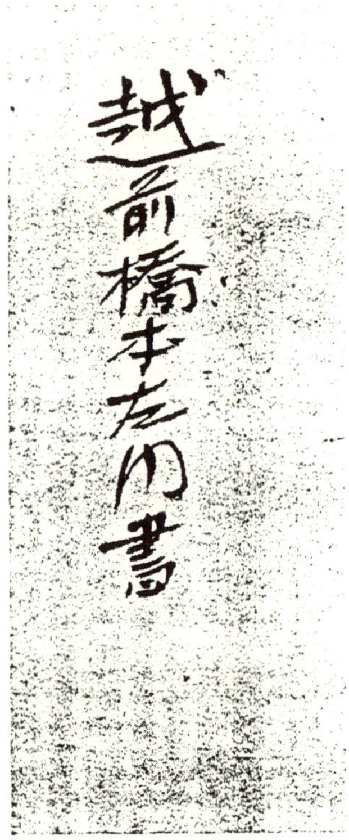

徳富蘇峰は橋本左内を不世出の英傑と喩えたが、
その左内が獄中から松陰へ贈った詩（左上）。
松陰はこの詩稿を包紙に入れ「越前橋本左内書」と上書（右上）した。

The left is two poem to Shouin Yoshida from Sanai Hashimoto and the right is a piece of paper inscribed by Shouin Yoshida with the words “a paper of Echizen’s Sanai Hashimoto” was wrapped around his poems.

曾て英籌を聴いて鄙情を慰む、君を要して久しく同盟を訂せんと欲す。
碧翁の狡弄何んぞ恨を限らん。春帆をして太平を颿せしめざりしを。
右人嘗て君の詩を傳へて云ふ。「昨夜太平の海、快風布帆を馳す」と故に轉結及ぶ。
磊落軒昂意氣豪なり、聞くならく夫君膽毛を生ずと、想ひ看る痛飲京城の夕、腕を扼して頻りに睨す日本刀。

無　名　氏

橋本左内；獄中で吉田松陰へ贈る詩

Poems dedicated to Shouin Yoshida in jail from Sanai Hashimoto

越前藩の英傑、橋本左内と吉田松陰は、互いにその才識を伝えきくばかりで生涯会うことがなかった。しかし安政の大獄で左内刑死の直前の数日、棟こそ違ったが同じ伝馬町の獄舎に収監されたので、左内は松陰に詩二首を贈って敬意を表した。松陰も留魂録で左内を賞賛し、会うことが出来なかったことを残念がっている。

Sanai Hashimoto (1834 - 1859), an extraordinary character in the Echizen Domain, and Shouin Yoshida knew each other only by hearing of their respective talents, but had never met each other in their lives. For several days just before the death of Sanai Hashimoto, however, though in different buildings, they were confined in the same jail. Sanai Hashimoto regarded Shouin Yoshida with respect as evidenced by these two poems to him. Shouin Yoshida also touched upon Sanai Hashimoto in the "Ryukonroku (Soulful Minute)" he wrote while in jail. He admired Sanai Hashimoto greatly and was disappointed at the circumstances that preventing them from meeting each other.

松陰に師事または幕末政治運動に関与した主な門下生。

久坂玄瑞（25歳）禁門の変で自刃
高杉晋作（29歳）奇兵隊総督、病没
吉田稔麿（24歳）池田屋事件で重傷、自刃
入江九一（28歳）蛤御門の変で戦死
寺島忠三郎（22歳）蛤御門の変で自刃
有吉熊次郎（23歳）八幡隊隊長、蛤御門の変で自刃
松浦松洞（26歳）尊皇攘夷運動に従事、自刃
赤根武人（29歳）奇兵隊第三代総督、処刑
前原一誠（49歳）干城隊副総督、萩の乱で刑死
玉木彦介（25歳）藩内訌戦で戦死
阿座上正蔵（19歳）蛤御門の変で重傷、自刃
駒井政五郎（29歳）御楯隊小隊司令、北海道で戦死
時山直八（31歳）奇兵隊参謀、北越戦争で戦死
飯田正伯（38歳）獄死
松山松介（27歳）池田屋事件で重傷、自刃
大谷茂樹（28歳）回天軍総督、俗論派によって処刑
木戸孝允（44歳）第一回地方長官会議議長、西南戦争で死去

正木退蔵（51歳）干城隊士、外交官
岡彦太郎（62歳）報国団創設、内閣書記官
山田顕義（49歳）整武隊総督、司法大臣
品川弥二郎（58歳）御楯隊隊長、内務大臣
伊藤博文（69歳）討幕運動に従軍、内閣総理大臣
尾寺新之允（70歳）奇兵隊士、伊勢大神宮大宮司
野村和作（68歳）鴻城隊総督、逓信大臣
山県有朋（85歳）奇兵隊軍監、内閣総理大臣
松本鼎（69歳）御楯隊士、元老院議官
滝弥太郎（65歳）奇兵隊第二代総督、佐波郡郡長

Shouin Yoshida's principal disciples

Genzui Kusaka(25 years old): suicide at the Kinmon Incident
Sinsaku Takasugi(29 years old):death of sickness
Toshimaro Yoshida(24 years old):suicide at the Ikedaya Incident
Kyuuichi Irie(28 years old):die on the Hamagurigomon Incident
Chuzaburou Terashima(22 years old):suicide at the above Incident
Kumajirou Ariyoshi(23 years old):suicide at the above Incident
Shoudou Matsuura(26 years old):suicide by the sword
Taketo Akana(29 years old):execution
Issei Maebara(49 years old):death by execution at Hagi Rebellion
Hikosuke Tamaki(25 years old):death in the Domain internal battle
Shouzou Azagami(19 years old):die on the Hamagurigomon incident
Seigorou Komai(29 years old):death in battle at Hokkaidou.
Naohachi Tokiyama(31 years old):death in Hokuriku Battle
Shouhaku Iida(38 years old):death in prison
Shousuke Matsuyama(27 years old):suicide at the Ikedaya incident
Shigeki Ohtani(28 yeard old):execution by vulgar faction
Kouin Kido(44 years old):death in the Southwest Rebellion

Taizou Masaki(51 years old):Diplomat
Hikotarou Oka(62 years old):Cabinet Secretariat
Akiyoshi Yamada(49 years old):Minister of Justice
Yajirou Shinagawa(58 years old):Minister of Home Affairs
Hirobumi Itou(69 years old):Prime Minister
Shinnojyou Odera(70 years old):Great Chief Priest of Ise Shito Shrine
Wasaku Nomura(68 years old):Minister of Posts & Telecommunications
Aritomo Yamagata(85 years old):Prime Minister
Kanae Matsumoto(69 years old):Senator
Yatarou Taki(65 years old):County Chief of Saba county

くさか げんずい　久坂玄瑞　1840～64(天保11～元治1)幕末期の志士。(系)長州藩医久坂良迪の子。(名)通武，のち義助，初名誠，字は実甫，号を江月斎，玄瑞は通称。‖吉田松陰の松下村塾に学び秀才の名が高かった。松陰の妹を妻として過激な尊王攘夷論を唱える。1862(文久2)脱藩上洛して公武合体派に反対して行動し，薩摩藩士有馬新七 らと京都所司代襲撃を計画したが，寺田屋事件で有馬らが斬られ，計画は挫折。同年12月には高杉晋作 らとともに江戸品川御殿山の英国公使館焼打ちを決行。'63上洛して攘夷親征の朝議決定を推進し，帰藩して攘夷決行の準備をすすめ下関の外国船砲撃事件に活躍。しかし，同年8月18日の政変によって長州藩は京都から追われる。翌'64(元治1)池田屋事件で同志が多く斬られたのに憤激し，真木保臣（和泉)らと長州藩兵をひきいて上洛して禁門の変をおこし，御所付近で激戦中負傷，鷹司邸内で自刃した。(墓)萩市の保福寺。(著)「江月斎日乗」(「維新日乗纂輯」1，1925)。(参)武田勘治「久坂玄瑞」1944。

たかすぎ しんさく　高杉晋作　1839～67(天保10～慶応3)幕末期の志士。(系)長州藩士高杉小忠太の子，家禄150石。(名)春風，字は暢夫，通称晋作・東一・和助，変名は谷梅之助・谷潜蔵，号を東行・西海一狂生・東洋一狂生。‖藩校明倫館に学び，吉田松陰 の松下村塾に入る。のち江戸に出て昌平黌に学び，帰藩後明倫館で講義をした。1861(文久1)小姓役に進み藩主に従って江戸に出，長井雅楽の航海遠略策を批判，一方翌年7月幕艦に便乗して上海で太平天国を実見する。帰国直後に長州藩の尊攘派同志と品川御殿山の英公使館焼打をして江戸を逃れた。京都で落髪し隠遁するが，'63藩主から馬関における攘夷実行を命ぜられ，奇兵隊を組織して外国勢と戦う。同年〈8月18日の政変〉で京都を追われ，その挽回を策して進撃を主張する来島又兵衛らを制止しようとし，かえって京坂へ出奔して脱藩の罪を問われ野山の獄入りとなる。'64(元治1)前年の攘夷への報復である四国連合艦隊の下関砲台占拠の講和の使者に起用された。同年禁門の変後幕府の長州征伐に敗れた藩が，和議をすすめたことに反対し九州に亡命。やがて下関に帰り挙兵し，諸隊の応援を得て藩政府に勝利，藩論を討幕に転換させた。その後長州再征には全藩兵を指揮し幕軍に連勝したが，翌'67(慶応3)4月に病死した。'91(明治24)贈正四位。(著)東行先生五十年祭記念会編「東行先生遺文」1916，「高杉晋作全集」全2巻，1974。(参)奈良本辰也「高杉晋作」1965，百年祭奉賛会編「東行－高杉晋作」1966。

よしだ としまろ　吉田稔麿　1841～64(天保12～元治1)幕末期の志士。(系)長州藩足軽吉田清内の長男。(生)長門。(名)秀実，通称栄太郎，字は無逸，号を風萍軒，変名松村小介・松里勇。‖1853(嘉永6)江戸に上り藩邸に出仕。'56(安政3)帰藩し吉田松陰 の松下村塾に学ぶ。高杉晋作 ・久坂玄瑞 ・入江九一 らと並んで村塾の四天王と称される。松陰の死後は京都・江戸において尊攘運動に奔走。'64(元治1)同志とともに京都三条池田屋で密議中，新撰組に襲撃され重傷を負い自刃した。

Genzui Kusaka(1840_1864)

A samurai of the Choushuu Domain(now Yamaguchi prefecture) and a leading figure in the proimperial and anti−shougunate movement of the early 1860s. A disciple and brother−in−law of Shouin Yoshida, Genzui Kusaka was much influenced by his radical loyalist doctrines. Impatient with Choushuu moderate political policy, in 1862 he decided to join other imperial loyalists in plan to expel foreigners from Japan.

Shinsaku Takasugi(1839_1867)

A retainer of the Choushuu Domain(now Yamaguchi prefecture) and a central figure in the movement to overthrow the Tokugawa shougunate. From 1857 he studied at the Shouka Sonjyuku, the school run by the proimperialist Shouin Yoshida. In 1862 he traveled to Shanhai, where he witnessed the Taiping Rebellion and the foreign presence in China. In 1863 Choushuu fired on foreign ships in the Shimonoseki Strait. He organized a militia called the Kiheitai to defend the domain,but in 1864 Western forces demolished Choushuu coastal fortifications.

Toshimaro Yoshida(1841_1864)

A samurai of the Choushuu Domain(now Yamaguchi prefecture). From 1856 he studied at the Shouka Sonjyuku, the school run by the proimperialist Shouin Yoshida. He was reputed to be the Big Four in the school with Genzui Kusaka, Shinsaku Takasugi and Kyuichi Irie. In 1864 he was seriously injured at the Ikedaya in Kyoto by Shinsengumi and committed suicide.

いりえ きゅういち　入江九一　1838～64(天保9～元治1)幕末期の志士。㊔弘毅，字は子遠，のち河島小太郎。‖長州藩士として吉田松陰 の腹心となって行動，1859(安政6)獄にある松陰の救助をはかり奔走中に捕えられる。'63(文久3)主命により杉山松介らと京都で活動，ついで高杉晋作 と奇兵隊創設に努力する。'64(元治1)7月，禁門の変に際し，久坂玄瑞・寺島忠三郎らと山崎天王山に屯し，その参謀となったが，19日鷹司邸で飛弾にあたって負傷し，切腹した。

まつうら しょうどう　松浦松洞　1837～62(天保8～文久2)幕末期の志士。(系)魚商人の子。(生)長門国萩郊外松本。㊔温古，通称亀太郎，別号を知新・無窮。‖萩藩士根来主馬の家臣となる。幼時から画を好み沼西涯に師事する。1856(安政3)吉田松陰 の教えをうけ，尊攘運動に尽力する。'58京都から江戸に出て，アメリカ行きを企てたが失敗，翌年帰国。'59松陰が江戸へ檻送される時その肖像を描き，その面影を今に伝えている。'62(文久2)久坂玄瑞らと京都へ出，同藩士長井雅楽の公武合体，開国説に反対して暗殺を計画したが説得されて断念し，自らは栗田山で割腹した。1911(明治44)贈正五位。

ありよし くまじろう　有吉熊次郎　1842～64(天保13～元治1)幕末期の志士。(系)山口藩士有吉伝十郎の弟。㊔良朋，熊次郎は通称，字は子徳。‖幼少より吉田松陰の門に入り，長じて高杉晋作と親交をもつ。1863(文久3)久坂玄瑞 とともに周防国山口で八幡隊を編成，その隊長となる。'64(元治1)禁門の変に加わり敗れて自刃した。

てらじま ちゅうざぶろう　寺島忠三郎　1843～64(天保14～元治1)幕末期の志士。㊔昌昭，字は子大，号を刀山・甃不休斎，別名牛敷春三郎・中島三郎・児島百之助。‖長州藩士。1858(安政5)吉田松陰 を敬慕し，その門下に入り，松下村塾で学ぶ。安政の大獄にあい，松陰が獄に入ると奔走して，減刑を図る。'62(文久2)脱藩，以後尊攘運動に身を投じて活躍。'63久坂玄瑞・轟武兵衛らと共に攘夷の期を定めよとの上書を提出。'64(元治1)禁門の変の時，鷹司邸で自刃した。1911(明治44)贈従四位。

Kyuichi Irie(1838_1864)
A samurai of the Choushuu Domain(now Yamaguchi prefecture) and also called "Shien". After he studied at the Shouka Sonjyuku, Kyuichi Irie behaved well like Shouin Yoshida's right hand man. He performed Hara－Kiri(seppuku) in Kyoto.

Shoudou Matsuura(1837_1862)
A samurai of the Choushuu Domain(now Yamaguchi prefecture)
From 1856 he studied at the Shouka Sonjyuku, the school run by the proimperialist Shouin Yoshida. The portrait of Shouin Yoshida was drawn by him

Kumajirou Ariyoshi(1842_1864)
A samurai of the Choushuu Domain(now Yamaguchi prefecture)
He studied at the Shouka Sonjyuku, the school run by the proimperialist Shouin Yoshida. In 1863 he organized the Hachimantai with Genzui Kusaka and conducted as the commander.

Chuzaburou Terajima(1843_1864)
A samurai of the Choushuu Domain(now Yamaguchi prefecture).
From 1858 he studied at the Shouka Sonjyuku, the school run by the proimperialist Shouin Yoshida. After Ansei Purge, he joined the campaign of the "Reverse the Emperor and expel the barbarians".

あかね たけと　赤根武人　1839～66(天保10～慶応2)幕末期の志士。㊋町医者松崎三宅の子，のち赤根雅平の養子。㊐周防国玖珂郡。㊔赤禰とも書く。通称幹之助。‖僧月性 および郷塾克己堂に学び，のち京都に出て梅田雲浜 に師事。また江戸の斎藤弥九郎に剣を学ぶ。安政の大獄で雲浜が捕えられた際，吉田松陰 の命によってその破獄を企てる。のち帰郷して尊皇攘夷を唱え，1863(文久3)下関海峡を通過する外国艦船への長州藩の砲撃に加わり，ついで奇兵隊が組織されるとその総監となる。'64(元治1)四国連合艦隊との戦闘に参加。'65(慶応1)高杉晋作 の討幕のための挙兵に際し，赤根は奇兵隊温存のために消極的態度をとった。高杉の挙兵で藩論が討幕に一変するや，捕えられて，'66斬罪された。㊫末松謙澄「防長回天史」1911。

まえばら いっせい　前原一誠　1834～76(天保5～明治9)明治前期の政治家。㊋萩藩士佐世彦七の長男。㊐長門(山口県)。㊔八十郎，のち彦太郎，字は子明，号を梅窓。‖1857(安政4)吉田松陰 に入門，長崎に留学後西洋学所に学ぶ。'62(文久2)久坂玄瑞 らと脱藩，'63七卿方御用掛，'64(元治1)高杉晋作 らと挙兵し藩権力を掌握，'65(慶応1)干城隊頭取役。戊辰戦争では北越に参謀として出兵，のち徴士越後府判事，'69(明治2)参議のち兵部大輔となるが，翌年病のため辞任，帰国。'74の佐賀の乱にはじめは県令の請に応じ県下士族を説得したが，'76神風連の乱がおこると，奥平謙輔らと萩で挙兵，捕われて処刑された。1916(大正5)贈従四位。㊫妻木忠太「前原一誠伝」1934。

ときやま なおはち　時山直八　1838～68(天保9～明治1)幕末・維新期の志士。㊋時山茂作の長男。㊔養直，通称松太郎，号を梅南・白水山人，変名萩野鹿助・玉江三平。‖長州藩士。藩校明倫館，ついで松下村塾で学ぶ。1859(安政6)江戸に出て藤森弘庵 ・安井息軒 に師事する。'60(万延1)帰藩以後尊王攘夷運動に挺身する。'62(文久2)京都長州藩邸の諸藩応接掛，'64(元治1)帰藩し浪士取締役，同年奇兵隊に入り参謀となる。'68(明治1)戊辰戦争に従軍し各地を転戦，越後朝日山で戦死した。

Taketo Akane(1839_1866)
A samurai of the Choushuu Domain(now Yamaguchi prefecture). After he studied from priest Gesshou (1817_1858), who was the priest of Myouenji Temple, Taketo Akane studied under Unpin Umeda in Kyoto. He had a great esteem for Shouin Yoshida at the Ansei Purge, and jointed the Kiheitai to defend the domain.

Issei Maebara(1834_1876)
A samurai and statesman of the Choushuu Domain(now Yamaguchi prefecture). In 1857 he studied at the Shouka Sonjyuku, the school run by the proimperialist Shouin Yoshida. When the Boshin Civil War, series of battles that led to overthrow of the Tokugawa shougunate and the restoration of imperial rule, happened, he jointed as the staff officer. After Meiji Restoration, he was promoted to the position like a justice, a vice minister(Sangi). In 1876 he was executed at the Hagi Rebellion.

Naohachi Tokiyama(1838_1868)
A samurai of the Choushuu Domain(now Yamaguchi prefecture). After studied Hanko Meirinkan, Choushu Domain Academy for education of children and it's retainer, Tokiyama studied at the Shouka Sonjyuku, the school run by the proimperialist Shouin Yoshida. He jointed the Kiheitai as the staff officer, after he joined Boshin Civil War and death in the battle in Echigo(now Niigata prefecture).

きど たかよし　木戸孝允　1833〜77（天保4〜明治10）幕末・維新期の政治家。㊛長州藩医和田昌景の子、同藩桂九郎兵衛に養われる。㊓長門国萩。㊔通称桂小五郎，のち貫治，準一郎。1865（慶応1）木戸と改姓。号を松菊。‖1849（嘉永2）吉田松陰に師事。'52江戸に出て，剣術を斎藤弥九郎に，西洋砲術を江川太郎左衛門に学ぶ。相州警衛に参加，海防に志し，有備館舎長となるなど長州藩士内の指導者となり，志士として活動。'62（文久2）京都に出て藩主毛利敬親をたすけ，久坂玄瑞・高杉晋作らとともに藩論を尊王攘夷から，さらに倒幕へまとめることに力を尽くした。'63年8月18日の政変により，禁門警固の任を解かれた長州藩兵が三条実美らとともに帰国した後も京に留まり，'64（元治1）池田屋事件では新撰組の刃を危うく逃れ，また，禁門の変後も京に潜伏，芸妓幾松（のちの夫人松子）のたすけにより危難を脱した。'65（慶応1）大村益次郎らと長州軍制を改革，翌年坂本龍馬*の斡旋により西郷隆盛・大久保利通らと薩長連合の密約を結び，倒幕勢力の結集をはかり，'67大久保らと倒幕挙兵の計画をすすめた。王政復古後，西郷・大久保と共に維新の三功臣として徴士，ついで参与となり五箇条の誓文の起草に加わるなど，明治新政権の中枢に参画した。早くより版籍奉還の必要を説き，廃藩置県を提唱，また下級士族の不満をそらすため征韓論をとなえた。'72（明治5）岩倉遣外使節団の副使となり，帰国後，国憲制定の急務であることを論じ，征韓論に反対。'74台湾出兵に際してもこれに反対し下野するなど開明的絶対主義者としての立場を堅持した。'75大阪会議によって板垣退助とともに参議に復し，第1回地方官会議議長となる。つねに大久保の専制主義と板垣らの自由民権派の間に立っていた。西南戦争の最中に死去した。㊟「木戸孝允日記」全3巻，1929〜31，「木戸孝允文書」全8巻，1932〜33（ともに「日本史籍協会叢書」所収）。㊕伝記編纂所編「松菊木戸公伝」全2巻，1927。

やまだ あきよし　山田顕義　1844〜92（弘化1〜明治25）明治前期の陸軍軍人（中将）・政治家。㊔通称市之允，号を空斎・養浩斎・韓峯人など。‖長州藩士。松下村塾に学び，禁門の変に参加。戊辰戦争に東北諸藩および箱館の征討に従軍。1869（明治2）兵部大丞，'71岩倉遣外使節に随行。'73東京鎮台司令官となり，同年清国特命全権公使兼任（赴任しなかった）。'74佐賀の乱を鎮定。'77西南戦争の鎮定に功があり，中将となった。'78元老院議官，'79参議兼工部卿，'83司法卿。他方'78より刑法草案審査委員となり法典編纂に与かった。'85内閣制度創設に伴い第1次伊藤博文内閣の司法相。黒田・第1次山県・第2次松方の各内閣でも司法相を歴任。'89日本法律学校（のちの日大）を創立した。㊕日本大学編「山田顕義伝」1963。

Takayoshi Kido(1833_1877)

A statesman of the Meiji period.　Also known Kido Kouin.
Until 1865 he was known Katsura Kogorou. He received an orthodox education at the Meirinkan, the domain academy, and he then attended the private academy of Shouin Yoshida, where he was introduced to imperial royalism. With Takamori Saigou and Toshimichi Oukubo, one of the “three heroes” of the Meiji Restoration of 1868.
As representative of the Choushuu domain(now Yamaguchi prefecture) he negotiated the secret alliance with the Satsuma domain(now Kagoshima prefecture) that eventually overthrew the Tokugawa shougunate. His initiatives between 1868 and 1871 as a Meiji government official brought about the abolition of the feudal system and the creation of a centralized bureaucratic state.
As associate ambassador to the United States and Europe with Iwakura Mission, he was able to study Western political and education system. He promoted policies of centralization and modernization, most notably as councilor in 1870_1876.
In his last years Takayoshi Kido oversaw the young emperor Meiji education.

Akiyoshi Yamada(1844_1892)

A statesman and military deputy general of the Meiji period.
From 1857 he studied at the Shouka Sonjyuku, the school run by the proimperialist Shouin Yoshida. He jointed Kinmon incident and Boshin Civil War. He accompanied to the United States and Europe with Iwakura Mission. Yamada rendered distinguished service in the Seinan Sensou (Satsuma rebellion), he was promoted the deputy general of the military. He was the Minister of Justice, the first Itoh Cabinet with consecutively other Cabinets. In 1889 he established Nippon Law School(now Nippon University).

しながわ やじろう　品川弥二郎　1843～1900（天保14～明治33）幕末・明治期の政治家。㊋長州藩士品川弥市右衛門の子。㊓長門（山口県）。‖14歳のとき，吉田松陰 の松下村塾に入門。尊王攘夷運動に挺身し，長州藩倒幕派の1人として活躍した。1868（明治1）戊辰戦争には奥羽鎮撫総督参謀として従軍，'70普仏戦争視察のため渡欧，'73外務省書記官としてドイツに駐在した。'76帰国。'77内務大書記官，'80内務少輔，'82農商務大輔。'84子爵，'85特命全権公使としてドイツ駐在，'87帰国して宮中顧問官，'88枢密顧問官となった。'91松方正義 内閣の内相に就任，'92第2回総選挙には猛烈な選挙干渉をおこない，責任を負って辞任した。同年西郷従道 ・佐々友房 らと国権主義的な国民協会を結成して副会頭となったが，その後党勢は意のごとくならず，'99帝国党への改組を機に京都に隠遁した。㊜村田峯次郎「品川子爵伝」1910，奥谷松治「品川弥二郎伝」1940。

いとう ひろぶみ　伊藤博文　1841～1909（天保12～明治42）明治時代の指導的政治家。㊋百姓林十蔵の子，萩の足軽伊藤直右衛門の養子。㊓周防（山口県）。㊔幼名利助，のち俊輔，号を春畝。‖はじめ松下村塾に学び，木戸孝允 に従い尊王攘夷運動に参加。1863（文久3）井上馨 らとひそかに渡英した。四国連合艦隊の下関砲撃の報を聞いて帰国，列国と講和を結ぶのに尽力。以後討幕運動にしたがい，薩長連合成立とともに高杉晋作 のもとに接薩副使となる。維新政府の成立にさいして参与・外国事務局判事・大阪府判事・兵庫県知事・大蔵小輔兼民部小輔・工部大輔となり，'71（明治4）岩倉具視 遣外使節団の副使として欧米を視察，帰国後は征韓論を制圧し，参議兼工部卿となり，大久保利通 の死後は内務卿として政府部内に地歩を固め，さらに'81〈明治14年の政変〉により対立者大隈重信 を政府から追放し，最高指導者となった。'82憲法取調べのため渡欧し，プロシア憲法を学んで帰国。以後，華族制度・内閣制度の創設，大日本帝国憲法・皇室典範の制定・枢密院設置など，天皇制確立のために努力した。'85内閣制度創設とともに初代総理大臣となり，また枢密院議長として政治を運営した。'92第2次内閣を組織し，行政管理・条約改正・海軍拡張を行ない日清戦争を強行。'98第3次内閣を組織したが，憲政党の反対にあい半年で崩壊。このことから政党組織の必要を感じ，1900立憲政友会を組織し，総裁となる。同年第4次内閣を組織したが翌年辞職，三たび枢密院議長となる。日露戦争後，'06日韓協約を結び，初代韓国統監となり併合強行への一歩をふみだした。'09満州（中国東北地方）視察と日露関係調整のため中国へ渡るさい，ハルビン駅頭で朝鮮独立運動家安重根に暗殺された。㊕「伊藤公全集」全3巻，1927。㊜平塚篤編「伊藤博文秘録」全2巻，1929～30，春畝公追頌会編「伊藤博文伝」全3巻，1940，岡義武「近代日本の政治家」1960，「伊藤博文関係文書」全9巻，1973

Yajirou Shinagawa(1843_1900)
A statesman of the Meiji period.
In 1859 he studied at the Shouka Sonjyuku, the school run by the proimperialist Shouin Yoshida. In 1870 he visited Europe, then resided as a secretary in Germany from 1873 to 1876. In 1884 viscount. In 1885 he visited again as the ambassador extraordinary and plenipotentiary in Germany. In 1891 he was inaugurated as the Minister of Home Affairs of the Matsukata Cabinet.

Hirobumi Itou(1841_1909)
A preeminent statesman of modern Japan.
He was born in Choushuu Domain(now Yamaguchi prefecture). His father was the adopted son of a low ranking samurai family.
In 1858 he studied at the Shouka Sonjyuku, the school run by the proimperialist Shouin Yoshida. In 1863 Choushuu officials awarded Itou samurai status and despite Japan's policy of national seclusion, sent him to England with Kaoru Inoue. While abroad he abandoned his anti Western stance and came to favor the diplomatic and commercial opening in Japan. In 1870 he went to the United States to study Western currency system. Returning to Japan in 1871, he was made Director of the Tax Division and then Vice Minister of Public Work. In 1875 he presided as chairman of the first Assembly of prefectural Governors. The death of Takayoshi Kido in 1877 and the assassination of Toshimichi Oukubo in 1878 signaled a change in Japanese political leadership. Upon the establishment of a modern cabinet system in 1885, Itou became the first prime minister, serving concurrently as imperial household minister and the chairman of the Constitutional Commission. In1889 he was granted the title "Genkun". In 1909 ,during a tour of Manchuria, he was assassinated in Harbin by An Chun Gun, a Korean nationalist.

のむら やすし　野村靖　1842〜1909(天保13〜明治42)幕末・明治期の志士・政治家。㊍長州藩士野村嘉伝次の子，入江杉蔵の弟。㊔通称和作，のち靖之助，号を欲庵・香夢庵主。‖1857(安政4)吉田松陰門下に入り，のち尊攘運動に挺身。'62(文久2)御殿山英館焼打ちに加わる。禁門の変ののち御楯隊を率いて藩の内戦，幕長戦争に参加。維新後，'71(明治4)宮内大丞，外務大書記となり，岩倉具視らに随行して欧米にわたる。帰国後，神奈川県令，駅逓総監，逓信次官をへて，'91駐仏公使などを務めた。'94第2次伊藤内閣の内相，'96第2次松方内閣の逓相に就任。1900枢密顧問官。

やまがた ありとも　山県有朋　1838〜1922(天保9〜大正11)明治・大正期の陸軍軍人(元帥)・政治家。㊓長門(山口県)。㊔小輔・狂介，維新後に有朋と改名。‖松下村塾に学び，藩命によって京都・江戸・鹿児島等を巡り，各藩の尊攘派志士と交わった。1863(文久3)奇兵隊の軍監となり，'64(元治1)奇兵隊を率いて藩内の俗論党と戦い，さらに第2次征長の役に際し幕軍と戦った。戊辰戦争に際しては北陸鎮撫総督兼会津征討越後国総督の参謀として転戦。維新後ヨーロッパに派遣され，帰国後，兵部少輔・同大輔・陸軍大輔となり，軍制の確立，徴兵令の制定などにあたった。'73(明治6)陸軍卿となり，西南戦争には征討参軍となる。その後，大久保利通・木戸孝允の死，板垣退助・大隈重信らの失脚によって伊藤博文とともに明治政府の最高指導者となる。'82参謀本部長から現職のまま参事院議長に転じ，'83内務卿，'85内閣制度による最初の内相となり，翌年農商相を兼ね，この間，地方制度の制定を通じて内務官僚の支配権を確立した。'88第1次内閣を組織し，その後陸軍大将にすすみ，'93枢密院議長。'94日清戦争に際しては第1軍司令官，大本営監軍兼陸相。'93ロシアに赴きロバノフと日露協定を結ぶ。'98元帥府に列せられ，この年第2次内閣を組織し，文官任用令改正・軍部大臣現役武官制を実現した。日露戦争には参謀総長となる。1907公爵。以後は表面に出ず，元老として政界を操縦した。大正期に入ると藩閥勢力に対する批判はきびしく，その絶対的な権力もゆるぎはじめ，'21(大正10)の皇太子妃選定問題(宮中某重大事件)によって右翼方面からも攻撃を受け，失意のうちに死んだ。終生政党を嫌悪し，官僚政治の保守に努めた典型的な藩閥政治家であった。㊟「懐旧記事」全5巻，1898，「山県有朋意見書」1966。㊜徳富猪一郎編「公爵山県有朋伝」全3巻，1933，岡義武「山県有朋―明治日本の象徴」1958，藤村道生「山県有朋」1961。

Yasushi Nomura(1842_1909)
A samurai of the Choushuu Domain(now Yamaguchi prefecture)and also called "Wasaku". He is a younger brother of Kyuichi Irie.
After he studied at the Shouka Sonjukyu, the school run by the proimperialist Shouin Yoshida from1857, jointed the Kinmon Incident.
In 1891 he held the post of the Japanese Minister in France.
In 1894 he took up his post with the Minister of the Communications at the second Itou Cabinet.

Aritomo Yamagata(1838_1922)
A political leader of the Meiji and Taishou periods.
Architect of the modern Japanese army, he also played a major role in building the political institution of Meiji Japan. He was born in Hagi, a castle town of Choushuu(now Yamaguchi prefecture), into a family of low ranking samurai. In 1858 he studied at the Shouka Sonjyuku the school run by the proimperialist Shouin Yoshida.
In 1870 he was appointed assistant vice minister of military affairs following a year abroad to study European military system, and in 1873 he assumed leadership of the Army Ministry, which had replaced the Ministry of Military Affairs the previous year.
He is credited with the enactment of the conscription ordinance of 1873,the suppression in 1877 of the Seinan Sensou (Satsuma Rebellion)led by Takamori Saigou, and the 1878 reorganization of the army along Prussian lines. Aritomo Yamagata resigned as army minister in 1878 and became the chief of the General Staff.
He was named to his first term as prime minister (1889_1891) in the same year that he was promoted to the rank of full general. During the last 20 years of his life, Aritomo Yamagata was the most influential member of the group of elder statesman known as "Genrou".

本章：留魂録

" Soulful Minute"

本章における『留魂録』逐語訳は作家・古川薫氏(文献 7) によるものである。
ここに英訳併記に際し、氏のご厚意と徳間書店のご了解を得て掲載した。
The word-for-word translation from original [Ryukonroku] archaic words has Been accomplished by Mr. Kaoru Furukawa, bibliography 7, a Japanese novelist. English translator would like to express the sincerest appreciation for his courtesy and Tokuma Shoten Publishing Company Ltd.

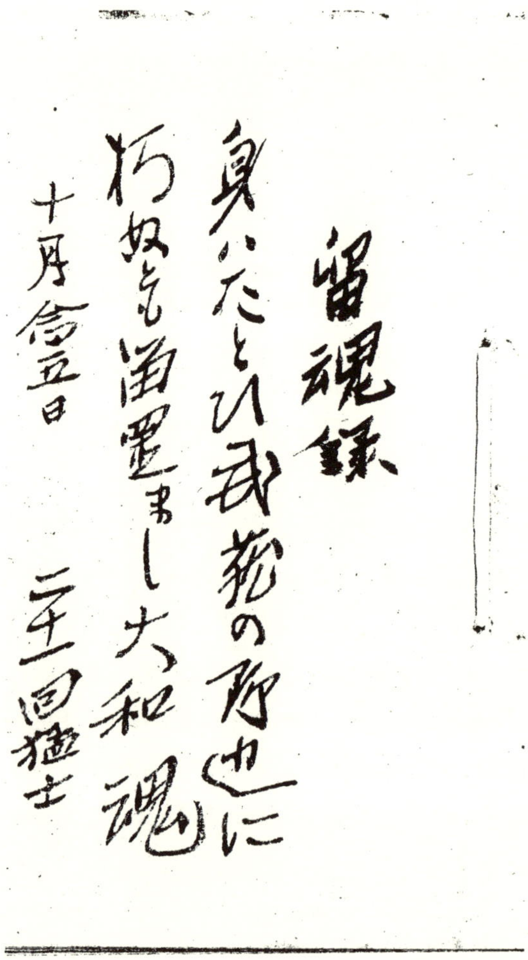

留魂録

身はたとひ武蔵の野辺に
朽ぬとも留置まし大和魂

十月念五日　　二十一回猛士

留魂録

“身はたとひ武蔵の野辺に朽ちぬとも留め置かまし大和魂”

十月二十五日

二十一回猛士

Soulful Minute

{Miwa, tatoe,Musashinono nobeni, kuchinutomo
todomeokamashi Yamato damashii}

“ Even if my physical body decays in the Musashino Plain
may my Yamato (Japan) Spirit remain as it is forever in Japan”

October 25, 1859

A samurai of undying loyalty.

一余去年已来心蹟百変挙テ数ヘ難シ就中
趙ノ貫高ヲ希ヒ楚ノ屈平ヲ仰ク諸知友ノ知
ル所ナリ故ニ子遠カ送別ノ句ニ燕趙多士一貫高
荊楚深憂只屈平ト云モ此事也然ルニ五月
十一日関東ノ行ヲ聞シヨリハ又一ノ誠字ニ工夫
ヲ付タリ時ニ子遠死字ヲ贈ル余是ヲ用ヒス
一白綿布ヲ求テ孟子至誠而不動者未之

有也ノ一句ヲ書シ手巾ヘ縫付携テ江戸ニ来リ
是ヲ評定所ニ留メ置シモ吾志ヲ表スル也
去年来ノ事恐多クモ　天朝幕府ノ間誠意
相孚セサル所アリ天苟モ吾カ區々ノ悃誠ヲ諒シ
給ハヽ幕吏必吾説ヲ是トセント志ヲ立タレモ
蚊蝱負山ノ喩終ニ事ヲナスコト不能今日ニ至
ル亦吾徳ノ菲薄ナルニヨレハ今将誰ヲカ尤
メ且怨ンヤ

一、余去年已来心跡百変、挙げて数へ難し。就中、趙の貫高を希ひ、楚の屈平を仰ぐ、諸知友の知る所なり。故に子遠が送別の句に「燕趙多士一貫高、荊楚深憂只屈平」と云ふも此の事なり。然るに五月十一日関東の行を聞きしよりは、又一の誠字に工夫を付けたり。時に子遠死字を贈る。余是れ用ひず、一白綿布を求めて、孟子の「至誠にして動かざる者は未だ之れ有らざるなり」の一句を書し、手巾へ縫ひ付け携へて江戸に来り、是れを評定所に留め置きしも吾が志を表するなり。去年来の事、恐れ多くも、天朝・幕府の間、誠意相孚せざる所あり。天苟も吾が区々の悃誠を諒し給はば、幕吏必ず吾が説を是とせんと志を立てたれども、蚊虻山を負ふの喩、終に事をなすこと能はず、今日に至る、亦吾が徳の菲薄なるによれば、今将た誰れをか尤め且つ怨まんや。

留魂録

Soulful Minute

第１章

私は昨年いらい実にさまざまな思いがうつり変わって、それは数えきれないほどである。なかでもとくに私がかくありたいと願ったのは、趙の貫高であり、また楚の屈平であることは諸君のすでに知るところだ。

だから入江杉蔵は私が江戸送りになると知って、「燕や趙にすぐれた士は多いが貫高のような人物は一人しかいなかったし、荊や楚にも深く国を憂う人は屈平だけだった」という送別の詩を贈ってくれたのである。

しかしながら五月十四日に東送の命令を聞いてからは、「誠」という一字について考えてみた。するとたまたま杉蔵がこんどは「死」の字を私に示し、死を覚悟するように説いてくれた。

私としてはそのことを考えないことにし、一枚の白木綿の布を求めて、孟子の「至誠にして動かざる者は未だ之れ有らざるなり」の一句を書いて、手拭に縫い付け、江戸にたずさえてきた。

そしてこれを評定所に留めおいたのも自分の志を表わすためであった。

昨年の情勢の推移を見るに、恐れ多くも朝廷と幕府のあいだには、互いに誠意が通じないところがあり残念に思われる。私の小さくてつまらないながら一途につらぬこうとする誠意をわかってもらえたなら、幕府の役人も私の説を聞いてくれるだろうと志を立てたのである。

しかし、私ごとき蚊や虻のような小さな虫は、結局は，幕府の力に押しつぶされて，幕府の俗吏どもがそれをにぎりつぶしてしまい、ついになすことなく今日にいたった。これも私の徳が薄いためだから、今さらだれをとがめ、怨むことがあろうか。

Chapter 1

Since last year, extremely various and innumerable ideas have floated in my mind.
It is a matter of common knowledge among my comrades that I would like to be the like of Kankou of Zhao and Kutsugen of Chu in particular.
So, having known that I would be brought to Edo (Tokyo), Sugizou Irie (one of the disciples of Shouin Yoshida) composed a farewell poem for me and sent it to me to the effect that although there were so many excellent figures in Yan era and Zhao era, it was only Kankou who was excellent in the true sense of the word, and it was only Kutsugen who was anxious about the future of Jing and Chu from the bottom of his heart. (Zhao, Chu, Yan, and Jing are the names of countries in ancient China)

However, since May 14,1859 when I knew that I would be brought to Edo to be punished with death, I have considered carefully the single word "Makoto (faithfulness)".

Then, this time, Sugizou Irie showed me the word "death" accidentally, and tried to persuade me to be prepared for death. However, I had decided not to think of death.

I wrote a phrase composed by Mongzi (a Chinese thinker in ancient times) on a white cotton cloth sheet to the effect that there has been nobody who has not been moved by sincerity; I brought this to Edo and submitted it to the supreme court of the Shogunate (Japanese Government in those days) to express my resolution.

Seeing the change of the situation in the last year, with due respect I may say, it seems, to my regret, that the Imperial Court and the Tokugawa Shogunate failed in making known their

貫高；前漢の人。趙王張敖の宰相。前漢の初代皇帝劉邦(BC247～195){高祖}が趙の国を訪れた時、胡坐をかいたままで趙王を罵倒し辱めたので、60余歳であった貫高は、趙王のために高祖を殺害したいと申し出て、逆に趙王共々捕らえられた。高祖はこれを壮士として許し、王は釈放されたが、貫高は獄中で自殺した。

Guan Gao; A minister of Zhang Ao, King of Zhao county, in the age of the Earlier Han Dynasty . Liu Bang (BC247 ~ 195), also called Gaozu, the first Emperor of the Dynasty, when visiting Zhao county, insulted Zhang Ao by sitting with his legs crossed. Guan Gao, a man of 60-odd years old, who saw Gaozu insult Zhang Ao, proposed killing of Gaozu to Zhang Ao, but they were arrested by Liu Bang instead. Later on, however, Liu Bang noticed that Guan's proposal was resulted from his devotion to his lord, Zhang Ao, and forgave them.
Zhang Ao was released, but Guan Gao committed suicide in jail.

屈原；戦国時代の楚の国の政治家、大詩人(BC340～278)。楚の懐王の時代に三閭大夫（さんりょたいふ）に就任。国務に精励したが、懐王の讒言、そねみに会い追放された。襄王が即位すると更に迫害され、長期間放浪を繰り返し、楚の国が秦の始皇帝に占領された後、汨羅（べきら）の淵に身を投げて自殺した。

Qu Yuan; A statesman and great poet of Chu country in the Age of the Warring States. (BC340 ~ 278).Qu Yuan took office as minister of King Huai in Chu and attended diligently to states affairs, but was banished by King Huai who believed the false charges caused by the jealousy of the other retainers. After the accession of King Rang to the throne, again, Qu Yuan was more persecuted and led a long and repetitive wandering life.
After Chu country was occupied by Shi Huangdi (BC259 ~ 210), Qu Yuan committed suicide at Miluo abyss (now Jiangxi Sheng in China).

sincerity to each other. I resolved that if my sincerity to attain my high ideal was understood by petty officials of the Shogunate, even if it was regarded as a trifle thing by them, they would listen to my ideal.

However, as the proverb says, "A small insect such as a mosquito or horsefly cannot bear a mountain on its back." I was crushed in the end beneath a mountain called the Shogunate, and petty officials of the Shogunate shelved my ideal.

After all, I haven't acted my part well, resulting in my meeting the present situation. This may be caused by my lack of discretion. Therefore, I neither blame anyone nor have an ill will against anyone.

一 七月九日初テ評定所呼出アリ三奉行出座
尋鞫ノ件両条アリ一曰梅田源二郎長門下
向ノ節面会シタル由何ノ密議ヲナセシヤ二曰
御所内ニ落文アリ其手跡汝ニ似タリト源二郎
其外申立ル者アリ覚アリヤ此二条ノミ夫
梅田ハ素ヨリ奸骨アレハ余与ニ志ヲ語ルコト
ヲ欲セサル所ナリ何ノ密議ヲナサンヤ吾性
光明正大ナルコトヲ好ム豈落文ナントノ隠昧
ノ事ヲナサンヤ余是ニ於テ六年間幽囚中ノ
苦心スル所ヲ陳シ終ニ大原公ノ西下ヲ請ヒ
鯖江侯ヲ要スル等ノ事ヲ自首ス鯖江
侯ノ事ニ因テ終ニ下獄トハナレリ

一、七月九日、初めて評定所呼出しあり、三奉行出座、尋鞠の件両条あり。一に曰く、梅田源次郎長門下向の節、面会したる由、何の密議をなせしや。二に曰く、御所内に落文あり、其の手跡汝に似たりと、源次郎其の外申立つる者あり、覚えありや。此の二条のみ。夫れ梅田は素より奸骨あれば、余与に志を語ることを欲せざる所なり、何の密議をなさんや。吾が性公明正大なることを好む、豈に落文なんどの隠昧の事をなさんや。余、是に於いて六年間幽囚中の苦心する所を陳じ、終に大原公の西下を請ひ、鯖江侯を要する等の事を自首す。鯖江侯の事に因りて終に下獄とはなれり。

まなべ あきかつ　間部詮勝　1802～84(享和2～明治17)幕末期の老中。㊋間部詮熙の3男，間部詮允の養子。㊔初名詮良，通称鉞之進，下総守，薙髪して松堂と号す。‖1814(文化11)襲封し越前国鯖江5万石を領した。'31(天保2)寺社奉行加役となり，'37大坂城代に進み，'38京都所司代をへて，'40年1月西丸老中に任ぜられた。しかし老中水野忠邦*と意見が合わず免ぜられた。以後，文雅の道に入り，また蘭学者と交際するなど外国の知識を得た。'58(安政5)6月再び老中となり，勝手掛・外国掛として，外交問題などの解決に腕をふるった。9月上洛して攘夷の志士を逮捕し(安政の大獄)，幕府にたいする疑念氷解の勅諚を得た。しかし翌年帰府ののち，大老井伊直弼と不和になり，12月に老中を辞職した。'62(文久2)在任中不宜として1万石の減封，謹慎を命ぜられたが，'65(慶応1)許された。

うめだ うんぴん　梅田雲浜　1815～59(文化12～安政6)幕末期の志士。㊋若狭国小浜藩士矢部岩十郎義比の次男，祖父の生家梅田氏の嗣子。㊔初名は義質，梅田氏となり定明，通称源次郎，別号を湖南・東塢。‖藩校順造館で学んだ後，同藩の儒者山口管山について山崎闇斎学を修め，1841(天保12)関西や九州諸国を遊歴し，のちに近江国大津の上原立斎に学び同地に湖南塾を開く。'43京都木屋町二条に移り，立斎の長女しんと結婚。森田節斎・梁川星巌らとの親交がはじまる。'50(嘉永3)からはじめた対外意見の建言は極貧の生活を送る中で書いたが，'52幕府の忌諱にふれて追放され，浪人儒者となる。'53ペリー来航に際しては頼三樹三郎・吉田松陰，水戸浪士らと尊王攘夷を唱えて奔走した。京都方面で星巌らと画策中，妻子は貧困の中で病死した。尊王攘夷と同時に大和と長州藩との交易の斡旋にも尽力。安政年間(1854～59)の将軍継嗣問題では，一橋慶喜の擁立につとめ公卿間に入説を行ない，幕府の開国の動きを止めるため大老井伊直弼排斥運動もすすめる。このため'58(安政5)9月幕吏に捕えられた。12月京都から江戸に檻送され，小倉藩邸に預けられたが，脚気を患い，翌年9月幽囚中に病死した。

七月九日に初めて評定所から呼び出しがあった。三奉行が出座し、次の二点について私を尋問した。

その一つは梅田源次郎が長州に行ったとき面会したというが、いかなる密議をしたか。今一つは御所内に落文があったが、その筆跡がお前のによく似ていると源次郎その他は言っている、覚えがあるかということだった。

梅田源次郎という人物は、がんらい奸智にたけており、共に志を語りたくないと思っていた私が、何で彼と密議をかわすことがあろうか。また私は公明正大に行動することを信条としている。落文などという陰にかくれた言論活動はけっしてしない。

上記二点をあきらかにしたのみ、私は六年間にわたる幽囚生活のあいだ、あれこれと苦心したことを陳述し、ついに大原公の西下をさそい、間部要撃を計画したことなどを自供してしまった。この間部要撃計画の自首によって、私は獄に投じられることになったのである。

Chapter 2

On July 9, 1859, I was summoned to the supreme court of the Shogunate for the first time. 3 magistrates attended and interrogated me about the following 2 points:

1. The meeting between Genjiro Umeda and I when he visited Choushuu (Yamaguchi Prefecture at the present time).
2. A letter purposely dropped in the Palace.

Regarding the first point, they regarded the meeting as a secret one and demanded that I disclose the contents of the meeting.

Regarding the second point, the magistrates told me that Genjiro Umeda and other persons testified that the handwriting of the letter looked like my handwriting and asked me whether I had done it.

Since I have regarded Umeda as a truly crafty man, he is the last man to whom I speak out my mind. Accordingly, it is outside the realm of possibility that I held a secret meeting with him. I live every day following my principle, that is, honorable behavior. I have never performed such a cloaked verbal deed as purposely dropping a letter.

After making these two points clear, I touched upon my hard experiences while I was confined for over six years, and at last, I confessed to my plan to ambush Akikatsu Manabe, a senior official, after inviting Court Noble Shigenori Ouhara to Choushuu. In the end, I was imprisoned because of my confession of the ambush plan.

一吾性激烈怒罵ニ短シ務メテ時勢ニ従ヒ人情ニ適スルヲ主トス是ヲ以テ吏ニ対シテ幕府違勅ノ已ムヲ得サルヲ陳シ然ル後当今的当ノ処置ニ及フ其説常ニ講究スル所ニシテ具ニ対策ニ載スルカ如シ是ヲ以テ幕吏ト雖モ甚タ怒罵スルコト不能直ニ曰ク汝陳白スル所悉ク的当トモ思ハレズ且卑賤ノ身ニシテ国家ノ大事ヲ議スルコト不届ナリ余亦深ク抗セズ是ヲ以テ罪ヲ獲ルハ万々辞セサル所

ナリト云テ已ミヌ又幕府ノ三尺布衣国ヲ憂ルコトヲ許サズ其是非敢テ弁争セサルナリ聞ク薩ノ日下部以三次ハ対吏ノ日当今政治ノ欠失ヲ歴詆シテ如是ニテハ往先三五年ノ無事モ保シ難シト云テ鞠吏ヲ激怒セシメ乃曰ク是ヲ以テ死罪ヲ得ルト雖モ悔サルナリト是吾ノ及サル所ナリ子遠ノ死ヲ以テ吾ニ責ルモ亦此意ナルベシ唐ノ段秀実郭曦ニ於テ彼カ如ク誠悃朱泚ニ於テハ彼カ如ク激烈然ラハ則英雄自ラ時措ノ宜シキアリ要ハ内省不疚ニアリ抑亦人ヲ知リ幾ヲ見ルコトヲ尊フ吾ノ得失当ニ蓋棺ノ後ヲ待テ議スヘキ、

一、吾が性激烈怒罵に短し、務めて時勢に従ひ、人情に適するを主とす。是を以て吏に対して幕府違勅の已むを得ざるを陳じ、然る後当今的当の処置に及ぶ。其の説常に講究する所にして、具さに対策に載するが如し。是を以て幕吏と雖も甚だ怒罵すること能はず、直に曰く、「汝陳白する所悉く的当とも思はれず、且つ卑賤の身にして国家の大事を議すること不届なり」。余亦深く抗せず、「是を以て罪を獲るは万万辞せざる所なり」と云ひて已みぬ。幕府の三尺、布衣、国を憂ふることを許さず。其の是非、吾れ曾て弁争せざるなり。聞く、薩の日下部以三次は対吏の日、当今政治の欠失を歴詆して、「是くの如くにては往先三五年の無事も保し難し」と云ひて、鞠吏を激怒せしめ、乃ち曰く、「是を以て死罪を得ると雖も悔いざるなり」と。是れ吾れの及ばざる所なり。子遠の死を以て吾れに責むるも、亦此の意なるべし。唐の段秀実、郭曦に於いては彼れが如くの誠悃、朱泚に於いては彼れが如くの激烈、然らば則ち英雄自ら時措の宜しきあり。要は内に省みて疚しからざるにあり。抑々亦人を知り機を見ることを尊ぶ。吾れの得失、当に蓋棺の後を待ちて議すべきのみ。

くさかべ いそうじ　日下部伊三次　1814 〜 58
(文化11〜安政5)幕末期の志士。㊋海江田納斎連の子。㊔信政、のち翼、号を九皐。‖薩摩藩士の父が水戸藩領多賀郡にあった時に生まれ、徳川斉昭 に招かれ水戸藩に仕える。のち1855(安政2)薩摩藩士に復する。'58幕府が日米修好通商条約に調印すると上洛して攘夷の勅諚を得るために活動する。薩摩・水戸の両藩に関係する地位を利用し、梅田雲浜 ・鵜飼吉左衛門らと暗躍の中心となる。水戸藩への攘夷勅諚が下るやその写しをもって木曽路をへて江戸の水戸屋敷へ伝達する。安政の大獄で捕えられ江戸伝馬町の獄で病死した。

私は性格が激しく　ののしられるとたちまち怒りを発する。それが自分でもわかっているから、日ごろはつとめて時流に従い、人々の感情に適応するように心がけてきた。

幕吏に対してもそれをもって臨み、幕府が朝廷の意思にそむいているのも、やむを得ない事情があったと相手の立場を認めた上で、これからとるべき適当な処置は何であろうかという方向に論を進めた。

そこで私が説こうとするのは、常に講究していることで、すでに『対策一道』に書いたとおりである。

そうした私の姿勢に対しては幕吏もさすがに怒罵することができなかったが、ただちに次のようなことを言った。

「お前の陳述することがすべて正しいとは思えない。かつ卑しい身分のくせに国家の大事を論ずるなどは不届である」

私はそれにも強く抗弁せず、ただ「このことが罪になるというのなら、それを避けようとは思わない」とだけ述べておいた。

幕府の法によれば、庶民が国を憂うことを許していない。

その是非について私はこれまで弁じたり争ったりしたことはなかった。

聞くところによると薩摩の日下部伊三次は、取り調べのとき当今の幕政の欠陥を徹底的に論じ立て、「こんなことでは幕府の安泰も三年か五年程度しか保てまい」と言ったため役人は激怒した。しかも日下部はさらに「これで死刑になっても悔いることはない」と言ってのけた。

私などには遠く及ばないところだ。杉蔵が私に死を覚悟せよと説いたのはこの意味かもしれない。

唐の段秀実は、郭曦には誠意を示し、朱泚には激烈に対して改心させた。英雄は時と所によって、それにふさわしい態度をとった。大事なことは、おのれをかえりみてやましくない人格を養うことだろう。

そして相手をよく知り、機を見るということもよく考えておかなければいけない。私の人間としての在り方がよいか悪いかは、棺の蓋をおおった後、歴史の判断にゆだねるしかない。

Chapter 3

I have a violent temper. Accordingly, I, when abused, would show anger at once. Since I am aware of this personality of mine, I have endeavored to follow the trend of the times as much as possible and to adapt myself to people's feeling.

I coped with officials of the Shogunate, too, with the same attitude.

That is, after recognizing the standpoint of the Shogunate acting against the intention of the Imperial Court based on an unavoidable situation, I struggled with how to cope with the measures which would be taken by the Shogunate. I was going to persuade officials of the Shogunate of the philosophy I always pursued, the same as the contents of "Taisaku Ichidou" (Road Leading to Ideal) which I published. Although the Shogunate's official didn't hurl abusive language at me, he said immediately to me. "I don't think all of your statements are completely correct. It is outrageous that you, only a low-born person, discuss the important matters of the country." I didn't protest strongly against his accusation, but I only made a comment: "If this leads to punishment, I will not avoid it."

The law of the Shogunate forbids the common people to be concerned about the future of our nation. I have neither talked about nor argued whether the common people should be concerned about the future of our nation or not.

I heard that Isouji Kusakabe of Satsuma Domain, when investigated, pointed out the defects in the recent Shogunal administration thoroughly and said, "Judging from the present state of affairs, periods of peace in the Shogunate may be maintained only for 3 or 5 years." This statement enraged the official. What is more surprising, Kusakabe said calmly, "Even if I

段秀実；唐時代の人(719 ~ 783)。字は成公。玄宗の時、安西府に将として赴任以来、
粛宗、代宗時代に累進出世し、徳宗時代に司農卿となった。名将郭子儀(697 ~ 781)の子、郭晞(? ~ 794)が親の威光を借り乱暴な振舞いに及んだため、訓戒を与え改心させた。また奸臣朱泚(742 ~ 784)が謀叛を企て段秀実に加担を誘ったが、これを厳しく面罵し退けたため、殺害された。[本文中の郭曦は詳細不明であるが,文献(88)より文宗に仕えた郭子儀の従兄弟(?_839)と思われる]

Duan Xiushi; A bureaucrat of Tang Dynasty (719 ~ 783).
Duan Xiushi had been promoted to the position of Minister in the De Emperor era since the start for his new post as an officer of Anxi county in the Xuan Emperor era. When Guo Xi (? ~ 794), a son of the famous General Guo Ziyi (697 ~ 781), did violence toward neighborhood sheltering himself under the influence of his father, Duan Xiushi led him into better ways with strong reprimands. In addition, wheb Duan Xiushi was tempted into rebellion by Zhu Ci (742 ~ 784), a villainous retainer, he rejected the temptation. Consequently, he was assassinated by Zhu Ci. [Details of Guo Xi in this text are not known, but according to the bibliography No.88, he seems to be a cousin of Guo Ziyi]

am sentenced to death because of this statement, I will not regret it." I am far behind him compared with his stout heart. It may be for this reason that Sugizou Irie tried to persuade me to be prepared for death.

It is said that Shuujitsu Dan (Xiushi Duan) in Tangchao era treated Kakugi (Guoyi) in good faith and Shusei (Zhu Xing) with violence in reforming them. Heroes should take a suitable measure depending on the time and place. It is especially important for me in this case to do everything with a clean conscience. It is also important to know one's opponents and take the first opportunity to carry it into execution. Time will tell whether my life style has been good or not after I am put in a coffin.

一　此回ノ口書甚草々ナリ、七月九日一通リ申立タル後九月五日十月五日両度ノ呼出モ差タル鞠問モナク、十月十六日ニ至リ口書読聞セアリテ直ニ書判セヨトノ事ナリ、余カ苦心セシ墨使応接航海雄略等ノ論一モ書載セス、唯数ケ所開港ノ事ヲ程克申延テ国力充実ノ後御打拂可然ナト吾心ニモ非ル迂腐ノ論ヲ書付テ口書トス、吾言テ益ナキヲ知ル故ニ敢テ云ハス不満ノ甚シキ也、甲寅ノ歳航海一条ノ口書ニ比スル時ハ雲泥ノ違ト云フヘシ

一、此の回の口書甚だ草々なり。七月九日一通り申立てたる後、九月五日、十月五日、両度の呼出しもさしたる鞫問もなくして、十月十六日に至り、口書読み聞せありて、直ちに書判せよとの事なり。余が苦心せし墨使応接、航海雄略等の論、一も書載せず。唯だ数個所開港の事を程克く申し延べて、国力充実の後、御打払ひ然るべくなど、吾が心にも非ざる迂腐の論を書付けて口書とす。吾れ言ひて益なきを知る、故に致へて云はず。不満の甚だしきなり。甲寅の歳、航海一条の口書に比する時は雲泥の違ひと云ふべし。

評定所で作成されたこのたびの供述書はまことに簡単なものである。七月九日にひと通り申し立てた後、九月五日、十月五日両度の呼び出しのときも大した尋問はなく、十月十六日にいたって、供述書の読み聞かせがあり、ただちに署名せよとのことだった。

私が苦心したアメリカ使節との応接、航海雄略論などについてはひとことも書いておらず、ただ数カ所に開港のことをほどよく申し述べて、国力が充実したあとで外国を打ち払うのがよいなどと、私の心にもない愚にもつかない論を書き付けて、これを供述書にしている。言っても仕方がないとわかったので、もうあえて抗議はしないことにした。

はなはだ不満である。

安政元年（一八五四）に、私がペリーの軍艦で海外密航をくわだで捕えられたときの供述書にくらべると雲泥の差がある。

Chapter 4

The written statement made by the supreme court of the Shogunate at this time was extremely simple. On July 9, I explained what I did briefly. After that, when I was summoned to the court on September 5 and October 5, I was not interrogated so much. On October 16, an official asked me to put my signature on the written statement immediately after reading it aloud.

In the written statement made by the supreme court, there were no records on the meeting with the American mission I had undertaken with great pains, nor on my view regarding the magnificent scheme of debouchment by voyage. The statement touched on the opening of ports only in several parts for mere form's sake and described an absurd theory to the effect that we should drive away foreign warships after completing our armaments, which is much removed from my ideas.

Since I realized that there was nothing to be gained by resisting officials of the Shogunate, I decided not to resist them actively. However, I am very dissatisfied. The written statement this time was quite different from the time I was arrested in 1854 on suspicion of an attempt to stow away to America on the Perry squadron in their particulars.

一七月九日一通リ大原公ノ事鯖江要駕ノ事等
申立タリ初メ意ラク是等ノ事幕ニモ已ニ諜知
スベケレハ明白ニ申立ルヲ却テ宜シキナリト已ニシテ
逐一ロヲ開キシニ幕ニテ一圓知ラサルニ似タリ
因テ意ラク幕ニテ知ラヌ所ヲ強テ申立テ
多人数ニ株連蔓延セハ善類ヲ傷フコト
少ナカラズ毛ヲ吹テ瘡ヲ求ルニ斉シト是ニ

於テ鯖江要撃ノ事モ要諫トハ云替タリ又
京師往来諸友ノ姓名連判諸士ノ姓名等
成丈ハ隠シテ具白セズ是吾後起人ノ為メニスル
区々ノ婆心ナリ而シテ幕裁果シテ吾一人ヲ罰シテ
一人モ他ニ連及ナキハ実ニ大慶ト云ヘシ同志
ノ諸友深ク考思セヨ

一、七月九日、一通り大原公の事、鯖江要駕の事等申立てたり。初め意へらく、是れ等の事、幕にも已に諜知すべければ、明白に申立てたる方却つて宜しきなりと。已にして逐一口を開きしに、幕にて一円知らざるに似たり。因つて意へらく、幕にて知らぬ所を強ひて申立て多人数に株連蔓延せば、善類を傷ふこと少なからず、毛を吹いて瘡を求むるに斉しと。是に於いて鯖江要撃の事も要諫とは云ひ替へたり。又京師往来諸友の姓名、連判諸氏の姓名等成るべき丈けは隠して具白せず、是れ吾れ後起人の為めにする区々の婆心なり。而して幕裁果して吾れ一人を罰して、一人も他に連及なきは実に大慶と云ふべし。同志の諸友深く考思せよ。

おおはら しげとみ　大原重徳　1801～79（享和1～明治12）幕末・維新期の攘夷派の公卿。㊅権中納言重尹の5子。㊔幼名常麿，字は徳義。‖1809（文化6）11歳で光格天皇の侍童となる。尊王の志をもち'58（安政5）徳川幕府の日米修好通商条約の勅許に岩倉具視・中山忠能らとともに反対した。のち水戸の徳川斉昭のもとへ脱京を企てたが失敗。'62（文久2）和宮が将軍徳川家茂夫人として降嫁すると，勅使として島津久光とともに江戸へ下り，幕政改革について勅命を伝達。翌'63寺田屋事件に関する一項削除の勅書改竄の罪に問われて蟄居。翌年赦される。'65（慶応1）兵庫開港に反対，'66同志の公家22人とともに御前会議で朝政革新を主張するなど，尊攘派として活躍，そのため'67閉門を命ぜられる。'70（明治3）参与，笠松裁判所総督，刑法官知事，議定上局議長，さらに集議院長官などを歴任した。

七月九日、ひと通り大原公のこと、間部要撃策のことなど申し立てた。これらは幕府においてすでに探知しているであろうから、こちらから明白に申しておくほうがよかろうと初めのうち私は思ったのである。そこで逐一そのことを自供したのだが、幕府は何も知っていないようだった。

幕府が知らないことを強いて申し立て、多くの人々に災厄を及ぼし、無関係の人を傷つけるのでは、毛を吹きわけて傷口を見つける譬にもひとしいと思いなおした。だから間部要撃の件についても「要撃」でなく［要諫」と言いなおした。

また京師に往来する諸友の姓名や間部要撃のとき連判状に署名した人々の姓名も隠して供述しなかった。これは後から起ち上がる人のためを思う私のささやかな老婆心であった。果して幕府の裁決は、私一人を罰して、他には一人も波及しなかった。実に喜ぶべきことだと思っている。

Chapter 5

On July 9, 1858, I briefly touched upon the invitation of Court Noble Sigenori Ouhara to the Choushuu domain and an attempt to ambush Akikatsu Manabe. This is because I supposed that the Shogunate had detected and known of our schemes, so I thought that it would bring a favorable result for me to disclose the scheme voluntarily at an early stage. Accordingly, I confessed it in detail, but I found that the Shogunate had not known anything about our scheme.

Later, I reflected that my conduct had been like "parting the hair to find a wound", that is, I had voluntarily disclosed what the Shogunate had not known, resulting in bringing misfortune on many people and injuring persons who had had nothing to do with my scheme.

Therefore, I amended the word, ambush to the word remonstrance regarding my scheme of ambushing Akikatsu Manabe. Of the friends who came to Kyoto (the capital of Japan at that time) to see me often and the comrades who signed on the compact under joint signatures to ambush Akikatsu Manabe, I didn't disclose their names at all. This is the manifestation of my solicitude for fearing that those who were planning to take action were arrested. Just as I thought, it was only I who received a verdict of guilty by the Shogunate. I was very glad to know that my confession did not affect any of my comrades.

一要諫一條ニ付事不遂時ハ鯖侯ト刺違テ死シ
警衛ノ者要遮スル時ハ切拂ヘキトノ事実ニ
吾カ云サル所ナリ然ルニ三奉行強テ書載シテ
誣服セシメント欲ス誣服ハ吾肯テ受ンヤ是ヲ
以テ十六日書判ノ席ニ臨テ石谷池田ノ両
奉行ト大ニ争辨ス吾肯テ一死ヲ惜ミンヤ

両奉行ノ権詐ニ伏セサルナリ是ヨリ先九月
五日十月五日両度ノ吟味ニ吟味役具ニ
申立タル旨死ヲ決シ要諫ス必シモ刺違切拂等ノ
策アルニ非ス吟味役具ニ是ヲ諾シテ而モ且
口書ニ書載スルハ権詐ニ非スヤ然氏事已ニ
爰ニ至レハ刺違切拂ノ両事ヲ受ケサルハ却
テ激烈ヲ欠キ同志ノ諸友亦惜ムナルヘシ
吾ト云氏亦惜シマサルニ非ス然氏反復是ヲ
思ヘハ成仁ノ一死區々ニ一言ノ得失ニ非ス今
日義卿奸権ノ為ニ死ス天地神明照
鑑上ニアリ何惜ムコトカアラン

一、要諫一条に付き、事遂げざる時は鯖侯と刺違へて死し、警衛の者要蔽する時は切払ふべきとの事、実に吾が云はざる所なり。然るに三奉行強ひて書載して誣服せしめんと欲す。誣服は吾れ肯へて受けんや。是を以て十六日書判の席に臨みて、石谷・池田の両奉行と大いに争弁す。吾れ肯へて一死を惜しまんや、両奉行の権詐に伏せざるなり。是れより先き九月五日、十月五日両度の吟味に、吟味役まで具さに申立てたるに、死を決して要諫す、必ずしも刺違へ・切払ひ等の策あるに非ず。吟味役具さに是れを諾して、而も且つ口書に書載するは権詐に非ずや。然れども事已に爰に至れば、刺違へ・切払ひの両事を受けざるは却つて激烈を欠き、同志の諸友亦惜しむなるべし。吾れと雖も亦惜しまざるに非ず、然れども反復是れを思へば、成仁の一死、区々一言の得失に非ず。今日義卿奸権の為めに死す、天地神明照鑑上にあり、何惜しむことかあらん。

第6章

間部「要諫」についてだが、諫言が取り上げられないときは間部と刺し違えて死に、護衛の者がこれを防ごうとすれば切り払うつもりだったとは、絶対に言っていない。ところが三奉行は強いてそれを記載し、私を罪におとしいれようとした。

そうした無実の罪にどうして服すことができようか。

そこで私は十六日、供述書に署名する席上、石谷・池田の両奉行と大いに論争した。私は死を惜しんでいるのではない。両奉行の権力にたのんだ詐術に伏したくなかったのだ。

これより先、九月五日、十月五日両度の取り調べのさい、吟味役にそのことをつぶさに申し立てた。死を覚悟して要諫するつもりであり、かならずしも刺し違え、切り払うなどは考えていなかったのだと。吟味役はよくわかったと答えたにもかかわらず、供述書には「要撃」として書き込んでいる。これも権詐というものではあるまいか。

だが、事はもうここまできた。刺し違え、切り払いのことを私があくまで否定したのでは、かえって激烈を欠き、同志の諸友も惜しいと思われるであろう。自分もまた惜しいと思わないわけではない。

しかしながら繰り返しこれを考えると、志士が仁のために死ぬにあたっては、このような取るに足らぬ言葉の得失など問題ではない。

今日、私は権力の奸計によって殺されるのである。神々はあきらかに照覧されているのだから、死を惜しむところはないであろう。

Chapter 6

I would like to take this opportunity to touch upon the ambush of Akikatsu Manabe. I didn't tell the three magistrates, for the life of me, that if Akikatu Manabe wouldn't have accepted my remonstrance, I would have killed him and died upon his sword and if his guards had been going to prevent my action, I would have killed them. However, the three magistrates dared to record that I planned to ambush and kill him. They tried to charge me unjustly. Why must I be falsely accused?

I will persist in pleading my innocence.

Then, on October 16, I substantially disputed the record of both magistrates, Ishitani and Ikeda, before signing the written deposition. I was not reluctant to lose my life. I was ashamed to lie down on the deceit fostered by both magistrates who were hiding behind their authority.

I asserted this in detail to the interrogator when an interrogation was made on September 5 and October 5. I insisted that although I would remonstrate against Akikatsu Manabe at the risk of my life, I wouldn't kill him and die on his sword. In spite of the interrogator's answer, "I understand very well', he used the word, "ambush", in the written deposition. This is also a kind of dishonesty hidden behind his authority, isn't it?

But, things have already come so far. I feared that if I denied everything to the last, including my will to kill Akikatsu Manabe and die on his sword and kill the guards, the magistrates and interrogator wouldn't have noticed my burning passion for my country. All of my comrades will regret it. I also feel it is regrettable.

奉行（magistrate and/or commissioners)

お上の命を奉じて事を執行すること。転じてその担当者。

平安時代、調停の諸儀式を取り行う為、臨時の奉行が設けられたが、鎌倉時代以降、次第に重要な武家職制となった。江戸時代は職制の整備と共に中央職と遠国職に各種の奉行が置かれた。中央職では寺社奉行、江戸町奉行、勘定奉行などが知られている。

Administrative officials of pre_modern Japan. The term originally meant "to carry out orders received from a superior". During Heian period (794_1185) {Bugyou } were appointed on a temporary basis to perform ceremonies at the imperial court. Kamakura shougunate appointed {Bugyou} more formally to oversee such administrative functions as the judiciary, shougunal household affairs, temples and shrines, and civil engineering projects. When civil and judicial administration was rationalized under the Tokugawa shougunate (1603_ 1867),{Bugyou} became middle ranking administrators with well defined duties.

However, I consider this repeatedly, concluding that for a noble-minded patriot who is about to die for a perfect virtue, it is nonsense to consider which expression of my mind is advantageous. I fell prey to the enemy's plot, and today, I will be killed by that power.

Since God knows everything, I should not regret my death.

一吾此回初メ素ヨリ生ヲ謀ラズ又死ヲ必セズ
唯誠ノ通塞ヲ以テ天命ノ自然ニ委シタルナリ
七月九日ニ至テハ略一死ヲ期ス故ニ其詩ニ云
継盛唯当甘市戮倉公寧復望生還其後
九月五日十月五日吟味ノ寛容ナルニ欺カレ
又必生ヲ期ス亦頗ル慶幸ノ心アリ此心吾此身
ヲ惜ム為メニ発スルニ非ズ抑故アリ去臘大晦
朝議已ニ幕府ニ貸ス今春三月五日吾公ノ駕
已ニ萩府ヲ発ス吾策是ニ於テ尽キ果タレバ死ヲ
求ムルコト極テ急ナリ六月ノ末江戸ニ来ルニ及テ
夷人ノ情態ヲ見聞シ七月九日獄ニ来リ天下
形勢ヲ考察シ神国ノ事猶ナスベキモノアルヲ
悟リ初テ生ヲ幸トスルノ念勃々タリ吾若シ

死セズンバ勃々タルモノ決シテ汨没セザルナリ
然レドモ十六日ノ口書三奉行ノ権詐吾ヲ死地ニ
措ントスルヲ知リテヨリ更ニ生ヲ幸フノ心ナシ
是亦平生学問ノ得力然ルナリ

一、吾れ此の回初め素より生を謀らず、又死を必せず。唯だ誠の通塞を以て天命の自然に委したるなり。七月九日に至りては略ぼ一死を期す。故に其の詩に云ふ、「[1]継盛唯当レ甘二市戮一、倉公寧復望二生還一」と。其の後九月五日、十月五日、吟味の寛容なるに欺かれ、又必生を期す、亦頗る慶幸の心あり。此の心吾れ此の身を惜しむ為めに発するに非ず。抑々故あり。去臘大晦、朝議已に幕府に貸す。今春三月五日、吾が公の駕已に萩府を発す。吾が策是に於いて尽き果てたれば、死を求むること極めて急なり。六月の末江戸に来るに及んで、夷人の情態を見聞し、七月九日獄に来り、天下の形勢を考察し、神国の事猶ほ為すべきものあるを悟り、初めて生を幸とするの念勃々たり。吾れ若し死せずんば勃々たるもの決して汨没せざるなり。然れども十六日の口書、三奉行の権詐、吾れを死地に措かんとするを知りてより更に生を幸ふの心なし。是れ亦平生学問の得力然るなり。

第７章

私はこのたびのことに臨んで、最初から生きるための策をめぐらさず、またかならず死ぬものとも思っていなかった。ただ私の誠が通じるか通じないか、それを天命にゆだねるつもりだったのである。

七月九日になって、ほぼ死を覚悟するにいたったので、次のような詩をつくった。

継盛唯だ当（まさに）に市戦を甘んずべし
倉公寧くんぞ復た生還を望まんや

その後、九月五日、十月五日になって吟味が寛大に見えたことにあざむかれ、生きる期待を抱き、大いに喜んだ。

これは私がこの身を惜しんだからではない。それには次のようなわけがあるのだ。

昨年の暮、大晦の朝廷の決定は幕府の措置を認めて攘夷を猶予し、公武合体の上で攘夷しようということだった。今春、三月五日、長州藩主もそれに従って萩を出発した。 私がとなえてきたこともこれで万策尽きたので、死を求める気持が強くわきおこっていた。

しかるに六月の末、江戸にきて外国人の状態を見聞し、七月九日に下獄してからも天下の形勢を考察するうちに、日本国の未来のためになお私がしなければならないことがあると思い、ここで初めて生きることを激しく願うようになったのだ。　　私がもし死ななかったら、この心にわき立つ気慨はけっして沈みはしないだろう。

だが、十六日に見せられた供述書によって、三奉行が権力的詐術によって私を殺そうとしていることを知ってからは、生を願う気持はなくなった。

これも私の平生の学問によって得た力によるものであろう。

Chapter 7

Upon occasion, I have neither evolved a scheme for surviving, nor I have assumed I would surely die. I intended to entrust God with the question of whether people understand my sincerity or not.

Since I came to be prepared for death almost on July 9 at last, I composed the following poem to the effect that

General Keisei was proud to accept a death sentence and so am I.
Who knows but that the Lord of Sou didn't expect to return alive.

After that, since their inquiries on September 5 and October 5 looked generous, I had a great expectation of returning alive. This is not because I was reluctant to lose my life. This was caused by the development of the following affair.

The last day of the last year, the Imperial Court decided to approve the measures that were taken by the Shogunate, that is, carrying out of the exclusion of foreigners after the achievement of the union of the Imperial Court and the Shogunate. The Lord of Choushuu domain also departed Hagi (a city of the present Yamaguchi Prefecture) this spring on March 5 in line with the decision of the Imperial Court. Having no way left to achieve what I have advocated for a long time, I felt a strong desire for death.

However, as a result of having watched foreign countries leveling unacceptable demands at our country since I came to Edo in the end of June and observed the trend of public affairs in our country since I was thrown into jail on July 9, I came to think that I should do something for the future of Japan, and the life impulse beat strongly in my heart for the first time. If I could live, so long as I live, this noble spirit seething in my heart will never fade.

楊継盛；明時代の忠臣(1516～1555)。世宗の時、大将軍仇鸞(?～1552)の罪状を挙げて糾弾し、また厳高(1480～1567)の十罪を弾劾して投獄され処刑された。遺体は市中にさらされた。同日彼の妻も後を追い縊死（自ら首をくくって死ぬこと）した。

Yang Jisheng; A loyal retainer of Ming Dynasty (1516 ~ 1555).

Yang Jisheng stridently denounced the Greatest General Qiuluan (? ~ 1552) with a list of his crimes and impeached Yan Gao(1480 ~ 1567) for serious crimes in the Shi emperor era. As a result, he was put in prison and was executed. His dead body was pilloried in the streets.

On the same day, his wife also committed suicide by hanging herself.

倉公；前漢の医者、淳于意(BC205_?)のことであり、医術に対し精励刻苦したが、或る時罪を犯し罰せられた。この時、倉公の娘が身代わりを願い出たため、文帝がそれを憐れみ、死罪をのがれた。

Cang Cong; A medical doctor in the Earlier Han Dynasty, also called Chun Ganyi (BC205 ~ ?). Cang Cong had worked hard for medicine, but committed a crime once and was sentenced to be punished. His daughter, learning of his punishment, sent an application to Wen Emperor to be punished in her father's place. When Emperor felt pity for the daughter, and Cang Cong narrowly escaped the death penalty.

But, since knowing that the three magistrates intend to execute me, by deceiving me and hiding behind their authority using the deposition shown on October 16, I have calmly abandoned the intention to live furthermore. This may be thanks the power which I obtained through my continued learning.

一今日死ヲ決スルノ安心ハ四時ノ順環ニ於テ得ル
所アリ蓋シ彼ノ禾稼ヲ見ルニ春種シ夏苗シ秋
苅リ冬蔵ス秋冬ニ至レハ人皆其歳功ノ成ルヲ
悦ヒ酒ヲ造リ醴ヲ為リ村野歓声アリ未タ
曾テ西成ニ臨テ歳功ノ終ルヲ哀ムモノヲ
聞カス吾行年三十一事成ルコトナクシテ死シテ
禾稼ノ未タ秀テス実ラサルニ似タレハ惜ム
ヘキニ似タリ然トモ義卿ノ身ヲ以テ云ヘハ

是亦秀実ノ時ナリ何ソ必シモ哀マン何トナレハ
人寿ハ定リナシ禾稼ノ必ス四時ヲ経ル如キニ非ス
十歳ニシテ死スル者ハ十歳中自ラ四時アリ
二十ハ自ラ二十ノ四時アリ三十ハ自ラ三十ノ
四時アリ五十百ハ自ラ五十百ノ四時アリ十歳
ヲ以テ短トスルハ蟪蛄ヲシテ霊椿タラシメント欲
スルナリ百歳ヲ以テ長シトスルハ霊椿ヲシテ蟪
蛄タラシメント欲スルナリ斉シク命ニ達セストス
義卿三十四時已備亦秀亦実其秕タルト其
粟タルト吾カ知ル所ニ非ス若シ同志ノ士其
微衷ヲ憐ミ継紹ノ人アラハ乃チ後来ノ
種子未タ絶ヘス自ラ禾稼ノ有年ニ恥
サルナリ同志其是ヲ考思セヨ

一、今日死を決するの安心は四時の順環に於いて得る所あり。蓋し彼の禾稼を見るに、春種し、夏苗し、秋苅り、冬蔵す。秋冬に至れば人皆其の歳功の成るを悦び、酒を造り醴を為り、村野歓声あり。未だ曽て西成に臨んで歳功の終るを哀しむものを聞かず。吾れ行年三十、一事成ることなくして死して禾稼の未だ秀でず実らざるに似たれば惜しむべきに似たり。然れども義卿の身を以て云へば、是れ亦秀実の時なり、何ぞ必ずしも哀しまん。何となれば人寿は定りなし、禾稼の必ず四時を経る如きに非ず。十歳にして死する者は十歳中自ら四時あり。二十は自ら二十の四時あり。三十は自ら三十の四時あり。五十、百は自ら五十、百の四時あり。十歳を以て短しとするは蟪蛄をして霊椿たらしめんと欲するなり。百歳を以て長しとするは霊椿をして蟪蛄たらしめんと欲するなり。斉しく命に達せずとす。義卿三十、四時已に備はる、亦秀で亦実る、其の秕たると其の粟たると吾が知る所に非ず。若し同志の士其の微衷を憐み継紹の人あらば、乃ち後来の種子未だ絶えず、自ら禾稼の有年に恥ぢざるなり。同志其れ是れを考思せよ。

第8章

今日、私が死を目前にして、平安な心境でいるのは、春夏秋冬の四季の循環ということを考えたからである。

つまり農事を見ると、春に種をまき、夏に苗を植え、秋に刈りとり、冬にそれを貯蔵する。秋・冬になると農民たちはその年の労働による収穫を喜び、酒をつくり、甘酒をつくって、村々に歓声が満ちあふれるのだ。この収穫期を迎えて、その年の労働が終わったのを悲しむ者がいるということを聞いたことがない。

私は三十歳で生を終わろうとしている。
いまだ一つも成しとげることがなくこのまま死ぬのは、これまでの働きによって育てた穀物が花を咲かせず、実をつけなかったことに似ているから惜しむべきかもしれない。だが私自身について考えれば、やはり花咲き実りを迎えたときなのである。

なぜなら、人の寿命には定まりがない。農事が必ず四季をめぐっていとなまれるようなものではないのだ。
しかしながら人間にもそれにふさわしい春夏秋冬があるといえるだろう。十歳にして死ぬ者には、その十歳の中におのずから四季がある。二十歳にはおのずから二十歳の四季が、三十歳にはおのずから三十歳の四季が、
五十、百歳にもおのずからの四季がある。

十歳をもって短いというのは、夏蝉を長生の霊木にしようと願うことだ。百歳をもって長いというのは、霊椿を蝉にしようとするようなことで、
いずれも天寿に達することにはならない。

私は三十歳、四季はすでに備わっており、花を咲かせ、実をつけているはずである。それが単なるモミガラなのか、成熟した粟の実であるのかは私の知るところではない。

もし同志の諸君の中に、私のささやかな真心を憐み、それを受け継いでやろうという人がいるなら、それはまかれた種子が絶えずに、穀物が年々実っていくのと同じで、収穫のあった年に恥じないことになろう。

同志よ、このことをよく考えてほしい。

Chapter 8

It may be because I live in an environment in which four seasons circulate in the order of spring, summer, autumn and winter that I can feel tranquil now in spite of my imminent death.

That is, taking agriculture as an example, farmers sow seed in spring, plant seedlings in summer, harvest them in autumn and store the grain in winter. In autumn and winter, farmers make sake (rice wine) and sweet sake in celebration of e good harvest, and the village is filled with cheer. I have never heard that farmers feel sorrow for the end of their yearly work seeing this harvest season.

I am on the verge of death at the age of thirty.
I have accomplished nothing. I may be like a grain of rice which neither bloomed nor bore fruit; in spite of having been cared for a long time, I may die without accomplishing anything. It seems I should regret it. As far as I am concerned, however, I am now in flower and about to bear fruit.

This is because human life is not set. Unlike agriculture, a human lifetime proceeds regardless of the rotation of the seasons. However, every man ought to have four season.

A man who dies at the age of ten ought to have had his own four seasons naturally during the ten years naturally. A man who dies at twenty ought to have naturally earned his four seasons during his twenty years. People who die at thirty, fifty and one hundred ought to have naturally had their own respective four seasons during their lifetime.

Thinking that a lifetime of ten years is too short is like a summer cicada envying a sacred tree which enjoys a long life. The idea that

西成；秋に植物(穀物)が成熟することをいう。

政治史・政教を記した中国最古の経典「書経」(宋代から言われた名称で、初めは単に書、漢代では尚書)に{西成を平秩せしむ}とある。

蟪蛄；夏蝉のこと。蝉の命が短いたとえ。

「老子」と併称される道家の代表著書である「荘子」の逍遥遊篇に{蟪蛄,春秋を知らず}とある。

霊椿；長生する零木のこと。

同じく「荘子」の逍遥遊篇に“小知は大知に及ばず…云々”で説明している。

a lifetime of one hundred years is too long is like a sacred tree that envies a summer cicada. Both ideas do not serve us in living natural life span.

Now, I am thirty years old and have lived my four seasons. My flower ought to have bloomed, and the flower ought to have turned to something. I don't know it is mere chaff or a matured chestnut. If there is a man who feels sympathy my devoted passion to the country and has a mind to spread my idea among like-minded persons, my devotional passion to the country will carry on, as the sown seeds grow and carry on every year without becoming extinct.

If so, what I have done will come be rewarded.

Comrades! Please remember this.

一東口揚屋ニ居ル水戸ノ郷士堀江克之助余
未タ一面ナシト雖モ真ニ知己ナリ真ニ益友ナリ
余ニ謂テ曰昔シ矢部駿州ハ桑名侯ヘ御預
ケノ日ヨリ絶食シテ敵讐ヲ詛テ死シ果シテ
敵讐ヲ退ケタリ今足下モ自ラ一死ヲ期スル
カラハ祈念ヲ籠テ内外ノ敵ヲ拂ハレヨ一
心ヲ残留テ給ハレヨト丁寧ニ告戒セリ
吾誠ニ此言ニ感服ス又鮎沢伊太夫ハ水
藩ノ士ニシテ堀江ト同居ス余ニ告テ曰今足下
ノ御沙汰モ未測ラレネハ小子ハ海外ニ赴クモ
天下ノ事ニ於テハ天命ニ付センノミ但シ天下ノ
益トナルヘキ事ハ同志ニ托シ後輩ニ残シ
度コトナリト此言大ニ吾志ヲ得タリ吾
祈念ヲ籠ル所ハ同志ノ士甲斐ミシ吾
志ヲ継紹シテ尊攘ノ大功ヲ建テヨカシ
ナリ吾死スルモ堀鮎二子ノ如キハ海外ニ在
モ獄中ニ在モ吾同志タラン者顧ハ交ヲ
結ヘカシ又本所亀沢町ニ山口三輶ト云
医者アリ義ヲ好ム人ト見ヘテ堀鮎二子
ノ事ナド外間ニ在テ大ニ周旋セリ尤モ
及フヘカラサルハ未タ一面モナキ小林民部
ノ事二子ヨリ申遣タレハ小林ノ為メニモ亦
大ニ周旋セリ其人想フニ不凡ナラン且
三子ヘノ通路ハ此三輶老ニ托スヘシ

一、東口揚屋に居る水戸の郷士堀江克之助、余未だ一面なしと雖も真に知己なり、真に益友なり。余に謂つて曰く、「昔、矢部駿州は桑名侯へ御預けの日より絶食して敵讐を詛ひて死し、果して敵讐を退けたり。今足下も自ら一死を期するからは祈念を籠めて内外の敵を払はれよ、一心を残し置きて給はれよ」と丁寧に告戒せり。吾れ誠に此の言に感服す。又鮎沢伊太夫は水藩の士にして堀江と同居す。余に告げて曰く、「今足下の御沙汰も未だ測られず、小子は海外に赴けば、天下の事総べて天命に付せんのみ、但し天下の益となるべき事は同志に托し後輩に残し度きことなり」と。此の言大いに吾が志を得たり。吾れの祈念を籠むる所は同志の士甲斐々々しく吾が志を継紹して尊攘の大功を建てよかしなり。吾れ死すとも堀・鮎二子の如きは海外に在りとも獄中に在りとも、吾が同志たらん者願はくは交りを結べかし。又本所亀沢町に山口三輶と云ふ医者あり。義を好む人と見えて、堀・鮎二子の事など外間に在りて大いに周旋せり。尤も及ぶべからざるは、未だ一面もなき小林民部の事二子より申し遣はしたれば、小林の為めにも亦大いに周旋せり。此の人想ふに不凡ならん、且つ三子への通路は此の三輶老に托すべし。

あゆざわ いだゆう　鮎沢伊太夫　1824～68(文政7～明治1)幕末・維新期の志士。(系)水戸藩士高橋諸往の次男、志士高橋多一郎の弟。(名)国維，字は廉夫。‖弘道館舎長をした後，弘化年間(1844～47)前藩主徳川斉昭の幽閉を解こうとして禁錮の処分を受け，のち斉昭が国政に復帰すると，勘定奉行に抜擢される。'58(安政5)朝廷より水戸藩に密勅が下ると，開国の中止に奔走。このため安政の大獄で豊後国佐伯藩に禁錮。3年後に赦されると京都で尊攘派志士と画策。'64(元治1)武田耕雲斎らの挙兵に参加。西上の途中脱して京都に入り勢力挽回をはかる。'68(明治1)水戸に帰り，ついで東北戦争に従軍。10月旧幕派藩士に水戸城を襲撃され戦死した。

やべ さだのり　矢部定謙　1794～?(寛正6～?)江戸後期の幕政家。(系)堺奉行矢部定令の長男。(生)堺。(名)通称彦五郎，左近将監・駿河守。‖累進して，1831(天保2)堺奉行，'33大坂町奉行となる。大塩平八郎と交友し，平八郎の助言もあって，'33～'34の飢饉にあたり，米価を調節し，窮民の救済などにみるべき功績をあげた。'36勘定奉行，'38西丸御留守居役をつとめ，'40より小普請組支配となる。'41年4月町奉行，庄内藩・長岡藩・川越藩の三方領知替令にあたって，庄内藩で領民の反対運動がおこると，それを取り上げて再審を上書した。12月，水野忠邦と意見が合わず，罷免された。

第９章

東口揚屋（あがりや）にいる水戸の郷士・堀江克之助には未だ一度も会ったことはないが、真の知己であり、真の益友だと思っている。彼は私に次のようなことを伝えてくれた。

「昔、矢部駿州は桑名侯へお預けの身となったその日から絶食して、仇敵を呪いながら死に、果してその仇敵を退けることができた。今、あなたもみずから一死を期するからには、祈念をこめて内外の敵を払われよ。
その心をこの世に残しておかれるように」

この丁寧な戒めに、私は心から感服した。

また鮎沢伊太夫は、水戸藩士で堀江と同じ房につながれている。彼もまた私にこう伝えてきた。

「今、あなたにどのような判決が下るかは予測できない。自分は遠島と決まったので、島に送られたら、天下の事すべては天命にまかすほかはないと思っている。しかし天下の益になることは、同志に託し、後輩の者に残しておきたい」この言葉も大いにわが意を得たのである。

私もそうありたいのだ。

私が祈念をこめて願うのは、同志の人々が強い意欲をもって私の志を継ぎ、尊王攘夷の大功を立ててくれることである。

私が死んだあと、堀江・鮎沢両氏が島に流されていようと獄中にあろうと、わが同志たらん者は、彼らと交わりを結んでもらいたい。

本所亀沢町に山口三輪という医者がいる。義を好む人と見えて、堀江・鮎沢のことを獄外から支援している。さらに私がこの人に及ばないと思ったのは、両氏から頼まれて一面識もない小林民部についても尽力しているということだ。なかなか非凡な人物と思われる。堀江・鮎沢・小林三氏への連絡は、この三輪老に頼むとよい。

Chapter 9

I have never seen Yoshinosuke Horie(1810-1871), a samurai of the Mito Domain, who is in jail on the east side of this jail. However I would call him a friend as distinct from a mere acquaintance, and I regard him as a truly trustworthy person. He was so kind as to send me the following message:

"In earlier times, Sunshuu Yabe (1789-1842: Yabe Suruganokami- Sadakane, Edo district magistrate) began a fast as soon as he was in the custody of the Load Kuwana, feudal domain (a northern part of Mie Prefecture) and died while cursing against his sworn enemy. As a matter of fact, his sworn enemy was driven away. Now, you are resolved to die. If so, you should strive to drive all of your enemies away.
Please pass on your loyalty to posterity."

I was deeply moved by this kind admonition. Idayuu Ayuzawa (1824-1868), retainer of Mito Feudal Domain, is also in jail together with Horie. He also sent me the following message:

"Although I can't estimate what judgment will be delivered on you, since I have already received a sentence of exile to a distant island, it will be the best to leave the future of the State to Heaven's decree after I am exiled to the island. However, I would like to entrust a policy salutary to the State to the care of comrades and younger men."

I heartily agree with him regarding this view, too. I would also like to do so. I sincerely hope that comrades follow in my footsteps with a strong will and fulfill the movement to revere the Emperor and expel the barbarians.

After my death, I hope that even if Horie and Ayuzawa are exiled to a distant island or are in jail, those sharing my beliefs will

東口揚屋（Higashiguchi Agariya）

江戸伝馬町の獄舎は八つの房に分かれていた。
東口揚屋（水戸藩士堀江克之助、鮎沢伊太夫）、東奥揚屋（越前藩士橋本左内、高松藩士長谷川宗右衛門、長谷川速水親子）、西奥揚屋（長州藩士吉田松陰、勝野保三郎）、のほか西口揚屋、西の三間半、西の大牢、百姓牢、無宿牢などである。この内揚屋とは、御目見え以下の直参、陪臣、僧侶、医者が入る牢屋のこと。

contact them.

A physician by name of Sanyuu Yamaguchi lives in Kamesawa-cho in Honjyo. He seems to respect justice judging from the fact that he actively supports Horie & Ayuzawa from outside the jail. Furthermore Yamaguchi is superior to me in that he supports Minbu Kobayashi(1808-1859), too, at their request though Kobayashi is a total stranger to Yamaguchi. He seems to be a man above the common run of humanity. It will be better to contact Horie, Ayuzawa and Kobayashi through this physician, Sanyuu Yamaguchi.

一堀江常ニ神道ヲ崇メ天皇ヲ尊ヒ大道ヲ天
下ニ明白ニシ異端邪説ヲ排セント欲ス謂ラク
天朝ヨリ教書ヲ開板シテ天下ニ頒示スルニ如カズ
ト余謂ラク教書ヲ開板スルニ一策ナカルヘカラズ京師ニ
於テ大学校ヲ興シ上天朝ノ御学風ヲ天下ニ示シ又天下ノ
奇材異能ヲ京師ニ貢シ然ル後天下古今ノ正論確議ヲ
輯集〆書トナシ天朝御教習ノ餘ヲ天下ニ分時ハ天下ノ
人心自ラ一定スヘシト因テ平生子遠ト密議スル所ノ尊
攘堂ノ議ト合セ堀江ニ謀リ是ヲ子遠ニ任スルコト決ス、
子遠若シ能ク同志ト謀リ内外志ヲ協ヘ此事ヲ〆
少シク端緒アラシメハ吾ノ志トスル所モ亦荒セズト云
フヘシ去年勅諚綸旨等ノ事一跌スト雖モ尊皇攘
夷苟モ已ムヘキニ非レハ又善術ヲ設ケ前緒ヲ継紹
セズンハアルヘカラズ京師学校ノ論亦奇ナラズヤ

一、堀江常に神道を崇め、天皇を尊び、大道を天下に明白にし、異端邪説を排せんと欲す。謂へらく、天朝より教書を開板して天下に頒示するに如かずと。余謂へらく、教書を開板するに一策なかるべからず。京師に於いて大学校を興し、上天朝の御学風を天下に示し、又天下の奇材異能を京師に貢し、然る後天下古今の正論確議を輯集して書となし、天朝御教習の余を天下に分つ時は、天下の人心自ら一定すべしと。因つて平生子遠と密議する所の尊攘堂の議と合せ堀江に謀り、是れを子遠に任ずることに決す。子遠若し能く同志と謀り、内外志を協へ、此の事をして少しく端緒あらしめば、吾れの志とする所も亦荒せずと云ふべし。去年勅諚綸旨等の事一跌すと雖も、尊皇攘夷苟も已むべきに非ざれば、又善術を設け前緒を継紹せずんばあるべからず。京師学校の論亦奇ならずや。

第 10 章

堀江克之助は、常に神道をあがめ、天皇を尊び、大道を天下に明白にして、異端や邪説を排除したいと願っている。彼は、朝廷から教書を出版して、天下に配布するのがよいのではないかと言う。

私としては教書を出版するには一つの方法があると思う。すなわち京都に大学校を創立し、朝廷の学風を天下に示すほか天下のすぐれた才能、人材を京都に集め、彼らに天下古今の正論、確乎たる議論を編集させて本をつくり、朝廷で教習ののち天下に配布すれば人心はおのずから一定するであろう。

私かねてから入江杉蔵と密議していたのは尊攘堂創設のことであったが、それもあわせて堀江に相談し、この実行を杉蔵にまかすことに決めた。杉蔵がよく同志とはかり、内外に協力を訴えて実現の端緒をつかむことができれば、私が志したことも無駄にはならないと思う。

昨年、勅綻や論旨を求めようとしたくわだては挫折してしまったが、尊王攘夷運動はけっしてやめるべきではないから、しかるべき方法を考え、前人の志を受け継いでいかなければならない。

その為にも京都に大学校か興すというのはすぐれた論策ではあるまいか。

Chapter 10

Yoshinosuke Horie always worships Shintouism, respects the Emperor, and wishes to exclude some heretical doctrine and heterodoxy by explicating moral principles. He proposes the publication of a state message from the Imperial Court and its distribution across the whole country.

I have an idea about publishing a state message. That is, what we have to do first is to establish a university in Kyoto to let people know the academic traditions of the Imperial Court and gather excellent talents there; and second, to collect and edit rational arguments and debates made in both ancient and present times in Japan and publish them in book form; and third, to check and review the arguments and controversies at the Imperial Court and then distribute them throughout the country. This will lead to the unification of public sentiment.

It was to discuss the plan of establishing an academy for the movement to revere the Emperor and expel the barbarians that I some times had confidential meetings with Sugizoh Irie(1834-1864). I determined to consult this plan with Horie and entrust the carrying out of the plan to Sugizoh. If Sugizoh contrives this plan in detail together with comrades and asks influential persons inside and outside the feudal domain for their cooperation and succeeds in realizing the plan, what I have done with a firm belief will be realized in the future.

Although my attempt to ask for an Imperial order collapsed last year, since the movement to revere the Emperor and expel the barbarians must be continued by all means, it is necessary to come up with a proper method to pursue it. For this reason, too, I believe a proposal such as to establish a university in Kyoto is a reasonable one.

一 小林氏云京師ノ学習院ハ定日アリテ百姓町人ニ至ルマテ出席シテ講釈ヲ聴聞スルコトヲ許サル講日ニハ公卿方出座ニテ講師菅家清家及ヒ地下ノ儒者相混スルナリ然ラハ此基ニ因テ更ニ斟酌ヲ加ヘハ我等モ妙策ナルヘシ又懐徳堂ニハ霊元上皇宸筆勅額アリ此基ニ因リ更ニ一堂ヲ興スモ亦妙ナリト小林云ヘリ

小林ハ鷹司家ノ諸大夫ニテ此度遠島ノ罪科ニ處セラル京師諸人中罪責極テ重シ其人多材多藝唯文学ニ浮カラズ武事ノオアル人ト見エ西奥揚屋ニテ余ト同居ス後東口ニ移ル京師ヲ吉田ノ鈴鹿石州同筑州別テ知己ノ由亦山口ニ繭

モ小林ノ為ニ大ニ周旋シタレハ鈴鹿カ山口カノ手ヲ以テ海外ニテモ吾同志ノ士通信ヲナスヘシ京師ノ事ニ就テハ後来必ズカラ得ル所アラン

一、小林民部云ふ、京師の学習院は定日ありて百姓町人に至るまで出席して講釈を聴聞することを許さる。講日には公卿方出座にて、講師菅家・清家及び地下の儒者相混ずるなり。然らば此の基に因りて更に斟酌を加へば幾等も妙策あるべし。又懐徳堂には、霊元上皇宸筆の勅額あり、此の基に因り更に一堂を興すも亦妙なりと小林云へり。小林は鷹司家の諸大夫にて、此の度遠島の罪科に処せらる。京師諸人中罪責極めて重し。其の人多材多芸、唯だ文学に深からず、処事の才ある人と見ゆ。西奥揚屋にて余と同居す、後東口に移る。京師にて吉田の鈴鹿石州・同筑州別して知己の由。亦山口三輶も小林の為めに大いに周旋したれば、鈴鹿か山口かの手を以て海外までも吾が同志の士通信をなすべし。京師の事に就いては後来必ず力を得る所あらん。

れいげん てんのう　霊元天皇　1654～1732(承応3～享保17)在位1663～87。㊋後水尾天皇の第18皇子，後光明天皇の養子，母は新広義門院藤原基子。㊔識仁(さとひと)，高貴(あての)宮。‖1658(万治1)親王宣下，二品に叙せられる。'62(寛文2)元服，'63践祚，即位。朝儀旧典の復興を意とした。'69前関白藤原教平の娘房子を女御とする。のち皇后に冊立。'87(貞享4)朝仁親王(東山天皇)に譲位。1713(正徳3)薙髪し素浄と称した。遺詔により霊元院と追号。㊏京都市東山区今熊野泉山町の月輪陵。

第11章

小林民部が言うには、京都の学習院では、決められた日に、農民・町人にいたるまで講義を聴くことを許されているらしい。
その講義の日には公卿も出席し、講師には菅原家、清原家と地元の儒者もまじる。そういうことであればこれを基本として、さらに計画を練ればいくらでも妙策はあるだろう。また懐徳堂には、霊元上皇宸筆の勅額もあるので、これを基として一堂を興すのもよいではないかと小林は言っている。

小林民部は鷹司家の諸大夫で、このたび遠島の罪科（島流しの刑罰）に処せられている。京都関係で大獄に連座させられた人の中では、
その罪がきわめて重いとされている。彼は多才多芸だが、文学にはあまり深くないようだ。事を的確に処理する才能のある人らしい。　西奥揚屋で私と同室だったが、あとで東口に移った。

　小林は京都で吉田神社の神官である鈴鹿石州・同筑前とはとくに親しいという。また山口三輪も小林のために大いに尽力している。鈴鹿か山口に頼んで、小林とも通信をすることを同志にすすめたい。
京都のことに関しては、後年かならず力になってくれる人物である。

Chapter 11

According to Minbu Kobayashi, Gakushuuin, a school originally for the children of court nobles in Kyoto, allows the general public including farmers and merchants to attend lectures on fixed days. On those lecture days, court nobles also attend the lectures by such speaker as men of the Sugawara family, the Kiyohara family and Confucianists of the district. If so, and if further elaboration is made on the plan using this arrangement as a base, bright ideas are sure to come out of it.

In addition, Minbu Kobayasi said that since an Emperor tablet handwritten by Reigen Joukou, ex-Emperor (the 112th emperor), was installed in Kaitokudou (a private school in those days), it would also be a good idea to establish a college using the Emperor tablet as a symbol.

Minbu Kobayashi is a lord steward (formally the 5th court rank) of the Takatsukasa family. He was sentenced to be exiled to a distant island. It is said that he received the severer sentence among the comrades who were implicated in the crime relating to the Kyoto case. He is well-rounded and multi-talented, but seems to be short on literature. He seems to be able in managing matters precisely. He and I shared the same jail cell, but he moved to another jail later.

Kobayashi said that he was on good terms in particular with Sekishuu Suzuka and Chikushuu Suzuka who are Shinto priests of the Yoshida shrine in Kyoto. I know that Sanyuu Yamaguchi also makes every effort in his favor. For this reason, I recommend my comrades to communicate with Kobayashi through Suzuka or Yamaguchi. Suzuka and Yamaguchi will surely help the comrades involved in the Kyoto case in the near future.

一
讃ノ高松ノ藩士長谷川宗右衛門年来主君
ヲ諫メ宗藩水家ト親睦ノ事ニ付テ苦心セシ人
ナリ東奥揚屋ニアリ其子速水余ト西奥ニ同居ス
此父子ノ罪科何如未タ知ルヘカラス同志ノ諸友
切ニ記念セヨ予初テ長谷川翁ヲ一見セシ時獄
吏左右ニ林立ス法度語ヲ交ルコトヲ得ス翁
獨語スルモノヽ如メ曰寧為玉砕勿為瓦全
ト吾甚タ其意ニ感ス同志其之ヲ察セヨ

一、讃の高松の藩士長谷川宗右衛門、年来主君を諫め、宗藩水家と親睦の事に付きて苦心せし人なり、東奥揚屋にあり。其の子速水、余と西奥に同居す。此の父子の罪科何如未だ知るべからず。同志の諸友切に記念せよ。予初めて長谷川翁を一見せしとき、獄吏左右に林立す、法、隻語を交ふることを得ず。翁独語するものの如くして曰く、「寧ろ玉となりて砕くるとも、瓦となりて全かるなかれ」と。吾れ甚だ其の意に感ず。同志其れ之れを察せよ。

はせがわ そうえもん　長谷川宗右衛門　1801～70(享和1～明治3)幕末・維新期の尊王家。㊓讃岐国高松。㊔秀驍，本姓松崎氏。‖文政年間(1818～29)頃主家移封の内議が起こるや奔走してこれを阻止し，ついで広く天下の士と交わった。1853(嘉永6)米艦の渡来に際し海防論を草して水戸藩主徳川斉昭に献ずるとともに，三条実万を通して孝明天皇に奉じた。'58(安政5)水戸藩に密勅が下されると，密かに亡命し丸岡淪と変名して尊攘運動に参加，翌年安政の大獄に際し自首し，子の速水とともに永牢に処せられる。'62(文久2)赦にあい現職に復帰して藩政を担当した。

第12章

讃岐の高松藩士・長谷川宗右衛門は、かねがね主君を諫め、主家筋にあたる水戸藩との親睦に苦心してきた人だ。 今、彼は東奥揚屋におり、その子の速水は私と同じ西奥に入れられている。この父子がどのような罪で投獄されたのか、まだ知らない。実は、同志の諸君にぜひ心にとめておいてほしいことがあるのだ。

私が初めて長谷川翁と会ったとき、そこには獄吏が立ち並んでいて、言葉を交わすことができなかった。囚人同士の会話はひとことでも許されていないのである。

そのとき翁は独りごとのように言った。

「玉となって砕けるとも、瓦となって命を長らえることがあってはならない」。 私はこの言葉に深く胸を打たれた。

同志諸君、そのときの私の気持を察してもらいたい。

Chapter 12

Souemon Hasegawa is a retainer of Takamatsu domain in Sanuki. He was an adviser for his Lord, and had done everything he could to cultivate mutual friendship between his Lord and Mito Domain, their head family. Now, he is in jail on the deep east side, and his son, Sokusui Hasegawa, is also in the same jail on the deep westside as I am. I don't know with what charge they, father and son, were imprisoned. By the way, referring to them, I would like to tell you of the following episode of which I wish you to make a mental note.

When I saw the venerable sage Hasegawa for the first time in front of the jailers, we couldn't talk with each other because we were under close guard. Prisoners were prohibited to talk with each other. In front of me, the venerable sage murmured half to himself:

"Do not hang on to life as a roof tile,
when you can shatter as a jewel"

I was struck deeply by this words, I hope you, my comrade, can share my feelings at that time.

一右数條余徒ニ書スルニ非ス天下ノ事ヲ成スハ天下
有志ノ士ト志ト通スルニ非レハ得ス而メ右数人
余此回新ニ得ル所ノ人ナルヲ以テ是ヲ同志ニ
告示スナリ又勝野保三郎早已ニ出牢ス就テ
其ノ詳ヲ問知スベシ勝野ノ父豊作今潜伏スト
雖モ有志ノ士ト聞ケリ他日事平ヲ待テ物
色スベシ今日ノ事同志ノ諸士戦敗ノ餘傷残
ノ同志ヲ問訊スル如クスベシ一敗乃挫折スル
豈勇士ノ事ナランヤ切ニ囑ス〱

一、右数条、余徒らに書するに非ず。天下の事を成すは天下有志の士と志を通ずるに非ざれば得ず。而して右数人、余此の回新たに得る所の人なるを以て、是れを同志に告示するなり。又勝野保三郎早や已に出牢す、就きて其の詳を問知すべし。勝野の父豊作今潜伏すと雖も有志の士と聞けり。他日事平ぐを待ちて物色すべし。今日の事、同志の諸士、戦敗の余、傷残の同士を問訊する如くすべし。一敗乃ち挫折する、豈に勇士の事ならんや。切に嘱す、切に嘱す。

かつの まさみち　勝野正道　1808～58(文化5～安政5)幕末期の志士。㊔通称豊作，号を台山。‖幕臣阿部四郎五郎につかえる。水戸藩士と交わり，1858(安政5)仁科多一郎と変名し京都で活躍したが，水戸への勅書により，追及が厳しくなり，水戸郊外に潜伏中に病死した。

第13章

右の数条は、無駄に書きしるしたのではない。天下の大事を成功させるためには、天下の有志の士と互いに志を通じなければならない。そこで上記の数人は私がこのたび新たに知り得た人物なので、これを同志に告げておくのである。勝野保三郎はすでに出獄した。彼に詳しいことを尋ねるがよい。勝野の父豊作は今潜伏中だが、有志の士と聞いている。
いずれ事件が落着するのを待って探し出すことだ。

今日のことに関しては、同志の諸士よ、戦に敗れたあと、傷ついた同志に会い、前後の経緯を尋ねて今後の参考にせよ。一度敗れたからといって挫折してしまうのは勇士とはいえないのではあるまいか。

同志諸君、切に頼む。頼むぞ。

Chapter 13

I wrote the above several chapters for a certain purpose. In order to succeed in realizing a matter of grave concern to the state, it is essential for comrades over the whole country to communicate with each other.

As I became newly aware of the above persons, let me introduce them to all of you.

Yasusaburou Katsuno was discharged from jail. For details, ask him. Hohsaku Katsuno, father of Yasusaburou, lies hidden still now. I hear that he is of a similar mind to us. You should find him after the settling of the case.

My friends and comrades!

We were defeated this time. However, see injured comrades and inquire from them how the case came about in detail for future reference. The celebrated hero is never discouraged even if he is defeated once or twice.

My friends and comrades, please be courageous. I rely heavily on all of you.

一

越前ノ橋本左内二十六歳ニ〆誅セラル実ニ十月七日ナリ左内東奥ニ坐スル五六日ノミ勝保同居セリ後勝保西奥ニ来リ予ト同居ス予勝保ノ談ヲ聞テ益々左内ト半面ナキヲ嘆ス左内幽囚邸居中資治通鑑ヲ読ミ註ヲ作リ漢紀ヲ終ル

又獄中教学工作等ノ事ヲ論セシ由勝保予カ為メニ是ヲ語ル獄ノ論大ニ吾意ヲ得タリ予益々左内ヲ起シテ一議ヲ発センヿヲ思フ嗟夫

一、越前の橋本左内、二十六歳にして誅せらる、実に十月七日なり。左内東奥に座する五、六日のみ。勝保同居せり。後、勝保西奥に来り、予と同居す。予、勝保の談を聞きて益々左内と半面なきを嘆ず。左内幽囚邸居中、資治通鑑を読み、注を作り、漢紀を終る。又獄中教学工作等の事を論ぜし由、勝保予が為めに是れを語る。獄の論大いに吾が意を得たり。予益々左内を起して一議を発せんことを思ふ。嗟夫。

はしもと さない　橋本左内　1834～59(天保5～安政6)幕末期の志士。㊋福井藩医橋本長綱の子。㊔弘道・綱紀，字は伯綱，号を景岳・黎園，変名桃井伊織。‖1849(嘉永2)大坂に出て緒方洪庵の適塾に学び洋学及び医学を習得。'52家督をつぎ藩医となる。'54(安政1)江戸遊学を命ぜられ，藤田東湖・西郷隆盛らとも交わる。藩主松平慶永に認められ，'57には中根雪江・由利公正らとともに藩政改革の中心になる。横井小楠を政治顧問として招き，その重商主義的な富国強兵論に基づき開国貿易・殖産興業・軍備強化など絶対主義的な方向を目ざして藩政改革を行なった。将軍継嗣問題が起ると，藩主の意をうけ，一橋慶喜の擁立運動のため上洛。青蓮院宮・三条実万・鷹司政通らの公卿や諸大夫に出入りし説得に全力をあげたが，'58井伊直弼の大老就任によって失敗し，ひきつづき幕府の大弾圧によって藩主松平慶永も隠居謹慎を命ぜられ，左内も捕えられた。翌年江戸伝馬町の獄に送られて斬られた。近代国家への展望に基づくもっとも開明的な思想をもった人材として知られる。'91(明治24)贈正四位。㊢景岳会編「橋本景岳全集」全2巻，1943。㊜滋賀貞「景岳橋本左内」1931，山口宗之「橋本左内」1962。

第14章

越前の橋本左内は二十六歳（満25歳）で殺された。
実に十月七日のことであった。左内は東奥の牢に入れられたが、
わずか五、六日いただけで処刑されたのである。
　勝野保三郎は、そのとき左内と同室だった。
後に私がいる西奥に移ってきた勝野から話を聞いて、ますます左内と一度も会う機会がなかったことを残念に思ったのだ。
左内は自邸内に幽囚中、『資治通鑑』を読み、註をつくり、また『漢紀』三十巻を読破したという。

また獄中では教学や技術のことを左内が論じていたと勝野は私に話してくれた。獄中の論は大いにわが意を得た。

私はそれを聞いてさらに左内をよみがえらせ議論をしてみたいと強く思ったのだが、もう左内はいない。ああ！

Chapter 14

Sanai Hashimoto from Echizen Domain was executed only at the age of 26 (25 years old). He was executed on October 7.
Sanai Hashimoto was executed only several days after he was put in the east side jail. Yasusaburou Katsuno was put in a jail cell together with Sanai Hashimoto when he was executed.

I knew of Sanai Hashimoto from Yasusaburou Katsuno who moved to my jail cell after Sanai's death. I increasingly regret that I had not once chance to meet Sanai Hashimoto. He said that Sanai Hashimoto read "Shijitsugan" and then made notes for readers while he was under house arrest, and read through all thirty volumes of the "Kanki, Chinese classics".

In addition, Katsuno told me that while in jail, Sanai Hashimoto pointed out the necessity of education and technology. I thoroughly agree with these views of Sanai Hashimoto. After learning of these from Katsuno, I wish I could bring him back to life.

However, Sanai Hashimoto has gone, alas!

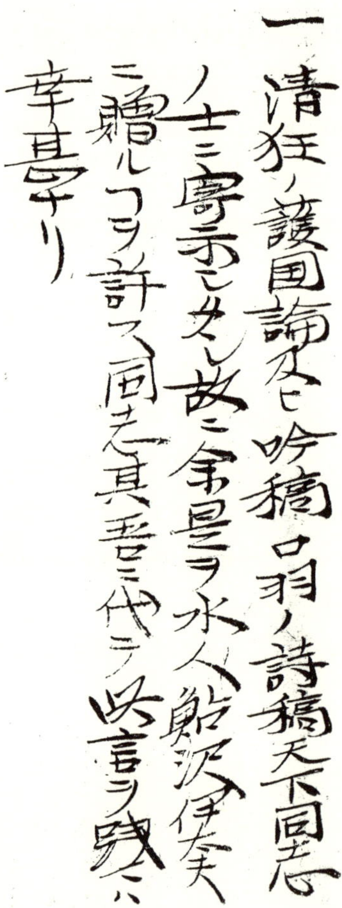

一　清狂ノ護国論及ヒ吟稿口羽ノ詩稿天下同志ノ士ニ寄示シタシ故ニ余是ヲ水人鮎沢伊太夫ニ贈ルコトヲ許ス同志其吾ニ代テ此言ヲ践ハ幸甚ナリ

一、清狂の護国論及び吟稿、口羽の詩稿、天下同志の士に寄示したし。故に余是れを水人鮎沢伊太夫に贈ることを許す。同志其れ吾れに代りて此の言を践まば幸甚なり。

げっしょう　月性　1817～58(文化14～安政5)　幕末期の志士・僧。㊔字は知円，号を清狂。‖周防国遠崎の妙円寺の住職。15歳の時学問を志して郷里を出る。その詩に〈男子立志出郷関，学若不成死不帰，埋骨何期墳墓地，人間到処有青山〉があり一世に名高く多くの人々に愛誦された。九州・京畿・北陸・関東をめぐり，詩文・仏教を学び，多くの名士らとも交わる。長州では執政浦靱負 ・福原越後 らに認められ吉田松陰 とも親交を結んで急進的な尊王攘夷の思想をもつにいたる。1856(安政3)本願寺に招かれて上洛して東山別院に住み，時務策などを献上する。さらに梅田雲浜 ・梁川星巌 らとも交わり，また紀州藩にのりこんで海防を説得するなど尊攘運動につくした。'57一旦帰郷したが，翌年病没した。㊘漢詩集「清狂詩鈔」。

第15章

僧月性の護国論および吟稿、ロ羽徳祐の詩稿、いずれも天下同志の人々に見せたいものと思う。それゆえ私はこれを水戸藩の鮎沢伊太夫に贈ることを約束した。同志のうちだれか私に代って、この約束を果してくれる人がいると有難いのだが。

Chapter 15

I am convinced that the theory of national defense and chant work written by Priest Gesshou (1817-1856) and poem composed by Tokusuke Kuchiba(1834-1859) are worth reading. I would like to show them to all of the comrades in the whole country. Consequently I promised to send these works to Idayuu Ayuzawa in Mito domain.

I would be pleased if someone among my comrades fulfils this promise on my behalf.

一　同志諸友ノ内小田村中谷久保久坂子遠兄弟等ノ事鮎沢堀江長谷川小林勝野等ヘ告知シ置ク也村塾ノ事須佐阿月等ノ事モ告置ケリ飯田尾寺高杉及ヒ利輔ノ事モ諸人ヘ告置ケリ是皆吾苟モ是ヲナスニ非ス

かきつけ終りては

心なることの種々かき置ぬ思残せることなかりけり

呼たしの声まつ外に今の世に待へき事のなかりけるかな

討れたる吾をあはれと見ん人は君を崇めて夷払へよ

愚かなる吾をも友とめつ人はわかとも友とめてよ人々

七たひも生かへりつゝ夷をそ攘はんこゝろ吾忘れめや

十月念六日黄昏書　二十一回猛士

一、同志諸友の内、小田村・中谷・久保・久坂・子遠兄弟等の事、鮎沢・堀江・長谷川・小林・勝野等へ告知し置きぬ。村塾の事、須佐・阿月等の事も告げ置けり。飯田・尾寺・高杉及び利輔の事も諸人に告げ置きしなり。是れ皆吾が苟も是れをなすに非ず。

かきつけ終りて後

心なることの種々かき置きぬ思ひ残せることなかりけり

呼びだしの声まつ外に今の世に待つべき事のなかりけるかな

討たれたる吾れをあはれと見ん人は君を崇めて夷払へよ

愚かなる吾れをも友とめづ人はわがとも友とめでよ人々

七たびも生きかへりつつ夷をぞ攘はんこころ吾れ忘れめや

十月二十六日黄昏書す

二十一回猛士

第16章

同志諸友のうち小田村伊之助、中谷正亮、久保清太郎、久坂玄瑞、入江杉蔵・野村和作兄弟たちのことは、鮎沢、堀江、長谷川、小林、勝野らへ話しておいた。

また松下村塾のこと、須佐・阿月などに私の同志が多いことも話し、飯田正伯、尾寺新之丞、高杉晋作および伊藤利輔のことも、これらの人たちに話しておいたのだが、

私としては軽い気持で諸君のことを告知したのではない。

書きつけが終ったあとで

心なることの種々かき置きぬ思ひ残せることなかりけり
呼びだしの声まつ外に今の世に待つべき事のなかりけるかな
討れたる吾れをあはれ（哀れ）と見ん人は君を崇めて夷払へよ
愚かなる吾れをも友とめづ（愛づ）人は
わがとも友とめでよ人々
七たびも生きかへりつつ夷をぞ攘はんこころ吾れ忘れめや

十月二十六日たそがれ書す

二十一回猛士

Chapter 16

I have given information on Inosuke Odamura, Masakatsu Nakatani, Seitaroh Kubo, Genzui Kusaka, Sugizou Irie and Wasaku Nomura brothers in particular to Ayusawa, Horie, Hasegawa, Kobayashi and Katsuno among our comrades.

In addition, I explained Shouka Sonjuku (the private school established by Shouin Yoshida) and informed them that many of my comrades live in Susa (Nagato) and Atsuki (Suou) districts.

In addition, I also gave information on Masahiro Iida, Shinnojyou Odera, Shinsaku Takasugi and Risuke Itou to them. I gave information on the above persons to them not on impulse but with a certain purpose.

[After finishing this note,]

"Having written all of weighing on my mind,
I have nothing to regret.
However, my heart is filled with desolation.
I have nothing to wait in the world
except for summons from an executioner.
If you moved to pity by me who is about to be killed,
revere the Emperor and expel the barbarians.
if you treat me as your friend, treat my comrades
as your friends.
Never forget my faith to expel barbarians by rising
from the dead 7 times."

at twilight on October 26, 1859

a samurai of undying loyalty

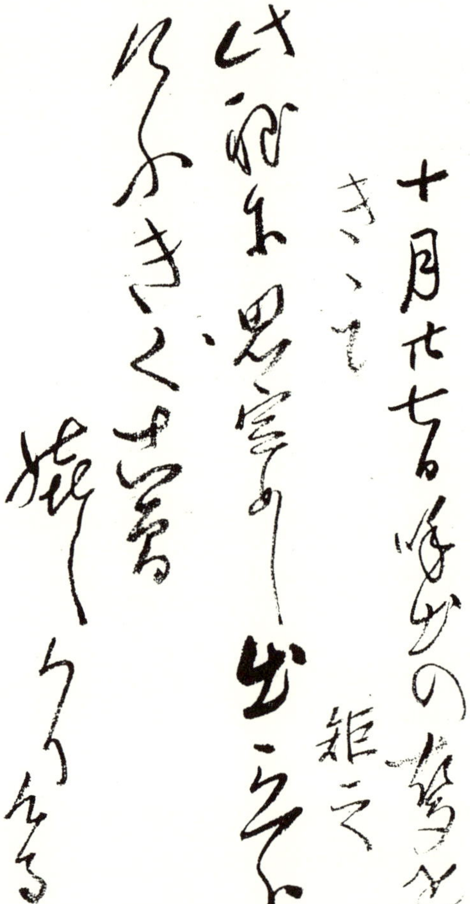

絶筆

十月二十七日呼出の声をききて

矩之

此程に思定めし出立ハ

けふきくこそ

嬉しかりける

絶筆

The last work of Shouin Yoshida.

R.L.Stevensonによる「吉田寅次郎」の記述。

英国の作家Robert Louis Stevenson(1850_1894)はエディンバラに生まれエディンバラ大学に入学、エンジニアである父の家業を継ぐべく機械工学を学んだが、法科に転じて1875年弁護士となった。しかし文学への興味絶ち難く、'79年一時アメリカに渡るも'80に帰国して創作活動に没頭。雑誌に紀行文、随筆、短編小説を投稿し始めた。'76年の「新アラビアンナイト」(The New Arabian Night)を皮切りに、'82年には「宝島」(Treasure Island), '86年には「ジキル博士とハイド」(Dr.Jekyll and Mr.Hide)など傑作を残した。

Stevensonによる「Yoshida Torajiro」の著作は明治11～12年頃(1878-79)当時英国出張中の松陰の弟子、松下村塾門下生の一人である正木退蔵（後に外交官）からの聞き書きを土台にしているが、一部の誤りを除き、ほぼ正確に吉田松陰の生涯を捉えている。著名な外国の作家が松陰の事績を記憶にとどめ、小稿とはいえ西洋にキチンと紹介していることは特別な意義がある。

特に文中、下田出国(踏海)事件では“この旅立ちは最も勇気を必要とする極地探検より、ユリシーズ(ギリシャ伝説における勇士オデッセイアのラテン名)の地獄への転落に近いものであり、前代未聞の壮挙であった。(中略)。この行動は日本では犯罪となり、人間社会からの抹殺を意味していた”....と述べている。

今回,主として海外に向けた本「留魂録」英完訳書発行に際し、125年前の上記のStevenson作「吉田寅次郎」稿を本書に再掲し、参考に供したい。

出典は本書のベースにもなっている山口県教育会編「吉田松陰全集」の別巻(昭和49年10月大和書房発行)に準拠しており、第15版Stevenson全集の[Familiar Studies of Men and Books] からの抽出である。
また、これによれば訳文は町田晃氏によるものである。

[Yoshida Torajiro] by R. L. Stevenson

Rovert Louis Stevenson (1850 - 1894), an English novelist, was born in Edinburgh, Scotland, and entered Edinburgh University, majoring in Mechanical Engineering in order to succeed his father in the family occupation. But he turned to the law department later and became an attorney. However, he couldn't get rid of his interest in literature that he had had since he was a boy. He went to America once in 1879, and after returning to England in 1880, he devoted himself to story writing from 1880. He began to contribute articles such as travel writings, essays and short stories to publishing companies. He wrote masterpieces such as "Treasure Island" in 1882 and "Dr. Jekyll and Mr. Hide" in 1886 with "The New Arabian Night" in 1876 as the start.

The literary work entitled"Yoshida Torajiro" and authored by Stevenson is based on the writings that he heard about from Taizou Masaki, one of disciples of Shouin Yoshida at the Shoukasonjuku School and later a diplomat, who stayed in London from1878 to 1879 on business. This literary work grasps the life of Shouin Yoshida except for a minor error.

It is worthy of note and especially significant that a famous foreign novelist wrote about the achievement of Shouin Yoshida and introduced him to the Western world exactly at that time even if it was done in a small piece of work.

R. L. Stevenson touched upon the incident of Shimoda in his writing as follows:

"This departure must have been as dreadful as descending into hell as Ulysses (Odyssey, a brave warrior in a Greek myth in Latin) did and would need greater courage than that in a polar expedition and an unheard - of heroic undertaking. (Some passages are

omitted.) This behavior might have constituted a crime and must have been crossed out from Human society in Japan at that time."

I would like to take this opportunity to publish the English version of "Soulful Minute" mainly as a reference to those outside Japan on Stevenson's work of 125 years ago, "Yoshida Torajiro. This manuscript can be traced to the *Complete works of Yoshida Shouin* edited by the Education Society in Yamaguchi Prefecture in October, 1974 (published by Yamato Shobo), which is the source upon which this manuscript is based. The message of R. L. Stevenson is abstracted from the *Complete works of Stevenson; Volume 15, Familiar Studies of Men and Books,* the Japanese translation of which is by Mr. Akira Machida.

吉田寅次郎

この頁(ぺーじ)の冒頭に掲げた人名は､おそらくイギリスの読者の知っている名ではなかろう。しかし、その名は、ガリバルディ①やジョン・ブラウン②の名と同じように、人口に膾炙(かいしゃ)されている名前になるべきだと思っている。いつの日にか、遠からずして、吉田の生涯の詳しい記述や、彼が日本の変革に及ぼした影響の程度については、さらに詳細なことが聞けるものと期待してよかろう。現在でも、この問題を熟知しているイギリス人がいるに相違ないし、また、おそらくこの小文が出れば、一層完全な正確な情報が提供されることになろう。正確には、私は本論の著書ではない、と言いたい。私は聡明(そうめい)な日本の紳士、マサキ・タイソー(正木退蔵)氏の話を典拠にして、この文を書くわけである。正木氏は、彼の心の栄誉にふさわしい感動を込めて、私に語った。私も幾分かは骨折り、草稿を彼に送って校訂してもらったりしたが、それでも、これは不完全な略述に過ぎないものである。

ヨシダ・トラジロー（吉田寅次郎）は、長州毛利家代々の兵学師範の養子になった。その名前 Yoshida-Torajiro は、各音節にほとんどフランス語のように等しいアクセントを置き、母音はイタリア語のように、子音は英語のように発音する。例外は j だけで、これはフランス語の発音、すなわち､zh―このように表記する案の方が適切に思える―の音である。吉田は、漢学―中国古典といってもよいかも知れないが―そして、父の専門の兵学に非常に通暁していた。築城術は彼の好む研究の一つであったし、また、少年時代から詩作も巧みであった。彼は熱烈にして知性的な憂国の士として生まれた。日本が置かれている状況は、彼の大きな関心事であった。彼はよりよき未来の設計図を頭に描きながらも、一方、自国の現状についての知識を増す機会があれば、決してこれをのがすことはしなかった。この

①(1802－1882) イタリアの愛国の志士。1848 年ローマ市民を扇動して法王を追う。のちアメリカに流寓した。
②(1800-1859)アメリカの急進的奴隷廃止論者。奴隷解放の反乱を起こし、絞首刑に処せられた。

YOSHIDA-TORAJIRO

THE name at the head of this page is probably unknown to the English reader, and yet I think it should become a household word like that of Garibaldi or John Brown. Some day soon, we may expect to hear more fully the details of Yoshida's history, and the degree of his influence in the transformation of Japan; even now there must be Englishmen acquainted with the subject, and perhaps the appearance of this sketch may elicit something more complete and exact. I wish to say that I am not, rightly speaking, the author of the present paper: I tell the story on the authority of an intelligent Japanese gentleman, Mr. Taiso Masaki, who told it me with an emotion that does honour to his heart; and though I have taken some pains, and sent my notes to him to be corrected, this can be no more than an imperfect outline.

Yoshida-Torajiro was son to the hereditary military instructor of the house of Choshu. The name you are to pronounce with an equality of accent on the different syllable, almost as in French, the vowels as in Italian, but the consonants in the English manner—expect the *j*,which has the French sound, or, as it has been cleverly proposed to write it, the sound of *zh*. Yoshida was very learned in Chinese letters, or, we might say, in the classics, and in his father's subject; fortification was among his favorite studies, and he was a poet from his boyhood. He was born to a lively and intelligent patriotism; the condition of Japan was his great concern; and while he projected a better future, he lost no opportunity of improving his knowledge of her present state. With this

目的のために、青年時代の彼は、徒歩で、時には3日間の食糧を背にして、絶えず遊歴していたが、これは、あらゆる俊傑に特有な勇敢で自立的な態度であった。このようにして旅をしながら、彼は詳細な日記をつけたが、この日記は失われてしまったのではないかと恐れられている。もしこの記録が、なんらかの点で、その人柄から当然期待できるようなものなら、日記が失われたことは、取り返しのつかない損失だといっても誇張ではあるまい。それはそれとして、吉田が遠くはるばると、この探求の遊歴をあくまでも強行したことは、日本人にとっても、今なお驚嘆に価することである。あの国の、あの時期の教養ある紳士は、親身な処遇を受けた場合、どこにおいても、挨拶の詩を残して立ち去ったものだ。同じように大いに遍歴の旅をした正木氏のある友人は、日本のきわめて遠隔の地に、吉田のそのような遊歴の足跡を発見している。

政治は、事前の準備は不必要と思われる、おそらく唯一の職業であろう。しかし、吉田の考え方は異なっていた。同胞の悲惨について、単にその救済策を発議するためだけでなく、一冊の書物を著そうとするかのような注意深さと探究心をもって研究した。彼のように熱烈で誠実な人にとって、自分の調査が極度に憂鬱（ゆううつ）なものだったことには、疑問の余地がない。彼が現状に不満を抱いていたことは、改革という目的に没頭した彼の熱烈さが如実に物語っている。他人なら落胆したようなことでも、そのためにかえって、吉田は仕事に対し情熱をかきたてたのだ。兵学を講じたとき彼の心を占めていたのは、第一に日本の防衛であった。日本の対外的な弱さは、跋扈（ばっこ）する夷人（いじん）の態度や、巨大な夷敵の軍艦の来訪をみれば明白なことであった。日本は包囲された国であった。かくして、吉田の愛国心は、みずから失敗を招いたといわれるような形をとった。これらのきわめて強力な夷人を打ち払おうと考えたが、かえって夷人を招じ入れることに役立ったことが、今では、彼の功績の一つになっているのである。しかし、自分の貞

end he was continually traveling in his youth, going on foot and sometimes with three days' provision on his back, in the brave, self-helpful manner of all heroes. He kept a full diary while he was thus upon his journeys, but it is feared that these notes have been destroyed. If their value were in any respect such as we have reason to expect from the man's character, this would be a loss not easy to exaggerate. It is still wonderful to the Japanese how far he contrived to push these explorations; a cultured gentleman of that land and period would leave a complimentary poem wherever he had been hospitably entertained; and a friend of Mr. Masaki, who was likewise a great wanderer, has found such traces of Yoshida's passage in very remote regions of Japan.

Politics is perhaps the only profession for which no preparation is thought necessary; but Yoshida considered otherwise, and he studied the miseries of his fellowcountrymen with as much attention and research as though he had been going to write a book instead of merely to propose a remedy. To a man of his intensity and singleness, there is no question but that this survey was melancholy in the extreme. His dissatisfaction is proved by the eagerness with which he threw himself into the cause of reform; and what would have discouraged another braced Yoshida for his task. As he professed the theory of arms, it was firstly the defences of Japan that occupied his mind. The external feebleness of that country was then illustrated by the manners of overriding barbarians, and the visits of big barbarian war ships: she was a country beleaguered. Thus the patriotism of Yoshida took a form which may be said to have defeated itself: he had it upon him to keep out these all-powerful foreigners, whom it is now one of his chief merits

潔な心情に忠実な者は、いつも終局においては、最高なもののために奮闘していたのだと認められるであろう。目覚めた人にあっては、一つの事態はそれだけで終始することなく、その結果が次の事態の原因となり、上向きの進歩を遂げながら、自然に次々と連続していくものである。この夷人たちの勢力と知識とは、分かつことのできないものであった。吉田は、外国の軍事力を羨望(せんぼう)することによって、その文化を羨望するようになった。軍事力において夷人に匹敵したいという願望から、文化においては彼等に比肩しうるようになりたいという欲求がわいた。かくして、彼は同じ著書の中で、京都の防衛を堅固にするとともに、京都の町に外人教師による大学を設立する計画を論考している。おそらく彼は、他国の悪いところを除いて長所を取り入れ、夷人の知識によって日本に利するところがあるようにし、しかも、自国の学術や美徳が、他国から犯されないようにと念願したのであろう。しかし、彼の願望の本質が正確にはどうであろうと、それを達成する手段は、困難でもあり、また、明白でもあった。誰(だれ)か眼識と理解力を備えた人が、役人の監視線を突破して新世界へ脱出し、その地においてこの異文明の研究をしなければならない。そして、誰が吉田よりもこの仕事に適材であり得たであろうか。その仕事は危険を伴わないわけではなかったが、彼は恐れなかった。それには、準備と洞察力とが必要であった。そして、彼が幼少のときから修練したことは、日本の最高の文化を身につけ、幾多の遊歴のうちに、観察の能力と習慣を身につけることではなかったであろうか。

彼は弱冠 22 歳であった。そして、ペリー提督が江戸の近くに碇泊しているという情報が長州に伝わったときには、上記のことはすべて、既に彼の心の中では明白になっていた。さて、ここに、憂国の士にとっての好機が到来した。長州のサムライの間では、特に大名の顧問役の間においては、吉田の一般教養や見識—開明的な者は進んでこれを受け入れようとした

to have helped to introduce; but a man who follows his own virtuous heart will be always found in the end to have been fighting for the best. One thing leads naturally to another in an awakened mind, and that with an upward progress from effect to cause. The power and knowledge of these foreigners were things inseparable; by envying them their military strength, Yoshida came to envy them their culture; from the desire to equal them in the first, sprang his desire to share with them in the second; and thus he is found treating in the same book of a new scheme to strengthen the defences of Kioto and of the establishment, in the same city, of a university of foreign teachers. He hoped, perhaps, to get the good of other lands without their evil; to enable Japan to profit by the knowledge of the barbarians, and still keep her inviolate with her own arts and virtues. But whatever was the precise nature of his hope, the means by which it was to be accomplished were both difficult and obvious. Some one with eyes and understanding must break through the official cordon, escape into the new world, and study this other civilization on the spot. And who could be better suited for the business? It was not without danger, but he was without fear. It needed preparation and insight; and what had he done since he was a child but prepare himself with the best culture of Japan, and acquire in his excursions the power and habit of observing?

He was but twenty-two, and already all this was clear in his mind, when news reached Choshu that Commodore Perry was lying near to Yeddo. Here, then, was the patriot's opportunity. Among the Samurai of Choshu, and in particular among the councillors of the Daimio, his general culture, his views, which the enlightened were eager to accept,

のだが—とりわけ、彼の予言者的魅力や男子のもつ燦然たる説得力が、多くの誠実な信奉者を得ていた。このように、彼はその地を去る許可と、ある口実によって、江戸で自分の職業に従事する特権を手に入れた。彼の地へ向って、彼は急いだ。やっと到着したときには、時は既に遅かった。ペリーはもはや抜錨し、船団は日本の水域からその姿を消していた。しかし、吉田はいったん仕事に着手すると、途中で引き返すような男ではなかった。この仕事に乗り出していたのだ。神よ、彼にその仕事を完遂させ給え。そのために、彼は公職を断念し、次の機会に備えて江戸に居残った。この行為によって、彼は上司である長州の大名に対して、ある態度を示したのだが、このことは、私には十分に説明することはできない。確かに、彼は、浪人、禄を剥奪された男、封建的放逐者となった。故郷の地に足を踏み入れれば、彼は確かに逮捕を免れることはなかったのだ。しかし、「彼は真に臣従の義務を損ねることはなかった」のであって、旧臣の行為に対し、主君がもはや責任を負わされることができないように、吉田は、みずからわが身を遠ざけたに過ぎないのだと、私は正木氏から戒められている。このことには、私に理解できないなにか微妙な封建的慣習があるのだ。

江戸においては、このように、政治的には明確に言いがたい身分であり、しかも、あらゆる生計の手段を絶たれていたが、彼は計画に共鳴する人々から温かく援助を受けた。その一人は、代々、将軍の顧問役を務めた家臣のサクマ・ショーザン(佐久間象山)で、彼から吉田は金銭以上のもの、すなわち金銭の価値以上のものを学び得た。佐久間は、堅実にして人格高潔、世論に対して慧眼を備えており、みずからは偉大な行為をなし得なくても、なし得る人々を心から賞賛し、歴史に感謝されるような人として推挙するような人物の一人であった。そういう人物は、おそらく想像以上に、偉大さを一層助長する力をもった人のようである。人々は、彼等のことを、夜になると主イエスを訪れたニコデモ①と関連づけて考えるのである。そし

---

①ユダヤ人のつかさで、隠れたキリストの弟子。(ヨハネ伝 3:1 参照)

and, above all, the prophetic charm, the radiant persuasion of the man, had gained him many and sincere disciples. He had thus a strong influence at the provincial Court; and so he obtained leave to quit the district, and, by way of a pretext, a privilege to follow his profession in Yeddo. Thither he hurried, and arrived in time to be too late: Perry had weighed anchor, and his sails had vanished form the waters of Japan. But Yoshida, having put his hand to the plough, was not the man to go back; he had entered upon this business, and, please God, he would carry it through; and so he gave up his professional career and remained in Yeddo to be at hand against the next opportunity. By this behaviour he put himself into an attitude towards his superior, the Daimio of Choshu, which I cannot thoroughly explain. Certainly, he became a *Ronyin*, a broken man, a feudal outlaw; certainly he was liable to be arrested if he set foot upon his native province; yet I am cautioned that "he did not really break his allegiance," but only so far separated himself as that the prince could no longer be held accountable for his late vassal's conduct. There is some nicety of feudal custom here that escapes my comprehension.

In Yeddo, with this nondescript political status, and cut off from any means of livelihood, he was joyfully supported by those who sympathised with his design. One was Sakuma-Shozan, hereditary retainer of one of the Shogun's councillors, and from him he got more than money or than money's worth. A steady, respectable man, with an eye to the world's opinion, Sakuma was one of those who, if they cannot do great deeds in their own person, have yet an ardour of admiration for those who can, that recommends them to the gratitude of history.

て、佐久間は、吉田に表面的な愛顧を与えるというより、実質的な援助を与え得る位置にあった。それは、佐久間がオランダ語を読むことができたし、自分の知識を他人に伝達することに熱心であったからである。

その若き浪人が、このようにして江戸で学問をしていたときに、ロシアの軍艦が長崎に滞留しているという情報が届いた。時を逸してはならなかった。佐久間は「長い一編の激励の詩」を餞別（せんべつ）とした。吉田は長崎へ向け、徒歩で出発した。彼の道は、故郷の長州を通っていたが、南の方の本街道は、藩主のいる所から離れていたために、逮捕は免れることができた。彼は詩に卓越していたのを利して、吟遊詩人（トルーベール）①のように自活の旅をした。紹介に役立てようと、自分の作品を携帯した。ある町へ着くと、剣術や詩、あるいは何か他の、世に認められている教養で名を知られている人の家を尋ねた。そこで彼の技芸（わざ）の程を披露（ひろう）すると、招じ入られて供応を受けた。そして辞去するときには、返礼の詩を残したものであった。このようにして、中世を通過して発見の航海を続け、19世紀にはいってきたのである②。長崎へ着いてみると、再度、時は既に遅すぎた。ロシア艦隊は立ち去ったあとであった。しかし、彼は不運にもかかわらず、この旅で得る所があった。しばらく滞在して、オランダ通詞たち―下層階級の者であったが、いろいろな機会に遭遇した人々であった―から断片的な知識を吸収した。それから、依然として決意にあふれて、来たときと同じように、徒歩で江戸へ帰ってきた。

このような引き続く失意のもとにあって、彼を支えたのは、彼自身の若さと勇気だけでなく、絶えず新しい門弟がたくさんいたからである。彼にはブルース③やコロンブスのような人の持つ執拗（しつよう）さがあったが、また、彼に特有の適応性もあった。彼はいわゆる世俗の成功ではなく、「行為の報酬」を求めたのである。どんな方向から阻止しても、彼は別の出口を見つけて出てくるであろう。引き続いて船艦に乗りそこね、おもな仕事は依然

---

①フランス中世の叙事詩人

②この文は、比喩的な記述で、松陰の旅が中世の吟遊詩人の遍歴のようであり、また、コロンブスのアメリカ大陸発見の航海にも似ていた。しかし、長崎へ来てみると、世は19世紀になっていて夷人の船艦が渡来する時代だという意。

③ウィリアム・S・ブルース（1867－？）のことであろう。彼はスコットランドの科学者、探検家、スティブンソンの生存中に南極探検を行っている。

They aid and abet greatness more, perhaps, than we imagine. One thinks of them in connection with Nicodemus, who visited our Lord by night. And Sakuma was in a position to help Yoshida more practically than by simple countenance; for he could read Dutch, and was eager to communicate what he knew.

While the young Rounin thus lay studying in Yeddo, news came of a Russian ship at Nangasaki. No time was to be lost. Sakuma contributed "a long copy of encouraging verses;" and off set Yoshida on foot for Nangasaki. His way lay through his own province of Choshu; but, as the highroad to the south lay apart from the capital, he was able to avoid arrest. He supported himself, like a *trouve're*, by his proficiency in verse. He carried his works along with him, to serve as an introduction. When he reached a town he would inquire for the house of any one celebrated for swordsmanship, or poetry, or some of the other acknowledged forms of culture; and there, on giving a taste of his skill, he would be received and entertained, and leave behind him, when he went away, a compliment in verse. Thus he traveled through the Middle Ages on his voyage of discovery into the nineteenth century. When he reached Nangasaki he was once more too late. The Russians were gone. But he made a profit on his journey in spite of fate, and stayed awhile to pick up scraps of knowledge from the Dutch interpreters—a low class of men, but one that had opportunities; and then, still full of purpose, returned to Yeddo on foot, as he had come.

It was not only his youth and courage that supported him under these successive disappointments, but the continual affluence of new disciples. The man had the tenacity of a Bruce or a Columbus, with a

として停滞していた。しかし、よりよい未来を築くために、彼が啓発し、覚悟を固めさせる日本人が一人でもいるかぎり、やはり彼は日本のために働いているのだと感じることができたのだ。さて、長崎から帰ってくるとすぐ、もっとも末頼もしい新しい探求者①が彼を探し出した。この男は平民階級の平侍（ひらさむらい）—生まれは紺屋（こうや）であったが、吉田の行動のことをどこからともなく②耳にして、その計画のことで驚嘆の念にかられていたのだ。この男は佐久間象山や長州の大名の顧問役たちとは、はるかに異なった探求者であった。刀を二本さす武士どころか、低い階層のうちに生まれ、学問による教養のない平凡な庶民であった。しかし、短い生涯のいかなる逆境においても、吉田から失（う）せることのなかったあの感化力、あの燦然とした説得力が、立派な学識のある者に対したのと同じように、この平侍の心をとらえ、魅惑し、そして変革したのであった。この男は即座に燃えさかり、真の熱狂者となった。彼の心は、ただ師を待っていたのだ。この新しい思想から、彼はたちどころに得るところがあった。彼も異国の見慣れぬ土地へ行き、日本を強くし、新しくしうるような知識を持ち帰ろうとしたのだ。ところで、この男により十分な準備をさせるために、吉田は漢文学を教授し、彼は学習し始めた。このことは、吉田にとって、もっとも誇りとすべき挿話であるが、その侍のみならず、日本の庶民の能力と美徳にとっても、さらに光栄とすべき挿話である。

さて、ペリー提督は、遂に下田へ引き返してきた。友輩たちが吉田を取り巻き、援助と相談と激励を与えた。ある者は、長さ３尺の非常に重たい太刀（たち）を送った。彼は狂喜して、遍歴の旅の間中それを腰に帯び—はるか遠い旅を共にした武器として—日本へ持ち帰ると誓った。長い書簡が、アメリカ士官あてに、漢文で用意された。それは佐久間によって修正、添削された。吉田は、ウリナキ・マンジ③（瓜中万二）の名で、そして侍の方はイチギ・コータ（市木公太）の名で署名をした。吉田は、著述のための用

①金子重輔のことであるが、このエッセイには金子という名は用いられていない。
②【原注】吉田は長崎への途上、その侍に路傍で出会い、語り合った。そこで二人は別れたが、侍はそのとき聞いたことばに非常に心を打たれたので、吉田が帰ると捜し出して、生命をその立派な目的のために捧げる決意を述べた。私は正木氏がこの話をしたときそばにいたので、作者の不在をかりて、あえてこの訂正を挿入する。—F.J.　そして、この相違に決着をつける者がいるはずもないから、私は二つの所説のあることを再述しておかざるをえない。—R.L.S.
③瓜中正二は、「ペリー日本遠征記」には、クワンズチ・マンヂとある。

pliability that was all his own. He did not fight for what the world would call success; but for "the wages of going on." Check him off in a dozen directions, he would find another outlet and break forth. He missed one vessel after another, and the main work still halted; but so long as he had a single Japanese to enlighten and prepare for the better future, he could still feel that he was working for Japan. Now, he had scarce returned from Nangasaki, when he was sought out by a new inquirer, the most promising of all. This was a common soldier, of the Hemming class, a dyer by birth, who had heard vaguely(1) of Yoshida's movements, and had become filled with wonder as to their design. This was a far different inquirer from Sakuma-Shozan, or the councillors of the Daimio of Choshu. This was no two-sworded gentleman, but the common stuff of the country, born in low traditions and unimproved by books; and yet that influence, that radiant persuasion that never failed Yoshida in any circumstance of his short life, enchanted, enthralled, and converted the common soldier, as it had done already with the elegant and learned. The man instantly burned up into a true enthusiasm; his mind had been only waiting for a teacher; he grasped in a moment the profit of these new ideas; he, too, would go to foreign, outlandish parts, and bring back the knowledge that was to strengthen and renew Japan; and in the meantime, that he might be the better prepared, Yoshida set himself to teach, and he to learn, the Chinese literature. It is an episode most honourable to Yoshida, and yet more honourable still to the soldier, and to the capacity and virtue of the common people of Japan.

And now, at length, Commodore Perry returned to Simoda. Friends

(1) Yoshida, when on his way to Nangasaki, met the soldier an talked with him by the roadside, they then parted, but the soldier was so much struck by the words he heard, that on Yoshida's return he sought him out and declared his intention of devoting his life to the good cause. I venture, in the absence of the writer, to insert this correction, having been present when the story was told by Mr.Masaki. –F.J. And I, there being none to settle the difference, must reproduce both versions –R.L.S.

具をたくさん用意していた。衣服には、観察にする知識をぎっしり詰め込んで再び帰国し、日本を偉大で幸福な国にするはずの用紙が、文字通り押し込まれていた。こうして準備が整うと、この二人連れの移住者は、江戸から歩いて出発し、日没ごろ下田についた。歴史のいかなる時期においても、旅が、いかなるヨーロッパ人に対しても、この勇敢な日本人に呈したのと同じ畏怖の顔付きを示したはずはない。最も勇気を有する極地遠征よりも、ユリシーズ①が地獄に降りたことの方が、この場合に一層類似している。二人の行為には、先例がないからである。それは国禁を犯すことであった。しかもそれは、人間界の境を越えて、二人を悪魔の国へ連れて行くことであった。異常な状況を考えて、二人が身震いをしたとしても、それは不思議なことではない。その侍は、「中国風の朗詠で」—これで彼が学問の成果を挙げていたことが分かるのだが—次の二行の適切な詩を朗誦したが、おそらくそれは二人の心情を述べたものであろう。

「今夜は知らず何れの処にか宿らん

平沙(へいさ)万里人烟(じんえん)を絶つ」②

海辺にすぐ近い小さな社で、彼等は横になって休息をとった。横になると睡魔が二人を襲った。目覚めたときには、日本における最後の朝の「東は既に白んでいた。」漁夫の舟を一艘(いっそう)手に入れると、潮の干満のため、はるか沖合いにいたペリーに向かって漕ぎ出した。彼等が船艦に乗り移った様子そのものが、決意をよく表していた。船艦に手をかけるや否や、二人は再び引き返すことができないようにするため、小舟を足で蹴り放してしまった。読者は、これでいっさいは首尾よくいったと思われたであろう。しかし、提督は、すでに将軍の政府（幕府）と条約を結んでいた。日本人が日本から脱出するのを援助してはならないというのが、約定の一つであった。そこで、吉田とその門人は、囚人として下田の番所に手渡された。その夜、夷人の秘事を探るつもりであった吉田は、—いやしくも、それが

---

①ギリシャ伝説におけるイサカの王で、トロイ戦争のときのギリシア軍の勇士。オデッセイのラテン名

②岑参の磧中作の転結。上の二句は、「馬を走らせて西に来り天に到らんと欲す　家を辞してより月の両回円かなるを見る」

crowded round Yoshida with help, counsels, and encouragement. One presented him with a great sword, three feet long and very heavy, which, in the exultation of the hour, he swore to carry throughout all his wanderings, and to bring back —a far travelled weapon – to Japan. A long letter was prepared in Chinese for the American officers; it was revised and corrected by Sakuma, and signed by Yoshida, under the name of Urinaki-Manji, and by the soldier under that of Ichigi-Koda. Yoshida had supplied himself with a profusion of materials for writing; his dress was literally stuffed with paper which was to come back again enriched with his observations and make a great and happy kingdom of Japan. Thus equipped, this pair of emigrants set forward on foot from Yeddo, and reached Simoda about nightfall. At no period within history can travel have presented to any European creature the same face of awe and terror as to these courageous Japanese. The descent of Ulysses into hell is a parallel more near the case than the boldest expedition in the Polar circles. For their act was unprecedented; it was criminal; and it was to take them beyond the pale of humanity into a land of devils. It is not to be wondered at if they were thrilled by the thought of their unusual situation; and perhaps the soldier gave utterance to the sentiment of both when he sang, "in Chinese singing" (so that we see he had already profited by his lessons), these two appropriate verses:

> "We do not know where we are to sleep to-night, In a thousand miles of desert where we can see no human smoke."

In a little temple, hard by the sea-shore, they lay down to repose; sleep

眠りといえるなら―背丈を伸ばして横になるには狭すぎ、直立するには低すぎる独房で眠った。説明を加えるには、余りにも大きな挫折がいくつもあるのだ。

佐久間は筆跡によって巻添えとなり、家郷に送還されて幽閉の身となったが、ほどなく釈放になった。吉田と従者は、長くみじめな囚われの苦渋を嘗めた。そして、侍の方は実際、まだ在獄中に皮膚病のため生涯を閉じた。しかし、吉田寅次郎のような人物は、繋留の身にすることは容易ではない。また、不運のために挫折することのない精神の持主を、牢獄に幽閉しようとしても無駄である。彼は不屈の積極性を発揮して、政府に対して上書を書き、また、自説を流布するための論説を書いた。この後者については禁制となっていたが、彼には常に看守が味方をしたために、その論説の撒布は困難なことではなかった。いかに彼の牢獄を次々と変え続けたとて、それは無駄なことであった。そのような計画を実行したことで、政府は新しい思想の伝播を早めたにすぎなかった。吉田は、人を改宗させるためには、新しい牢獄へ移って来さえすればよかったのだ。このようにして、彼自身は監禁の身でありながらも、信奉者の仲間を国中に確立し、また、広めていった。

幾つかの獄舎を移されたあと、遂に、将軍の牢獄から、主君である長州の大名の獄舎へ引き渡された。日本を脱出しようと企てたための刑期を勤め終え、浪人すなわち封建的放逐者として、些細な起訴で地方の藩に渡されることはありうることだと思う。しかし、それはそれとして、この転獄は吉田にとって非常に重要なことであった。大名の幕僚中の崇拝者たちの力によって、彼は内密で自宅に蟄居する特権を許されたのである。自宅では、仲間の改革者たちと意見の疎通を図るとともに、教育の仕事に従事しようとして、若年者の教育を引受けた。だからといって、彼が自由であったと考えてはならない。自由であるには余りに要注意人物であり過ぎた。

overtook them as they lay; and when they awoke, " the east was already white" for their last morning in Japan. They seized a fisherman's boat and rowed out—Perry lying far to sea because of the two tides. Their very manner of boarding was significant of determination; for they had no sooner caught hold upon the ship than they kicked away their boat to make return impossible. And now you would have thought that all was over. But the Commodore was already in treaty with the Shogun's Government; it was one of the stipulations that no Japanese was to be aided in escaping from Japan; and Yoshida and his followers were handed over as prisoners to the authorities at Simoda. That night he who had been to explore the secrets of the barbarian slept, if he might sleep at all, in a cell too short for lying down at full length, and too low for standing upright. There are some disappointments too great for commentary.

Sakuma, implicated by his handwriting, was sent into his own province in confinement, from which he was soon released. Yoshida and the soldier suffered a long and miserable period of captivity, and the latter, indeed, died, while yet in prison, of a skin disease. But such a spirit as that of Yoshida-Torajiro is not easily made or kept a captive; and that which cannot be broken by misfortune you shall seek in vain to confine in a bastille. He was indefatigably active, writing reports to Government and treatises for dissemination. These latter were contraband; and yet he found no difficulty in their distribution, for he always had the jailor on his side. It was in vain that they kept changing him from one prison to another. Government by that plan only hastened the spread of new ideas; for Yoshida had only to arrive to

おそらく、ある小範囲に限定され、警吏の監視つきで暮らしたのであろう。しかし、幽閉の身でこれほどの大事をなした彼にとって、ここでの生活は、大きな得る所の多い自由だと思えたであろう。

正木氏が、吉田と個人的な接触を結んだのは、この時期であった。それ故、当時 13 歳の少年の眼を通して、この俊傑の性格や習慣をよく見知し得るのである。吉田は醜く、おかしな程痘瘡(とうそう)の跡が残っていた。自然は初めから彼に物惜しみしたが、一方、彼の個人的な習性は、だらしないとさえいってよかった。衣服はぼろぼろであったし、食事や洗面のときには、袖(そで)で手をふいた。頭髪は 2 ヶ月に 1 回程度しか結わなかったので、見苦しいことがしばしばあった。このような様子であったから、彼が結婚しなかったことを信じることは容易である。ことば使いは激しく乱暴であったが、振舞いは温和で立派な教師であり、講義が難解なため門下生の頭上を素通りし、そのため彼等が唖然(あぜん)としたり、さらにしばしば笑うことがあっても、そのまま放置し気にもとめなかった。学問に対する情熱はすこぶる激しかったので、自然の眠りすら惜しんだ程であった。そこで、読書中に眠くなると、夏だと蚊(か)を着物の袂にとまらせ、冬なら履物(はきもの)を脱いで、裸足で雪の上を走ったものであった。彼は格別に悪筆であり、詩作はしたけれども、優雅なものには興味がなかった。美しい字を書くことが、公証人たるの特徴なのではなく、紳士として賛美すべき才芸(たしなみ)である国にあって、事態の近迫さと信念から生まれる情熱のために、文字が揺れ動いても、彼は意に介さなかった。賄賂(わいろ)については、それらしい様子だけでも我慢しようとはしなかった。賄賂は、日本においては、その近隣の国々と同じように、多くの悪の根源にあったからである。それで、ある商人が教育をしてもらいに子息を連れてきて、慣習[①]に従って、わずかばかりのお菓子料をそっと差し出すと、吉田は、その金銭を差し出した人の顔面に投げつけ、憤怒の情を爆発させたので、そのことが獄中に知れ渡るほどであった。正木が彼を

---

①【原注】その商人が、自分では受ける資格のない教育を息子に受けさせようとして、内密に努力していうのだということが、私には理解できた。—F.J.

make a convert. Thus, though he himself has laid by the heels, he confirmed and extended his party in the State.

At last, after many lesser transferences, he was given over from the prisons of the Shogun to those of his own superior, the Daimio of Choshu. I conceive it possible that he may then have served out his time for the attempt to leave Japan, and was now resigned to the provincial Government on a lesser count, as a Rounin or feudal rebel. But, however that may be, the change was of great importance to Yoshida; for by the influence of his admirers in the Daimio's council, he was allowed the privilege, underhand, of dwelling in his own house. And there, as well to keep up communication with his fellow-reformers as to pursue his work of education, he received boys to teach. It must not be supposed that he was free; he was too marked a man for that; he was probably assigned to some small circle, and lived, as we should say, under police surveillance; but to him, who had done so much from under lock and key, this would seem a large and profitable liberty.

It was at this period that Mr. Masaki was brought into personal contact with Yoshida; and hence, through the eyes of a boy of thirteen, we get one good look at the character and habits of the hero. He was ugly and laughably disfigured with the smallpox; and while nature had been so niggardly with him from the first, his personal habits were even sluttish. His clothes were wretched; when he ate or washed he wiped his hands upon his sleeves; and as his hair was not tied more than once in the two months, it was often disgusting to behold. With such a picture, it is easy to believe that he never married. A good teacher, gentle in act, although violent and abusive in speech, his

知った当時は、吉田は獄舎での苦渋のため、ひどく弱っていて、長さ３尺の贈られた刀も、彼には重すぎて持ち歩くにも苦労していた。それでも、菜園を掘り起こしに出たときも、常に帯刀していたものであった。このことは、なんとなく吉田という人物を特徴づけるものである。性格が弱い者なら、失敗の記念に過ぎないこの刀を見ることすら避けていたであろう。しかし、彼は、もし「あなたの失策を勇気をもって悲劇的なものにし得るなら、失策は成功となんら異なりはしないだろう」というソーロー①の考え方をしていた。彼は熱烈な将来への夢を抱いていたことを、当惑することなく回想することができた。もし事態が意に反して、目的を遂行できないと分かったとしても一それは、ただ、勇を鼓し不屈の決意をもって、別の目的に当たるための理由を強めるに過ぎなかったのだ。たとえ、刀を夷国に携えることができないとしても、その刀は、少なくとも、生涯をまったく日本のために捧げたことへの証拠となるべきものである。

これが、塾生たちの目に写った彼の姿であるが、塾生気質から語られたものではない。優雅さにこれほど無関心な男は、少年や婦女子にとっては、一顧に価しない存在なのである。実際、私たちは誰も、多少の差こそあれ、通学の経験があるから、吉田が門下生たちから物笑いの種にされたことに驚きはしないであろう。生徒には鋭いユーモアの感覚があるものだ。生徒は、書物の中で、英傑を理解し、尊敬することを習うのである。しかし、同時代の人の場合には、どんな特性をもっていても、殊に、よく争論し、薄汚れ、一風変わった教師に対しては、生徒は決して英雄らしさを認めようとはしないものである。しかし、歳月がたち、吉田の門弟たちが、理論的に完全無欠の人物を身近に見付けようと努力しても無駄だと知り、また、吉田の薫陶の意味をますます深く理解し始めると、門弟たちはこの滑稽な教師を、人類の中で最も高潔な人物として追憶するようになった。

この短いが充実した生涯における最後の行為は、既に間近に迫っていた。

---

①(1817-1862)アメリカの超絶主義の著述家。代表作は森林生活の随想的記録「ウォールデンの森」。

lessons were apt to go over the heads of his scholars, and to leave them gaping, or more often laughing. Such was his passion for study that he even grudged himself natural repose; and when he grew drowsy over his books he would, if it was summer, put mosquitoes up his sleeve; and, if it was winter, take off his shoes and run barefoot on the snow. His handwriting was exceptionally villainous; poet though he was, he had no taste for what was elegant; and in a country where to write beautifully was not the mark of a scrivener but an admired accomplishment for gentlemen, he suffered his letters to be jolted out of him by the press of matter and the heat of his convictions. He would not tolerate even the appearance of a bribe; for bribery lay at the root of much that was evil in Japan, as well as in countries nearer home; and once when a merchant brought him his son to educate, and added, as was customary (1), a little private sweetener, Yoshida dashed the money in the giver's face, and launched into such an outbreak of indignation as made the matter public in the school. He was still, when Masaki knew him, much weakened by his hardships in prison; and the presentation sword, three feet long, was too heavy for him to wear without distress; yet he would always gird it on when he went to dig in his garden. That is a touch which qualifies the man. A weaker nature would have shrunk from the sight of what only commemorated a failure. But he was of Thoreau's mind, that if you can "make your failure tragical by courage, it will not differ from success." He could look back without confusion to his enthusiastic promise. If events had been contrary, and he found himself unable to carry out that purpose – well, there was but the more reason to be brave and constant in another. If

(1) I understood that the merchant was endeavouring surreptitiously to obtain for his son instruction to which he was not entitled –F.J.

彼の事業のうちいくつかは成就した。オランダの教師たちが、既に長崎にはいることを許されていたし、日本の国は、全体としては、新しい学問を熱心に探求していたからである。しかし、改革は始まっていたけれども、将軍の権力によって妨害を受け、脅迫され、かつ危機に瀕していた。大老は—護衛の真中(ただなか)にありながら雪の中で暗殺されたのと同一人物であるが—学究の徒がオランダ人の所へ行くのを差し止めたばかりでなく、間諜(かんちょう)や探偵(たんてい)を使い、投獄や死罪によって、もっとも聡明で活動的な人物を日本から滅じていたのだ。それは、今にも倒壊しそうな国の古い物語—学問を投獄し、優位を断頭台に乗せ、羊と驢馬(ろば)のほか何も残らなくなると、その国が救われたことになる—そのような古い物語なのである。しかし、一個人が革命を処理しようとしてはならないし、一大老がいかに護衛者で身を固めていようと、吉田と彼の侍の従者のような人物を生んだ国を抑圧しようとしてはならない。大老タークイン①の暴虐は、将軍の統治が違法であることに、注意を向けるに役立つだけであった。人々は忠誠心を、江戸や将軍から、京都に閑居し長く忘れ去られているミカド（御門）の方に転じ始めた。そのためかどうかは別にして、この危機に際して、これら両統治者の関係が緊迫してくると、将軍の老中②は、正統の主催者に対しさらに恥辱を与えようとして京都に向かった。このことは、事件の成行きを早めるのにふさわしかった。御門を守護することは一種の宗教であったし、暴君的、流血的侵害に対抗することは、明らかにある種の政治的正義であった。吉田にとって、行動を起こすべき時期が到来したように思えた。彼自身は、まだ長州に幽閉の身であった。彼にとっては、知性以外に自由になるものはなく、将軍の老中に対しては、その知性で剣を磨いた。門下生の一団は、江戸から京都へ向かう途中のある村で、この暴君を待ち伏せし、嘆願書を差し出しておいて殺戮するつもりであった。しかし、吉田とその友輩たちは、厳重に監視されていた。そして、二人の共謀者—１８歳の少年①とそ

---

①ローマ初期の伝説的な王家の人で、暴政をしいた。
②老中間部詮勝のこと。安政５年に上洛し、条約問題等を奏上するとともに、志士たちを逮捕しようとした。

he could not carry the sword into barbarian lands, it should at least be witness to a life spent entirely for Japan.

This is the sight we have of him as he appeared to schoolboys, but not related in the schoolboy spirit. A man so careless of the graces must be out of court with boys and women. And, indeed, as we have all been more or less to school, it will astonish no one that Yoshida was regarded by his scholars as a laughing-stock. The schoolboy has a keen sense of humour. Heroes he learns to understand and to admire in books; but he is not forward to recognize the heroic under the traits of any contemporary man, and least of all in a brawling, dirty, and eccentric teacher. But as the years went by, and the scholars of Yoshida continued in vain to look around them for the abstractly perfect, and began more and more to understand the drift of his instructions, they learned to look back upon their comic schoolmaster as upon the noblest of mankind.

The last act of this brief and full existence was already near at hand. Some of his work was done; for already there had been Dutch teachers admitted into Nangasaki, and the country at large was keen for the new learning. But though the renaissance had begun, it was impeded and dangerously threatened by the power of the Shogun. His minister —the same who was afterwards assassinated in the snow in the very midst of his bodyguard – not only held back pupils from going to the Dutchmen, but by spies and detectives, by imprisonment and death, kept thinning out of Japan the most intelligent and active spirits. It is the old story of a power upon its last legs – learning to the bastille, and courage to the block; when there are none left but sheep and donkeys,

年①とその兄のあまりに遠い討伐の旅は、当局の疑惑をひき起こし、陰謀はそのすべてが露顕し、連累者全員が逮捕されるに至った。

江戸では―そこに檻送されたのであるが―吉田は再び厳重な監禁の身となった。しかし、この最後の試練の時においても、誰からも共鳴を得られないままではなかった。隣の独房に、南国薩摩の山国生まれの改革者クサカベ②（日下部以三次）という志士がいた。彼らは、実際には、異なった計画で投獄されていたのだが、意図するところは同一であった。日本のために、同じ信念と、同じ抱負を分かちあっていた。獄舎の壁を通して、幾度となく、長時間にわたって会話を交わした。そして間もなく二人を結びつけた共感は、深い心情から生まれたものであった。日下部の方が、先に奉行の前に引き出される運命になった。そして、判決が言い渡されると、吉田の窓の下を通って処刑場へ引かれていった。もし頭を振り向けたら、彼の仲間の囚人を連座させることになったであろう。しかし、彼は吉田を流し目で見ると、次の二行の漢詩を大声で朗吟して訣別を告げた。

「大丈夫寧ろ玉砕すべく
　何ぞ能く瓦全せん」③

こうして、薩摩の山国の藩士日下部は、現世の舞台からその姿を消した。彼の詩は古の名士の死に似ていた。

その後しばらくして、吉田も評定所へ姿を現さねばならなかった。彼の最後の場面は、それまでの生涯にふさわしく、しかも、彼の一生の栄誉を飾るものとなった。彼は機会をとらえて並みいる者に自分の計画を告白し、また、その計画を誇りと考えた。そして、聞き入る者たちへ、自国の歴史の中の一課を朗誦し、遂には、将軍の権力の不法と、その権力の行使を汚点とする数々の罪状を説いた。こうして、一度だけ、言うべきことを述べ終わると、彼は引き立てられ、処刑された。齢３１歳④。

兵法学者、勇敢な遍歴者（少なくとも願望としてはそうであった）、詩

---

①野村（入江）和作とその兄入江杉蔵。ただし、事実はこの分と多少異なる。
②名は信政。安政5年12月17日、伝馬町の獄で病死。実際には、松陰は彼と生前面識がなく、同囚から日下部の逸話を聞いたと伝えらえる。
③「大丈夫寧可㆓玉砕㆒、何能瓦全」（北斉書）
別文に「寧ろ玉となり砕くるとも瓦となりて全かるなかれ」とある、意味は同じ。なお、この詩を吟じたのは高松藩士長谷川宗右衛門であるという。
④数え年30歳が正しい。

the State will have been saved. But a man must not think to cope with a Revolution; nor a minister, however fortified with guards, to hold in check a country that had given birth to such men as Yoshida and his soldier-follower. The violence of the ministerial Tarquin only served to direct attention to the illegality of his master's rule; and people began to turn their allegiance from Yeddo and the Shogun to the long-forgotten Mikado in his seclusion at Kioto. At this juncture, whether in consequence or not, the relations between these two rulers became stained; and the Shogun's minister set forth for Kioto to put another affront upon the rightful sovereign. The circumstance was well fitted to precipitate events. It was a piece of religion to defend the Mikado; it was a plain piece of political righteousness to oppose a tyrannical and bloody usurpation. To Yoshida the moment for action seemed to have arrived. He was himself still confined in Choshu. Nothing was free but his intelligence; but with that he sharpened a sword for the Shogun's minister. A party of his followers were to waylay the tyrant at a village on the Yeddo and Kioto road, present him with a petition, and put him to the sword. But Yoshida and his friends were closely observed; and the too great expedition of two of the conspirators, a boy of eighteen and his brother, wakened the suspicion of the authorities, and led to a full discovery of the plot and the arrest of all who were concerned.

In Yeddo, to which he was taken, Yoshida was thrown again into a strict confinement. But he was not left destitute of sympathy in this last hour of trial. In the next cell lay one Kusakabe, a reformer from the southern highlands of Satzuma. They were in prison for different plots

人、憂国の士、教育者、学究の徒、改革への殉教者―このような多方面の役割を果たし、自国に貢献した人物で、70歳で死んだ者は多くはいない。彼は思想の点で、聡明にして先見の明があっただけでなく、実行の点においても、確かに最も熱烈な英傑の一人であった。看守たちを屈服させた支配力、燃えるような衰えを知らない熱中さ、敗北を克服しようとする執拗な心―この中のどれが最も顕著であるかは言い難い。彼は、企てた独自の計画には、いずれも失敗したけれども、全体として見た場合、彼の成功がいかに完璧(かんぺき)なものであるかを知るには、彼の国を見さえすればよい。彼の同士や門下生たちは、今では12年ばかり前になるが、あの最終的な改革に際して多数の指導者となった。また、その多くは、日本の為政者の中でも高い地位にあり、現在はそうではなくても、過日までは高位にいたのだ。そして、今日、私たちの周囲に、風変わりな異国の風采(ふうさい)をし、活発で聡明な学生を見かけるときには、吉田が徒歩で長州から江戸へ、江戸から長崎へ、そして長崎から江戸へと再び引き返したことを、彼が衣服に筆記用具を押し込みアメリカの船艦に乗り込んだことを、また、彼が獄舎で苦悶し、遂には生命までも投げ捨てた―それまでもなく、彼は祖国のために、現在の日本が大いに享受しているあの実益そのものを手に入れようとして、生命と力と余暇のすべてを捧げたのだが―これらのことを決して忘れてはならない。佐久間のようになって単に危害を免れるよりも、吉田となって死滅する方がすぐれている。薩摩の日下部は、次のように言っている。「大丈夫寧ろ玉砕すべし」と。

一言付け加えておかねばならない。これは英雄的な一個人の話であるとともに、ある英雄的な一国民の話だということを見損じないでほしいと願うからである。吉田のことを脳裏に刻み込むだけでは十分ではない。あの平侍のことも、日下部のことも、また、熱心さのあまり計画を漏らした長州の18歳の少年ノムラ(野村和作)のことも忘れてはならない。このよ

indeed, but for the same intention; they shared the same beliefs and the same aspirations for Japan; many and long were the conversations they held through the prison wall, and dear was the sympathy that soon united them. It fell first to the lot of Kusakabe to pass before the judges; and when sentence had been pronounced he was led towards the place of death below Yoshida's window. To turn the head would have been to implicate his fellow-prisoner; but he threw him a look from his eye, and bade him farewell in a loud voice, with these two Chinese verses; —

"It is better to be a crystal and be broken,
Than to remain perfect like a tile upon the housetop."

So Kusakabe, from the highlands of Satzuma, passed out of the theatre of this world. His death was like an antique worthy's.

A little after, and Yoshida too must appear before the Court. His last scene was of a piece with his career, and fitly crowned it. He seized on the opportunity of a public audience, confessed and gloried in his design, and, reading his auditors a lesson in the history of their country, told at length the illegality of the Shogun's power and the crimes by which its exercise was sullied. So, having said his say for once, he was led forth and executed, thirty-one years old.

A military engineer, a bold traveler (at least in wish), a poet, a patriot, a schoolmaster, a friend to learning, a martyr to reform, —there are not many men, dying at seventy, who have served their country in such various characters. He was not only wise and provident in thought, but surely one of the fieriest of heroes in execution. It is hard to say which is most remarkable – his capacity for command, which subdued his

うな広大な志を抱いた人々と同時代に生きてきたことは、歓ばしいことである。宇宙の比率からすれば、わずか数マイル離れた所で、私が日々の課業を怠っている間に、吉田は眠気を覚まそうと自ら蚊にさされ、自分を責めさいなんでいたのだ。そして、読者が一文の所得税を惜しんでいる間に、日下部は高潔な詩文を朗誦して、死に向かって歩を進めていたのである。

very jailors; his hot, unflagging zeal; or his stubborn superiority to defeat. He failed in each particular enterprise that he attempted; and yet we have only to look at his country to see how complete has been his general success. His friends and pupils made the majority of leaders in that final Revolution, now some twelve years old; and many of them are, or were until the other day, high placed among the rulers of Japan. And when we see all round us these brisk intelligent students, with their strange foreign air, we should never forget how Yoshida marched afoot from Choshu to Yeddo, and from Yeddo to Nangasaki, and from Nangasaki back again to Yeddo; how he boarded the American ship, his dress stuffed with writing material; nor how he languished in prison, and finally gave his death, as he had formerly given all his life and strength and leisure, to gain for his native land that very benefit which she now enjoys so largely. It is better to be Yoshida and perish, than to be only Sakuma and yet save the hide. Kusakabe, of Satzuma, has said the word: it is better to be a crystal and be broken.

I must add a word; for I hope the reader will not fail to perceive that this is as much the story of a heroic people as that of a heroic man. It is not enough to remember Yoshida; we must not forget the common soldier, nor Kusakabe, nor the boy of eighteen, Nomura, of Choshu, whose eagerness betrayed the plot. It is exhilarating to have lived in the same days with these great-heated gentlemen. Only a few miles from us, to speak by the proportion of the universe, while I was droning over my lessons, Yoshida was goading himself to be wakeful with the stings of the mosquito; and while you were grudging a penny income tax, Kusakabe was stepping to death with a noble sentence on his lips.

関防印：Kanbouin「日月佳」

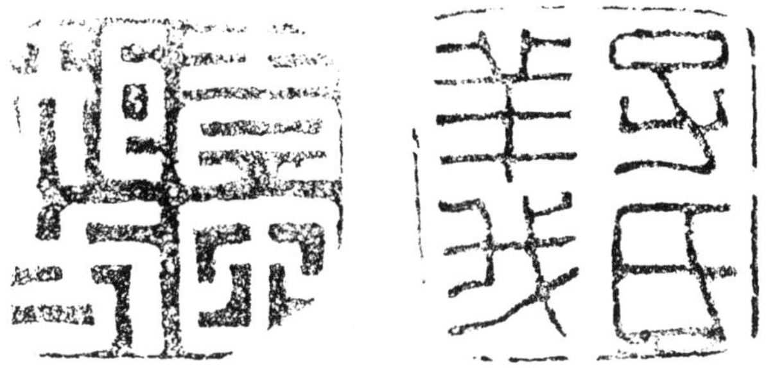

落款：Rakkan 松陰の名「吉田矩方」字「子義氏」

紺野大介先生『留魂録』英完訳本の刊行に寄せて

2002年12月
中国 北京日本学研究センター助教授
文学博士　郭連友

このたび、幕末の代表的思想家吉田松陰の代表作である『留魂録』が紺野大介先生により初めて翻訳され、刊行されることになった。海外の吉田松陰研究者の一人として、まず紺野先生の長年の研究や労作に衷心より敬意とお祝いを申し上げたい。

周知のように、松陰の事蹟が彼の弟子により海外に伝えられ、イギリスの文豪スティブンソンが松陰の幕府の海禁を破った「下田踏海」の壮挙に感動し、自ら『吉田寅次郎』を執筆し、そのお陰で、松陰の名前が以前から西洋人に知られていたのである。しかし、西洋では、松陰の著作に直接触れ、それを頼りに松陰の思想や行動をよく理解する人は管見の限りあまりいなかったようである。まさにこの点に着眼された紺野先生は橋本左内の『啓発録』（英完訳本）に継いで『留魂録』の英完訳を刊行した。先生のお仕事により日本と西洋との思想交流の空白がまた一つ埋められ、西洋人の日本理解に新たな架け橋が作られたと思われる。

西洋と対照をなすのは中国である。
日本と長い思想文化交流の歴史を持つ中国は特に近代に入ってから、一歩早く近代化を成し遂げた明治日本を自国の手本にした。政治、法律、教育などはもとより、日本の思想、文化も中国知識人の学習の対象となった。このような背景の中で、明治維新の先駆者として松陰がいちはやく中国に紹介された。黄遵憲の代表作『日本国誌』（1895年刊）、詩集『人境廬詩草』、康有為の『日本変政考』（1898年成立。1998年紫禁城出版社より刊行）、『日本書目誌』（1896年刊）、康同微の『日本変法由遊侠義憤考』（康有為序、1898年大同訳書局より刊行）、梁啓超の『自由書』（1899年）、『新民説』（1902年）などで、清末中国の改革者たちは中国改革の必要性から松陰の事蹟、思想、行動を意欲的に紹介し、中国にも松陰のような改革者の誕生を切望した。

このような時代の必要にあわせて、蘇峰の『吉田松陰』（明治26年初

绀野大介先生《留魂录》英文全译本出版寄语

2002 年 12 月
北京日本学研究中心副教授
文学博士　郭 连友

幕末最有代表性的思想家吉田松阴的代表作《留魂录》即将由绀野大介先生翻译出版。作为一名海外的吉田松阴研究者，我首先对绀野先生长年的松阴研究和呕心力作致以衷心的敬意和祝贺！

众所周知，松阴的事迹曾被他的弟子传到海外，英国文豪史蒂文森为松阴不顾幕府禁止出海的禁令毅然做出“下田踏海”的壮举所感动，亲自执笔写下了《吉田寅次郎》，因为这个缘故，松阴的名字很早就为西方人所熟知。然而，就笔者所知，在西方似乎还没有发现有人直接阅读松阴的著作，并通过这些著作来理解松阴的思想与行动。绀野先生正是着眼于这一点，继桥本左内的《启发录》的英文全译本之后又推出了这部吉田松阴的《留魂录》英文全译本。我认为绀野先生的研究填补了日本与西方思想交流的一个空白，为西方人理解日本架起了一座新的桥梁。

在松阴的影响方面中国则与西方形成了鲜明的对照。在思想文化方面与日本有着悠久交往历史的中国，进入近代以来，曾把率先进入现代化的明治日本视为自己学习的榜样。一时期日本的政治、法律、教育等自不待言，日本的思想文化亦成为中国知识分子学习的对象。在这种背景下，松阴作为明治维新的先驱者很早就被介绍到了中国。在黄遵宪的代表作《日本国志》(1895 年出版)、诗集《人境庐诗草》、康有为的《日本变政考》（1898 成立，1998 年由紫禁城出版社出版)、《日本书目志》(1896 年刊)、康同微的《日本变法由游侠义愤考》(康有为序。1998 年由大同译书局出版)、梁启超的《自由书》(1899 年)、《新民说》(1902 年) 等著作中，中国清末的改革者们出于中国改革的需要积极介绍松阴的事迹、思想和行动，热切期望中国也能出现松阴那样的改革者。

配合这种时代需要，以德富苏峰的《吉田松阴》(明治 26 年初版，1902 年中译本) 为首，松阴的代表作《幽室文稿》(选译本。中译本名为《松阴文钞》，梁启超翻译并注，1906 年由广智书局书版)、《吉田松阴遗墨》(上中下三卷，国民丛书社编辑，由商务印书馆出版、出版年不详）等纷纷被翻译成中文在中国出版发行。甚至有的思想家通过这些出版物在汲取松阴

版、1902年中訳本）を始め、松陰の著作『幽室文稿』（抜粋。中訳本題『松陰文鈔』、翻訳と批評は梁啓超、1906年広智書局より刊行）、『吉田松陰遺墨』（上・中・下三巻。国民叢書社編集、刊行年不明、商務印書館より刊行）が次々と中国語に翻訳、刊行された。それらの刊行物を通じて、松陰から多くの思想的栄養を吸収しながら、自らの思想を形作っていく思想家（たとえば梁啓超。詳細は拙稿参照）さえいた。その意味で、近代中国における松陰の影響は西洋と比べ物にならないほど大きいものがあったといえよう。

経済のグローバリゼーションが問われている現今、国と国との間の相互理解は今までと比べて一層重要性を増している。二国間におきる経済や外交などの諸問題の奥底を探れば、相手の国の歴史、思想、文化に対する誤解あるいは無知が原因であることはしばしばである。

紺野先生の『留魂録』の翻訳を契機に、世界各国の人々に松陰のみならず、日本人の思想、行動ないし日本歴史に親しんでもらい、過去の歴史経験や教訓の中から多くの知恵を学び取りながら、国内外の問題の解決に取り組んでもらうことを厚く期待して止まない。

思想养分的同时形成了自己的独特思想(如梁启超,详细情况请参照拙稿)。从这个意义上，可以说松阴在近代中国所产生的巨大影响与其在西方的影响简直不可同日而语。

在各国都在提倡全球经济一体化的今天，国与国之间的相互理解比以往显得更为重要。对于两国之间发生的经济或外交问题，追根寻源，往往大多就是由于对对方国家的历史、思想、文化的误解或无知所致。

我衷心希望世界各国人民能够以绀野先生的这部《留魂录》翻译为契机，了解日本人的思想、行為乃至日本的历史，从过去的历史经验和教训中汲取更多智慧的同时致力于解决国内外的各种问题。

「留魂録」英完訳書の上梓に寄せて。

財団法人 山口県教育会
会長　　河村太市

この度、吉田松陰の「留魂録」が、紺野大介先生によって英完訳され上梓の運びとなりましたことは、誠に大きな意義を有することであり、先ずは先生のご精進に対し深甚なる敬意を表させて戴きます。

日本の近代化についての関心の増大は、諸外国の研究者の中にも、松陰を研究対象としたり、あるいは松陰の著述を引用する向きを次第に増大させております。しかしながら松陰の著述を完全な形で翻訳した例は、寡聞にして知らないのでありますが、おそらく紺野先生の"Soulful Minute"をもって嚆矢とするのではないかと思います。

本書について第一に指摘させて戴きたいことは、松陰の厖大な著作の中から「留魂録」を選ばれた紺野先生のご見識であります。

選定された理由は、「はじめに」詳しく述べられておりますが、特に{松陰の魂の叫びが聞かれ、重い警鐘を現代の日本人に与えていること}、{"教育とは何か"を深く考察させていること}、また{その死生観は日本人のみならず外国の人々の共感も得られるだろう}といわれた言葉が注目されたのでありますが、取り分け、紺野先生が{限りない優しさと、言葉の最良の意味における愛情で我々に語りかけている}松陰の心情にうたれたためでありましょう。

紺野先生は、「留魂録」の中に、門人や周囲の人々への「細心の配慮」を読み取っておられるのであり、その読みの的確さが伺われるのであります。と申しますのは、松陰は「細心の配慮」を生活の信条としていたからであります。

松陰は、現に自分が置かれている状況を把握し、そこで求められていることに万全を致すことを心掛け、これを武士たるものの「平日の覚悟の筋」(「武教全書講録」開講主意)と表現しています。

安政6年(1859) 5月14日江戸召喚が伝えられてから、同月25日に出立するまでの約10日間に、「心事」の一々を詩文や書簡にするなど、万端の心準備をしているのであり、それは江戸獄に移ってからも続けられ、そして「平日の覚悟の筋」の仕上げとして、「留魂録」が執筆されているのであります。

それは紺野先生のいわれる「細心の配慮」の仕上げだったと言えましょう。

「留魂録」を「平日の覚悟の筋」ないし「細心の配慮」として捉えてみるとき、本書で「留魂録」が選定された新しい意義が見えてくるようにも思われるのであります。

本書について指摘させて戴きたいことの二つ目は、訳者に紺野先生を得た喜びであります。

先生は、先に橋本左内の「啓発録」を英完訳しておられ、同書は英語圏を初めとする多くの国々の著名人から高い評価を得ており、先生は翻訳者としましても高い力量をお持ちの方であります。

こうした翻訳の力量もさることながら、左内と松陰の関係を思いますとき、まさにその人を得たという喜びを感じるのであります。左内と松陰とは、安政6年の交、同じ江戸獄にありながらも遂に会うことが出来なかったのであります。しかし松陰は本書でも左内に言及しており（第 14 章）、是非会って議論したい人物として敬しているのであります。

そういうことで紺野先生を訳者とすることが出来ましたことは実に意義深いものがあると考えておるのであります。

最後になりましたが、今回の翻訳にあたり山口県教育会が編纂しました「吉田松陰全集」を底本としてご使用戴き、また本会発行の「吉田松陰」（山口県立博物館編）をご利用くださいましたことに対し感謝いたしますとともに、本書が広く普及されますよう祈念申し上げます。

{謝辞}

本書は「啓発録」同様、基本的には日本人以外の海外の方々に日本人を理解して頂くためになした小さな仕事であったが、以下大変多くの方々のご厚意ご助力に依存している。先ず全体を纏めるのに際し、山口県教育会編の「吉田松陰全集」を底本とし、図録、書幅などは山口県立山口博物館編の「吉田松陰」を多数引用させて戴いた。また理解を深めて戴くため松陰の留魂録直筆のコピーを等寸大で示した。これらのことをご快諾戴き跋文まで頂戴した教育会の河村太市会長に先ず御礼を申し上げたい。また日本人の方々のために、留魂録の逐語訳は松陰研究で高名な古川薫氏によるものを採用させて頂くことで、氏からご丁寧なお手紙とご諒解を得た。ここに感謝を評する次第である。加えて本件では徳間書店のご諒承を得た。また理解を深めるため必要に応じて「日本人名辞典」転写を図り、この断面では三省堂のご厚意とご諒承を戴いた。両社に感謝の意を表したい。また英完訳に際しては、米国の Georgetown 大学で日本語学、Washington 大学院で英語学の双方を修めた日本語研究者である Cheiron McMahill 氏、旧友でプロ翻訳家である高梨正伸氏にお力をお借りした。ここに改めて心から御礼申し上げる次第である。なお「留魂録」以外の和文 vs 英文は必ずしも対応していない。また R.L.Stevenson 著述「吉田寅次郎」を参考として付記するに際しての retype や作表は石野亮子嬢にお願いした。また中国人で「吉田松陰の研究」で東北大学から文学博士号を取得した日本学者、郭連友氏から論評を頂戴した。
あわせ御礼を申し上げたい。それに最後まで叱咤激励を戴いた日本学協会江種隆弘常務理事と出版社錦正社の中藤社長に感謝の意を表し筆を擱くこととしたい。

訳者しるす。

Acknowledgments

This translation and publication of "Soulful Minute" into English is aimed at introducing Japanese history abroad and having the Japanese understood by the people in overseas countries, just as was my translation of the "Treatise on Enlightenment" written by Sanai Hashimoto. I will feel greatly rewarded for my efforts if this book also helps to make present-day Japanese people newly appreciate the splendor of the Japanese of old times and incites them to strive to attain even some part of it.

Before everything, I am indebted to Mr. Taichi Kawamura, the chairman of the Foundation of Yamaguchi Prefectural Education Society. In making up many notes into a book, I could use a complete edition of Shouin Yoshida's works edited by the Yamaguchi Prefectural Education Society as my source material, and quote many pictures of paintings, calligraphic writings and an actual size copy of the manuscript of "Soulful Minute" from "Shouin Yoshida" edited by Yamaguchi Prefectural Museum through the kindness of Mr. Taichi Kawamura. I also would like to express my gratitude to Mr. Kaoru Furukawa, a famous scholar of Shouin Yoshida, for his consent to use his translation of "Ryuukonroku" from the archaic style of the Edo period into modern Japanese, and Tokuma Shoten Publishing Co., Ltd. and Sanseido Co., Ltd. for their understanding in quoting some excerpts of this translation.

With reference to translation, I am indebted to Ms. Cheiron McMahill, associate professor of English at Daito Bunka University, and my old friend Mr. Masanobu Takanashi, who is a professional translator, for their invaluable assistance in avoiding mistranslation and holding to the proper English syntax. I would like to take this opportunity to express my sincere appreciation to them.

Also I wish to extend my thanks to Miss Ryouko Ishino for her service in retyping the article of R. L. Stevenson and creating tables.

In addition, I would like to take this opportunity to express my sincere appreciation to Mr. Lianyou Guo, a Chinese scholar who received a doctorate in literature from Tohoku University for his research on Shouin Yoshida, for his review of the "Soulful Minute".My deepest gratitude goes to Mr. Takahiro Egusa for his good offices as well as to Mr. Masabumi Nakafuji, the President of Kinseisha Co., Ltd.
There is no one to one correspondence as a whole between Japanese phrases and English phrases in materials other than "Soulful Minute".

by translator

引用及び参考文献（Bibliography）

1).山口県教育会編：吉田松陰全集（岩波書店）S.9~S.11(1934_1936)

2).山口県教育会編：吉田松陰全集（岩波書店）S.13~S.15(1938_1940)

3).山口県教育会編：吉田松陰全集（大和書房）S.47~S.49(1972_1974)

4).山口県立山口博物館編：吉田松陰（山口県教育会）

5).(財）松風会編：吉田松陰撰集（松風会）

6).松陰神社社務所版：吉田松陰留魂録直筆墨筆写

7).古川薫：吉田松陰留魂録（徳間書店）

8).福本義亮：吉田松陰の最後（誠文堂新光社）

9).広瀬豊：吉田松陰言行録（三省堂）

10).徳富蘇峰：吉田松陰（岩波文庫）

11).広瀬豊：吉田松陰書簡集（岩波文庫）

12).川上喜蔵：宇都宮黙霖・吉田松陰往復書翰（錦正社）

13).河上徹太郎：吉田松陰（文藝春秋）

14).山口県立下関中学・英語同好会編：Yoshida Shoin（1937 年版）

15).玖村敏雄：吉田松陰の思想と教育（岩波書店）

16).奈良本辰也：吉田松陰集{日本の思想}（筑摩書房）

17).古川薫：松陰とその門下（新人物往来社）

18).奈良本辰也：吉田松陰{批評日本史}（思索社）

19).吉田常吉他：吉田松陰{日本思想大系}（岩波書店）

20).山口県教育会：吉田松陰遺墨帖（大和書房）

21).近藤啓吾：校註講孟箚記（日本学協会）

22).徳永真一郎：吉田松陰{物語と史跡をたずねて}（成美堂出版）

23).山岡荘八：{小説}吉田松陰（学研）

24).栗原隆一：松陰－その謀叛の系譜（エルム）

25).郭連友：アヘン戦争と吉田松陰（文芸研究 第 140 集抜刷）

26).郭連友：近代中国における吉田松陰認識（文化 第 62 巻 3,4 号 別刷）

27).郭連友：太平天国と吉田松陰の思想形成（日本史思想史学会編：史学）

28).郭連友：梁啓超と吉田松陰（日本思想史 60 号.近代日本と東アジア）

29).郭連友：吉田松陰の人間観形成と孟子の性善説（思想史研究第 33 号）
30).郭連友：吉田松陰の思想形成と近代中国に於ける吉田松陰認識
（東北大学文学博士号学位論文 1999）
31).諸橋轍次選書三：孟子の話（大修館書店）
32).吉田常吉：安政の大獄（吉川弘文館）
33).内閣文庫所蔵史籍叢刊：安政雑記（汲古書院）
34).日本史籍協会叢書：九条尚忠文書全四冊（東京大学出版会）
35).中根雪江：昨夢紀事（東京大学出版会）
36).景岳会編：橋本景岳全集（景岳会）
37).George M.Wilson: The Bakumatsu Intellectual in Action/Hashimoto Sanai in the Political Crisis of 1858 [Personality in Japanese History] (University of California Press, 1970)
38).福井郷土歴史博物館編：橋本景岳先生の生涯（生誕 150 年記念図録）
39).佐伯仲蔵・青木晦蔵：梅田雲浜関係資料（東京大学出版会）
40).吉田常吉：井伊直弼{人物叢書}（吉川弘文館）
41).日本史籍協会叢書：三条実万手録全二冊（東京大学出版会）
42).毛利敏彦：明治維新政治史序説（未来社）
43).小堀桂一郎：鎖国の世界的意味（日本学・名著刊行会）
44).土井良三：幕末五人の外国奉行（中央公論社）
45).Daisetz T,Suzuki: Zen and Japanese Culture(Princeton Univ.Press)
46).Inazou Nitobe: Bushido; The Soul of Japan(Tuttle Publishing Inc.)
47).司馬遼太郎：幕末（文春文庫）
48).司馬遼太郎：「明治」という国家（日本放送出版協会）
49).源了圓：郭連友・漆紅訳；日本文化与日本人性格的形成（北京出版）
50).司馬光：資治通鑑/全 294 巻の一部{文白対照全訳}（革命出版社）
51).三谷博：明治維新の革新と連続（山川出版社）
52).小西四郎：日本の歴史{19 開国と攘夷}（中公文庫）
53).角川書店偏：日本史探訪{19 開国か攘夷か}（角川書店）
54).B.A.Shilloney:日本の天皇制が生き延びた謎(世界の中の日本 V Ⅶ'66)

55).John Breen: "Emperor, State and Religion in Restoration Japan"
(Doctoral Dissertation, Cambridge University 1992)
56).尾崎秀樹：歴史の中の地図・司馬遼太郎の世界（文春文庫）
57).Donald Keene: Anthology of Japanese Literature(GroveWeidenfeld)
58).Shusaku Endo, translated by Van Gessel: The Samurai(NDP Corp)
59).H. Paul Varley: Japanese Culture(Hawaii Univ. Press)
60).羽生道英：幕末英傑風雲録（中公文庫）
61).山川菊栄：覚書・幕末の水戸藩（岩波文庫）
62).大平喜間多：佐久間象山{人物叢書}（吉川弘文館）
63).倉田信久：詳解・省諐録（倉田寛）
64).佐久間象山先生顕彰会：佐久間象山の生涯（同顕彰会）
65).橋本治：江戸にフランス革命を（青土社）
66).綱淵謙錠：「斬」（河出書房新社）
67).Samson, G：A history of Japan 1616－1867 (Stanford Univ. Press)
68).江戸漢詩撰：藤田東湖/佐久間象山/橋本左内/吉田松陰/西郷隆盛(岩波)
69).Aera Mook：幕末学のみかた（朝日新聞社）
70).足立和：黒船に乗っていた日本人（徳間書店）
71).田中彰編：幕末維新の社会と思想（吉川弘文館）
72).川口雅昭：松下村塾考（山口県地方史研究・第 80 号,1998）
73).北岡伸一：第三の開国と人材登用（学士会会報 No.830/2001-1）
74).佐藤一斎著/久須本文雄全訳註：言志四録（講談社）
75).芳賀登：幕末志士の生活（雄山閣）
76).Seidensticker, E :Low City, High City (Tokyo from Edo to the
Earthquake (Harvard Univ. Press)
77).綿貫哲雄：維新と革命{政治の貧困}（大明堂）
78).Atsuharu Sakai: Japan in a Nutshell Vol.2(Yamagata Printing Co.)
79).徳川斉昭著：弘道館記／The Kodokwanki or Kodokwan Record,
The Three English Version(The Meiji Japan Society 1937)
80).Philipp F. von Siebold: Nippon/First Edition published in part 1832.
81).紺野大介：日本固有古代文字ホツマツタエ考察（Tronware 68,2001）

82).横浜開港資料館：ペリー来航関係資料図録（横浜開港資料普及協会）
The Japan Expedition of Commodore M.C.Perry
83).宋元人注：四書五経[上中下巻]（中国書店）
84).Former US President Fillmore's letter to Perry, 10 September 1856
Houghton Library, Harvard University
85).ワシリイ・コロウニン著/大塚博人訳：幕末日本見聞録（大観堂出版）
86).和田英松/所功校訂：官職要解（講談社学術文庫）
87).三省堂編集所編：日本人名事典（三省堂）
88).劉特重等編：中国歴史人名大辞典[上下巻]（上海古籍出版社）
89).岩波・ケンブリッジ：世界人名辞典（岩波書店）
90).孟慶遠：中国歴史文化辞典（新潮社）
91).Edwin Reischauer et: Japan an Illustrated Encyclopedia(Kodansha)
92).徳富蘇峰：井伊直弼執政時代{近世日本国民史}（明治書院）Nov.1935
93).徳富蘇峰：神奈川条約締結篇{近世日本国民史}（明治書院）Dec.1934
94).徳富蘇峰：開国初期篇{近世日本国民史}（明治書院）April 1936
95).刑務協会篇：日本近世行刑史稿・上下巻（財・矯正協会）July 1945

著者略歴

紺野大介

科学技術者、企業経営者、大学教授、論説随筆家、幕末維新歴史研究家。1945年生まれ。東京大学で流体力学・流体工学・流体機械を中心に自然科学を学び、工学博士の学位を取得。この間、旧ソ連 Moscow 大学数理統計研究所に短期留学。また野村／Harvard Management School で「トップのための経営戦略講座」修得。1999年まで日本の重厚長大型及び軽薄短小型の大企業2社で研究開発本部長、新規事業本部長、取締役 CTO など重責を担った。

併任で日本機械学会論文審査委員、通産省・大型国家プロジェクト作業部会長、政令指定都市・新潟市の市長顧問、　最近では政府創設の国策会社「産業革新機構」創立時の key person として参画、初代取締役・産業革新委員など歴任。2000年以来今日まで1200名余の評価委員を擁する技術事業性評価の為の公益シンクタンク ETT の理事長＆CEO を務める。また自民党、民主党の政権時の国会議員団の要請により「中国の動静」等について講演。1994年以来、中国・清華大学・SKLT（摩擦学国家重点実験室）招聘教授、2008年からは北京大学・RICFRH（歴史学系中外関係史研究所）客座教授も務める。中国を代表する Top 2 大学の双方で教授職にある現在日本で唯一の人物でもあり中国要人とのパイプも太い。また伝統ある日中科学技術交流協会・常務理事も兼ねている。

一方、世界70ケ国を学術・ビジネスで歴訪。傍ら英国 Cambridge 大学など数大学、仏国 CEEJA（欧州日本学研究所）など海外の日本研究機関で武士道等に関する招待講演を実施。こうした体験を基に、世界に日本を理解戴くため日本人のエートス、価値観、閉鎖性、謙虚さ、潔さ、美意識等を幕末維新期の偉人に素材を求め、その著作を英完訳し海外大学や研究機関等に無償で配布・紹介している。1996年上梓された第一作目の橋本左内『啓発録』英訳書は、同年米国クリントン大統領から感謝状を授与。　2003年の吉田松陰『留魂録』英訳書に続き、2016年春、遂に幕末三部作となる佐久間象山『省諐録』英訳書（いずれも錦正社）を完成した。他に著作・『中国の頭脳・清華大学と北京大学』（朝日新聞）、『民度革命のすすめ』（東邦出版）等がある。[2016/03 現在]

Author Profile

Daisuke KONNO

Japanese Scientist, Engineer, Business Director ,Professor, Essayist and Editorial writer, and Researcher on the history of Japan's Bakumatsu period and Meiji Restoration.

Born in 1945, Dr. Konno studied engineering (with particular focus on fluid dynamics and fluid engineering) at the University of Tokyo, eventually earning a Ph.D. in Mechanical Engineering. In the meantime, he went abroad for short-term study at the Mathematical Statistics Institute of Moscow University in the former Soviet Union. He also attended the "Top Management Course" at the Nomura Harvard Management School.

Until 1999, he filled important positions such as Division Executive, Board Member and CTO in listed Japanese companies of all conceivable sizes. In the past, he concurrently held other posts including Reviewer of Papers for the Japan Society of Mechanical Engineering, Chair of the National Big Project at MITI, and more recently, the first Director as well as Industrial Innovation Committee Member and others as the key person and prime mover upon the creation of the national corporation "Innovation Network Corporation of Japan" by the Japanese government.

Since 2000, he has served as President and CEO of the Eureka Think Tank for evaluation of technical projects, an organization with over 1,200 evaluators. Concurrently, as Political Counselor to the Mayor of Niigata City, he has given lectures on "China's Movements" and other subjects upon request by prominent Dietmembers' groups from the Liberal Democratic Party and the Democratic Party.

Since 1994, he has served as Tenured Professor, State Key Laboratory on Tribology at Tsinghua University in China, and since 2008 as Guest Professor, RICFRH of History Dept. at Peking University. This makes him the only Japanese person to hold professorial posts at both of China's top two universities, and has yielded strong connections with high-ranking Chinese officials. He also serves as General Executive Board Member and Director of the Japan-China Science & Technology Exchange Association.

Meanwhile, he has visited 70 of the world's countries for academic or business purposes, and has given lectures on Bushido (The Way of the Samurai) at Cambridge University in England and other universities, European Center for Japanese studies, Alsace in France and elsewhere. To increase understanding of Japan in the world, he looks for Japanese attributes such as their ethos, reservedness, values, humility, graciousness, and aesthetic awareness in the great figures of the Bakumatsu and Meiji Restoration period, then translates their works into English and distributes or introduces them free at overseas universities and elsewhere. He received a letter of acknowledgement from US President Clinton for the first of these, the English translation of *Keihatsuroku* ("Treatise on Enlightenment") by Hashimoto Sanai, published in 1996. The second was *Ryūkonroku* ("Soulful Minute") by Yoshida Shoin, published in 2003, and at last, he accomplished a translation *Seikenroku* ("Record of Conscience") by Sakuma Shozan as the three Bakumatsu work in Spring 2016.

Other publications include *Chūgoku no Zunō – Seika Daigaku to Pekin Daigaku* ("Brains of China – Tsinghua and Peking Universities", Asahi Shimbun) and *Mindo Kakumei no Susume* ("Encouragement for Revolution in Cultural Standards", Toho Publishing). As of March,2016.

吉田松陰著「留魂録」英完訳書
"Soulful Minute"

平成15年10月24日　第一刷発行
平成28年 4月15日　第二刷発行

※定価は函等に表示してあります。

訳　者　紺野大介
装丁者　吉野史門
発行者　中藤正道
発行所　㈱錦正社
〒162-0041　東京都新宿区早稲田鶴巻町544-6
TEL　03（5261）2891
FAX　03（5261）2892
URL　http://www.kinseisha.jp/

落丁本・乱丁本はお取替えいたします。　印刷・㈱平河工業社　製本・㈱ブロケード

ISBN978-4-7646-0264-9

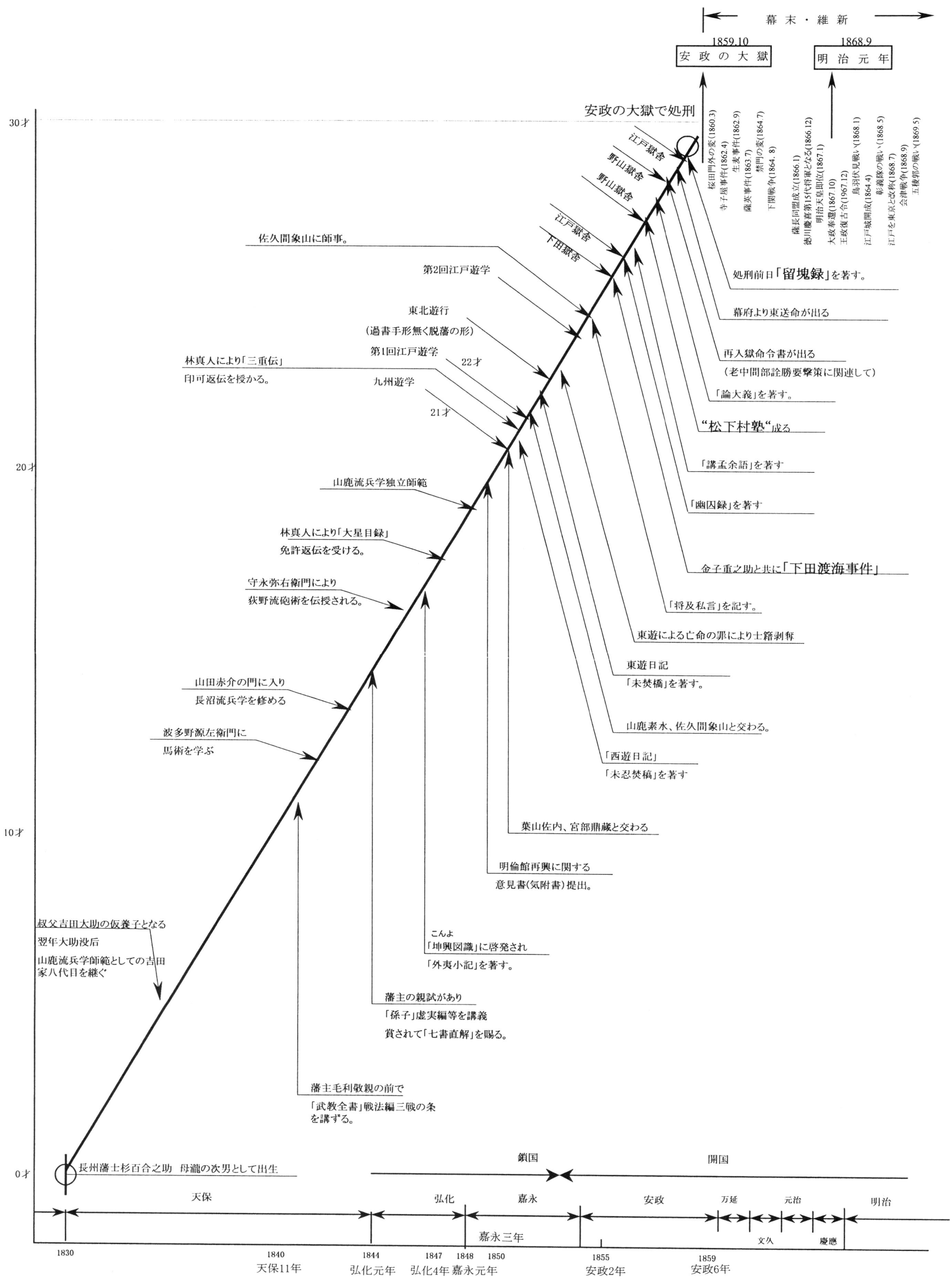

幕末・維新
1859.10
安政の大獄
1868.9
明治元年
安政の大獄で処刑
桜田門外の変(1860.3)
寺子屋事件(1862.4)
生麦事件(1862.9)
薩英事件(1863.7)
禁門の変(1864.7)
下関戦争(1864. 8)
薩長同盟成立(1866.1)
徳川慶喜第15代将軍となる(1866.12)
明治天皇即位(1867.1)
大政奉還(1867.10)
王政復古令(1967.12)
鳥羽伏見戦い(1868.1)
江戸城開成(1864.4)
彰義隊の戦い(1868.5)
江戸を東京と改称(1868.7)
会津戦争(1868.9)
五稜郭の戦い(1869.5)
30才
20才
10才
0才
江戸獄舎
野山獄舎
野山獄舎
江戸獄舎
下田獄舎
処刑前日「留魂録」を著す。
幕府より東送命が出る
再入獄命令書が出る
(老中間部詮勝要撃策に関連して)
「論大義」を著す。
“松下村塾“成る
「講孟余語」を著す
「幽囚録」を著す
金子重之助と共に「下田渡海事件」
「将及私言」を記す。
東遊による亡命の罪により士籍剥奪
東遊日記
「未焚稿」を著す。
山鹿素水、佐久間象山と交わる。
「西遊日記」
「未忍焚稿」を著す
葉山佐内、宮部鼎蔵と交わる
明倫館再興に関する
意見書(気附書)提出。
こんよ
「坤輿図識」に啓発され
「外夷小記」を著す。
藩主の親試があり
「孫子」虚実編等を講義
賞されて「七書直解」を賜る。
藩主毛利敬親の前で
「武教全書」戦法編三戦の条
を講ずる。
佐久間象山に師事。
第2回江戸遊学
東北遊行
(過書手形無く脱藩の形)
第1回江戸遊学
22才
林真人により「三重伝」
印可返伝を授かる。
九州遊学
21才
山鹿流兵学独立師範
林真人により「大星目録」
免許返伝を受ける。
守永弥右衛門により
荻野流砲術を伝授される。
山田赤介の門に入り
長沼流兵学を修める
波多野源左衛門に
馬術を学ぶ
叔父吉田大助の仮養子となる
翌年大助没后
山鹿流兵学師範としての吉田家八代目を継ぐ
長州藩士杉百合之助 母瀧の次男として出生
鎖国
開国
天保
弘化
嘉永
安政
万延
元治
明治
文久
慶應
嘉永三年
1830
1840
天保11年
1844
弘化元年
1847
弘化4年
1848
嘉永元年
1850
1855
安政2年
1859
安政6年

長州藩士　吉田松陰の30歳の生涯

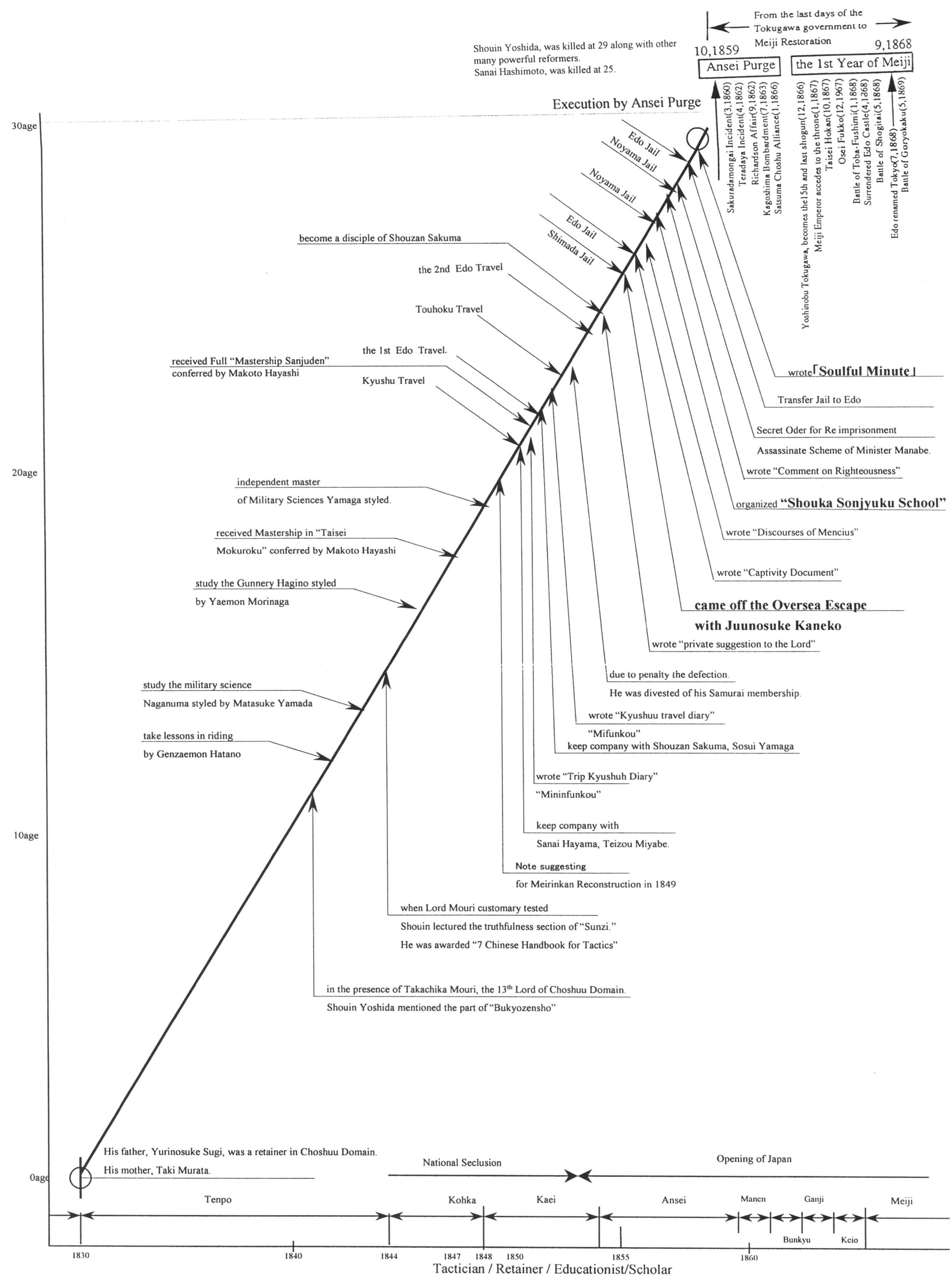
From the last days of the Tokugawa government to Meiji Restoration
10,1859
Ansei Purge
9,1868
the 1st Year of Meiji
Sakuradamongai Incident(3,1860)
Teradaya Incident(4,1862)
Richardson Affair(9,1862)
Kagoshima Bombardment(7,1863)
Satsuma Choshu Alliance(1,1866)
Yoshinobu Tokugawa, becomes the15th and last shogun(12,1866)
Meiji Emperor accedes to the throne(1,1867)
Taisei Hokan(10,1867)
Osei Fukko(12,1967)
Battle of Toba-Fushimi(1,1868)
Surrendered Edo Castle(4,1868)
Battle of Shogitai(5,1868)
Edo renamed Tokyo(7,1868)
Battle of Goryokaku(5,1869)
Shouin Yoshida, was killed at 29 along with other many powerful reformers.
Sanai Hashimoto, was killed at 25.
Execution by Ansei Purge
30age
20age
10age
0age
Edo Jail
Noyama Jail
Noyama Jail
Edo Jail
Shimada Jail
become a disciple of Shouzan Sakuma
the 2nd Edo Travel
Touhoku Travel
the 1st Edo Travel.
received Full "Mastership Sanjuden" conferred by Makoto Hayashi
Kyushu Travel
independent master of Military Sciences Yamaga styled.
received Mastership in "Taisei Mokuroku" conferred by Makoto Hayashi
study the Gunnery Hagino styled by Yaemon Morinaga
study the military science Naganuma styled by Matasuke Yamada
take lessons in riding by Genzaemon Hatano
wrote「Soulful Minute」
Transfer Jail to Edo
Secret Oder for Re imprisonment
Assassinate Scheme of Minister Manabe.
wrote "Comment on Righteousness"
organized "Shouka Sonjyuku School"
wrote "Discourses of Mencius"
wrote "Captivity Document"
came off the Oversea Escape with Juunosuke Kaneko
wrote "private suggestion to the Lord"
due to penalty the defection.
He was divested of his Samurai membership.
wrote "Kyushuu travel diary"
"Mifunkou"
keep company with Shouzan Sakuma, Sosui Yamaga
wrote "Trip Kyushuh Diary"
"Mininfunkou"
keep company with Sanai Hayama, Teizou Miyabe.
Note suggesting for Meirinkan Reconstruction in 1849
when Lord Mouri customary tested Shouin lectured the truthfulness section of "Sunzi."
He was awarded "7 Chinese Handbook for Tactics"
in the presence of Takachika Mouri, the 13th Lord of Choshuu Domain.
Shouin Yoshida mentioned the part of "Bukyozensho"
His father, Yurinosuke Sugi, was a retainer in Choshuu Domain.
His mother, Taki Murata.
National Seclusion
Opening of Japan
Tenpo
Kohka
Kaei
Ansei
Manen
Bunkyu
Ganji
Keio
Meiji
1830
1840
1844
1847
1848
1850
1855
1860
Tactician / Retainer / Educationist/Scholar

30 years long life of Shouin Yoshida (1830～1859)